Affective Teacher Education

Exploring Connections among Knowledge, Skills, and Dispositions

Edited by
Patrice R. LeBlanc and Nancy P. Gallavan

Published in partnership with the
Association of Teacher Educators

Rowman & Littlefield Education
Lanham • New York • Toronto • Plymouth, UK

Published in partnership with the
Association of Teacher Educators

Published in the United States of America
by Rowman & Littlefield Education
A Division of Rowman & Littlefield Publishers, Inc.
A wholly owned subsidiary of The Rowman & Littlefield Publishing Group, Inc.
4501 Forbes Boulevard, Suite 200, Lanham, Maryland 20706
www.rowmaneducation.com

Estover Road
Plymouth PL6 7PY
United Kingdom

British Library Cataloguing in Publication Information Available

Library of Congress Cataloging-in-Publication Data

Affective teacher education : exploring connections among knowledge, skills, and dispositions / edited by Patrice R. LeBlanc and Nancy P. Gallavan.
p. cm.
"Published in partnership with the Association of Teacher Educators."
Includes bibliographical references.
ISBN 978-1-60709-226-1 (cloth : alk. paper) — ISBN 978-1-60709-227-8 (pbk. : alk. paper) — ISBN 978-1-60709-228-5 (electronic)
1. Teachers—Training of. 2. Affective education. I. LeBlanc, Patrice R., 1954– II. Gallavan, Nancy P. III. Association of Teacher Educators.
LB1707.A44 2009
370.71'1—dc22 2008054610

∞™ The paper used in this publication meets the minimum requirements of American National Standard for Information Sciences—Permanence of Paper for Printed Library Materials, ANSI/NISO Z39.48-1992.
Manufactured in the United States of America.

Contents

Reviewers

EDITORS

REVIEW BOARD—FIRST REVIEWERS

EDITORIAL BOARD—SECOND REVIEWERS

Association of Teacher Educators Affective Education Commission Resolution

February 2006

Affective education seeks to enhance students' growth in attitudes, interest, character, values, and other areas within the social-emotional domain. It is evident in programs such as moral education, character education, conflict resolution, social skills development, self-awareness, and other related areas.

Whereas,

1. We believe that teacher education programs should impart the knowledge, skills, and dispositions that all educators need for affective education, in support of state and national standards.
2. We believe that development of the knowledge, skills, and dispositions is a process that requires support at all levels within the cultural milieu.
3. We believe that modeling the knowledge, skills, and dispositions of affective education must be provided by teacher educators who demonstrate a high commitment to the education of the whole person, in the cognitive, affective, and psychomotor domains.
4. We believe that affective education is manifested through formal and informal actions and interactions evident in all content, process, and contexts essential for teaching the whole child.
5. We believe that through attentive practice and reflection, educators should employ prosocial affective characteristics and curriculum, including but not limited to: respect, responsibility, flexibility, resiliency, collaboration, commitment, self-awareness, and self-efficacy.
6. We believe that quantitative and qualitative assessment of affective knowledge, dispositions, and skills must occur in real world settings.

Be it resolved that we recommend that ATE support teachers' and teacher educators' efforts in affective education in the following ways.

- Continue to offer workshops and other sessions at conferences related to affective education topics
- Increase publications on affective related topics
- Pursue opportunities for joint ventures between ATE and other teacher and teacher education professional organizations that support affective education

Members of the Association of Teacher Educators Affective Education Commission

Diana Bernshausen, 2003–2005

Nancy P. Gallavan, 2003–2009

Linda M. Holdman, 2003–2009

Marilyn Johnson, 2003–2009

Patrice R. LeBlanc, chair, 2003–2009

Jane McCarthy, 2003–2009

Gwendolyn Middlebrooks, 2003–2009

Terrell M. Peace, 2006–2009

Caroline Pryor, 2003–2009

Marvin Seperson, 2006–2009

Stephen Sherblom, 2003–2005

Regina M. Ryel Thomason, 2003–2009

Frances S. van Tassell, ex-officio member, 2003–2009

John White, 2003–2009

Foreword

Frances S. van Tassell

In any society, there are aspects of a person's life that impact his or her affective growth. Certainly, a nation's educational system inherently includes variables that either support or hinder the affective development of its students. As societies globally become more and more diverse in cultures, beliefs, practices, and values, the educational system seems to be more and more a part of the growth and development of affective human characteristics. It is for these reasons that, as the 2003–2004 president of the Association of Teacher Educators, I appointed a commission to study affective education. Association members who would be invited to participate and serve on this commission were thoughtfully and carefully selected. It was critical to involve persons who had demonstrated a passion for the affective aspects of the educational process. The individuals who have served on this commission for six years are passionate, strong voices for the education and development of the whole child. Now, proudly, we present the outcomes of the work of this prestigious group in this monograph.

As stated by Thomas Bellamy and John Goodlad in the April 2008 issue of *Phi Delta Kappan*, it is critical that students in all generations have an understanding of the tenets of democracy. It is for this reason that the affective component of the development of the whole child has our full attention. As has been historically supported by a number of theorists and educators cited here and throughout the chapters of this book, the mission of developing both the cognitive and the affective human capacities is inherent in the mission of public schooling. John Steinberg's (1998) history of affective education informs us of the vital importance affective education has played in our nation's development. Steinberg mentions Howard Gardner and his work (see Gardner, 1993) when describing the many intelligences human beings have, especially the intelligences associated with intrapersonal and interpersonal abilities. Steinberg also mentions Carl Rogers and his focus on personal concerns. As Rogers (1963) explained, we are continually in a pattern of human growth in our effort to achieve wholeness. It is the affective side of humanity that leads us to that sense of actualization that Rogers promoted in order to reach the wholeness that we inherently need. No review of the history of affective education would be complete without consideration of the work of Abraham Maslow (1970), who showed us the importance of a number of affective aspects of personal life. In Maslow's hierarchy, as we move from the most basic human needs to the goal of self-actualization, we are continually in the process of developing our affective selves. Also critical to the consideration of theorists and their views on affective education is the work of Erik Erikson (1963). Erikson taught us about the stages of psychosocial development and how each stage deals with the affective component of human development. From his initial stage of trust versus mistrust to the final stage of integrity versus despair, it is clear that as humans progress through the psychosocial stages, they are continually developing affective skills and understandings.

It is our hope that readers will receive support and encouragement from this publication in order to face the challenges and barriers sometimes erected that counter educators' attempts to develop the whole child, which, by necessity, include the affective side of life. Without attention to affective education, our nation's democratic purpose may be at risk. As Richard Neumann points out in the January 2008 issue of the *Phi Delta Kappan*, our historical adherence to democratic principles as the guide to our nation's survival is at risk. Educators at all levels are encouraged to understand and to develop in their students the dispositions (i.e., the affective aspects of the human condition) that are necessary to maintain democratic citizenship.

REFERENCES

Bellamy, G. T., & Goodlad, J. I. (2008). Continuity and change in the pursuit of a democratic public mission for our schools. *Phi Delta Kappan, 89*(8), 565–571.

Erikson, E. (1963). *Childhood and society* (2nd ed.). New York: Norton.

Gardner, H. (1993). *Multiple intelligences: The theory in practice*. New York: Basic Books.

Maslow, A. H. (1970). *Motivation and personality* (2nd ed.). New York: Harper and Row.

Neumann, R. (2008). American democracy at risk. *Phi Delta Kappan, 89*(5), 328–339.

Rogers, C. R. (1963). The actualizing tendency in relation to "motives" and to consciousness. In M. R. Jones (Ed.), *Nebraska symposium on motivation* (Vol. 11, pp. 1–20). Lincoln: University of Nebraska Press.

Steinberg, J. (1998). *A history of affective education*. Retrieved from www.eqtoday.com/archive/jpca.html.

Preface

Patrice R. LeBlanc and Nancy P. Gallavan

The purpose of this monograph is two-fold: to raise educators' awareness of current issues in the area of affective education, often referenced in the literature as social and emotional learning, and to provide possible guidelines to assist educators with their work. Balancing the continuing focus emphasizing and assessing academic progress and outcomes in education from prekindergarten classrooms through university graduate programs, a movement toward incorporating and accounting for more social and emotional learning is growing (Graczyk, Domitrovich, Small, & Zins, 2006). Through the Affective Education Commission, the Association of Teacher Educators (ATE) has been a part of that growth.

The ATE Affective Education Commission defined affective education as follows (LeBlanc & Sherblom, 2004, p. 1).

> The commission has globally defined affective education, based on input from the membership at a focus group session at the August 2004 conference and on discussions held at Commission meetings. Affective education draws upon knowledge bases that include moral education, character education, conflict resolution, social skills development, self-awareness, and other related areas. Within these knowledge bases there are skills and dispositions that preservice and inservice teachers must master, as mandated by state and national standards. Development of these skills and dispositions is a process that requires support within the cultural milieu. Assessment of the knowledge, skills, and dispositions occurs quantitatively and qualitatively, yet must be actualized in real world settings.

With this definition in mind, the Affective Education Commission completed many tasks to promote affective education during its six-year tenure.

The commission proposed the Association of Teacher Educators Resolution on Affective Education, which was approved by the Delegate Assembly in 2006. Additionally, members of the commission made multiple presentations at ATE conferences addressing a variety of affective education topics applicable to multiple contexts. The commission met regularly, and the culmination of its work is captured in this monograph, *Affective Teacher Education: Exploring Connections among Knowledge, Skills, and Dispositions.*

The monograph is composed of three distinct divisions: "Teacher Dispositions and Teacher Preparation Programs" (chapters 2, 3, and 4), "Teachers' Practices and Professionalism" (chapters 5 and 6), and "Quality Affective Educational Experiences for PK–12" (chapters 7, 8, and 9). The collection of chapters in each division is designed to provoke thinking about the many areas involved in affective education, or social and emotional learning, at all levels of education. As a precursor to these divisions, chapter 1 traces the history of affective education and describes specific positive outcomes that accrue from social and emotional learning. Beginning with chapter 1, the Affective Education Commission invites you to read and apply the new knowledge that you gain from each chapter to promote social and emotional learning.

REFERENCES

Graczyk, P. A., Domitrovich, C. E., Small, M., & Zins, J. E. (2006). Serving all children: An implementation model framework. *School Psychology Review, 35,* 266–274.

LeBlanc, P., & Sherblom, S. (2004). Affective Education Commission report to the president of the Association of Teacher Educators. Unpublished report.

Acknowledgments

We would like to express our heartfelt appreciation to Dr. Frances van Tassell for serving as our mentor in ATE and inviting our participation on the Commission on Affective Education, to the members of the commission for sharing our passions, and to the many fine educators who served in a variety of roles that contributed to bringing this monograph to completion.

1

The Importance of Social and Emotional Learning

David W. Johnson and Roger T. Johnson

ABSTRACT

Historically, social and emotional learning is the most important responsibility of schools. In order for effective social and emotional learning to exist in schools, certain conditions must be established. Schools first must establish positive interdependence in learning groups, classrooms, and the school as a whole. Positive relationships need to be developed among all school members. Social skills must be taught. Moral character must be induced. In order to achieve these goals, schools may wish to implement cooperative learning throughout all grade levels to ensure that the school is a learning community, teach students to resolve their conflicts of interests through integrative negotiations and peer mediation, and use the constructive controversy procedure to ensure students disagree and challenge each other's thinking.

PUBLIC EDUCATION IN A DEMOCRACY: HISTORY OF SOCIAL AND EMOTIONAL LEARNING

Thomas Jefferson and many other founders of American democracy believed that public schools were indispensable for creating competent, active, and engaged citizens/leaders. Jefferson believed that schools should cultivate *virtue* and patriotism. Samuel Adams believed teachers were responsible for nurturing a *moral sense* in students. Abigail Adams told her son John Quincy that learning math, science, and literature are of little value unless the person also develops virtue, honor, truth, and integrity. The founders believed that a free republic was the most powerful form of government but also the most fragile, because it requires a virtuous citizenry who can balance their personal needs with those of the republic as a whole. The majority of the people must be committed to doing what is best for the nation as a whole. The founders of the United States thus created universal, state-supported, and locally governed public schooling to (a) instill moral and ethical values in American children and youth, (b) ensure the American people would be responsible citizens, and (c) provide citizens the knowledge they need for national economic development and prosperity (Comer, 2004; Fuhrman & Lazerson, 2005). Public education was to consist of more than knowledge of basic skills, the classics, or reading, math, and science. Jefferson wanted a public education system that would ensure the average person would understand the current political, economic, and social issues, their relevance to his or her life, and what was needed to improve and sustain democracy. A similar emphasis on social and emotional learning existed in higher education (Boyer, 1987). The colonial college focused on building students' character and preparing them for civic and religious leadership. Teaching was viewed as a sacred calling honored as highly as the ministry. Students were entrusted to faculty tutors responsible for their intellectual, moral, and spiritual development.

The emphasis on social and emotional learning did not end with the founders of American democracy. In the last three decades of the nineteenth century, Colonel Frances Parker (Campbell, 1965), perhaps the leading American educator of the time, advocated the view that schools were responsible for teaching students an intense devotion to freedom, democracy, and individuality. He viewed mutual responsibility as the great, central principle of democracy. He believed that the two major motivations for learning were (a) the inherent joy in gaining competence and discovering the *truth* and (b) using what one learned to help others. In essence, he would ask students two questions: "What have you learned?" and "How have you used it to help your classmates?" Parker believed that students would fully develop their capacities only if cooperative learning was encouraged and competition and individualistic efforts were eliminated as motives in school tasks. Following in Parker's footsteps, in the first half of the twentieth century, John Dewey (1924) used his famous project method of instruction to stress the social and emotional aspects of learning and prepare students for problem solving and democratic living.

In the past several decades, however, a major enemy of traditional American education has been the essentialist view, known as the "back to basics" movement in the 1970s, that education should limit itself to basic subject matter (such as reading, math, and science) that is measurable by standardized tests. The essentialist emphasis is on motivating students through personal economic gain rather than through becoming contributing citizens of a democratic society. What advocates of essentialism ignore is that knowledge without virtue and integrity is dangerous and a potential menace to society. If schools graduate brilliant but dishonest people, individuals who have great knowledge but who do not care about others, or individuals who are great thinkers but who are irresponsible, society is harmed rather than benefited.

DIVERSITY AND SOCIAL-EMOTIONAL LEARNING

In addition to the fact that American public education was created to achieve social and emotional learning goals, the increasing diversity of public schools requires an emphasis on social and emotional learning. There are a wide variety of goals that schools are responsible for achieving related to diversity, such as reducing prejudice and creating positive attitudes toward diversity. In addition, students from markedly different cultures and backgrounds often attend the same school and, therefore, the school has to create a common culture that binds all members of the school together. Faculty and students must share a common culture that includes a common language, a large body of commonsense knowledge, and a similar knowledge of cultural heroes, popular tastes, and everyday customs and conversations (Jackson, 1968). Creating this common culture is one of the social and emotional goals of any school.

In this chapter we shall define social and emotional learning and how it relates to cognitive learning, identify four of the important steps in promoting social and emotional learning, and discuss each of the steps in some detail.

SOCIAL AND EMOTIONAL LEARNING: THE OTHER SIDE OF THE REPORT CARD

There is some confusion regarding the nature of social and emotional learning. *Social-emotional* is most often contrasted with *cognitive* in a way that implies that the two are separate aspects of learning. Cognitive usually refers to conceptualizing and intellectual functioning (i.e., the understanding and retention of subject matter knowledge and related skills such as how to read and do math problems). Social-emotional learning then refers to everything that is not cognitive, such as feelings, attitudes, values, interpersonal skills, work habits, and moral character. These variables are known as "the other side of the report card."

This dichotomy between cognitive and social and emotional learning is misleading for several reasons. First, all learning has both cognitive and social and emotional components. No matter what subject matter knowledge or skills students master, students will have feelings and attitudes about the results and process of instruction. In fact, a person's cognitive learning and social-emotional learning cannot be separated. To teach any concept, principle, or theory is to teach not only for its comprehension but also for an attitude toward it. Teaching students to read, for example, is of little use unless students also learn to enjoy, appreciate, and value reading. W. Edwards Deming (personal communication, 1991), the guru and one of the founders of total quality management, stated that if teachers achieved one goal, everything else would take care of itself. The goal is to instill in students a *love of learning*. He believed that if students loved to learn, the cognitive aspects of learning would take care of themselves and no standardized tests or other inspections of instructional success were needed.

Second, the processes by which instruction is conducted creates social and emotional outcomes regardless of the teacher's intentions. Teachers may focus on teaching math concepts and procedures, but whether they use cooperative, competitive, or individualistic learning procedures affects students' attitudes, values, social skills, and relationships simultaneously with their academic learning. Everything teachers do affects the social and emotional outcomes of learning. Social and emotional learning is inherent in everything that happens in the classroom and in the day-to-day flow of life in the school.

Third, there are courses, such as drug education and multicultural education, which are aimed at changing attitudes and values as well as teaching cognitive knowledge. Civics courses are aimed more at inculcating the motivation to be good citizens than teaching information. Drug education courses are aimed more at teaching attitudes toward healthy living than at teaching information about drugs. Multicultural education courses are often aimed more at teaching positive attitudes toward diversity than at teaching information about other cultures. Health classes are aimed more at inculcating attitudes toward healthy living than information about health. In teaching classes such as these, teachers need to know how to inculcate attitudes and values as well as how to present information.

Fourth, there are many social and emotional characteristics that are important for students to develop independently from specific subject matter. Personal competencies include understanding and managing emotions, acquiring self-motivation and persistence, managing impulses and moods, resisting negative influences, coping with stressful situations, delaying gratification, building self-efficacy and self-esteem, developing moral values and character, and making healthy choices. Interpersonal competencies include communicating effectively, building and maintaining trust, providing leadership, resolving conflicts constructively, engaging in prosocial actions that include reducing antisocial behaviors such as bullying and drug abuse, and being a good citizen (Elias, 1997; D. W. Johnson, 1973, 1974, 2009; D. W. Johnson & R. Johnson, 1996b, 2008a; Payton et al., 2000; Zins, Weissberg, Wang, & Walberg, 2004). Both personal and interpersonal competencies help the person build and maintain positive relationships with peers and adults. There are also attitudes that students need to develop, such as a love of learning, commitment to being a responsible citizen, desire to learn, liking scientific reasoning, liking of diversity, commitment to making the world a better place, and many others. Schools are more successful when students enjoy their educational experiences, laugh often, and have fun.

Fifth, children and adolescents need to be socialized into the role of "student" before cognitive learning can take place. Students need to be taught how to be *role responsible* (i.e., having the capacity to live up to general expectations of appropriate role behavior, such as promptness, cleanliness, respect for faculty) and having *role readiness* (i.e., the ability to meet the demands of many organizational settings with the proper cooperation). Learning how to fulfill the role of student includes learning appropriate work habits. Those work habits include completing work on time, using time wisely, meeting responsibilities, striving for quality work, continuously improving one's work, and striving to add value to each job one does. Knowing how to be a student and to adopt the appropriate work habits are predecessors of cognitive learning.

Finally, there are values underlying American democracy that schools are responsible for inculcating. Students are supposed to learn to value a pluralistic and democratic society, freedom of choice, equality of opportunity, equality before the law, the importance of being a participating citizen, free and open inquiry into all problems, self-reliance, a lack of ethnic prejudice, the joy of creativity, and the possibilities of entrepreneurism (D. W. Johnson & R. Johnson, 1996b, 2000).

Seeing cognitive and social-emotional learning as a dichotomy results in teachers having a false choice of emphasizing one or the other. Cognitive and social emotional learning are actually two parts of a whole that cannot be separated from each other. Since social and emotional learning is embedded in the processes of instruction and school life as well as in the content being presented, social and emotional learning goes on continuously regardless of what teachers do. The essentialist view of school, furthermore, neglects the fact that many courses were created to achieve social and emotional goals. Schools have to achieve some social and emotional goals, such as ensuring children and adolescents can fulfill the role responsibilities of being a student, before cognitive goals can be achieved; and there are adult responsibilities, such as citizenship, that can only be fulfilled if schools achieve social and emotional goals.

When teachers want to maximize social and emotional learning, there are several steps they need to take. Four of the steps are:

1. Creating a cooperative context.
2. Promoting positive relationships with peers and faculty.
3. Teaching students essential interpersonal and small group skills, especially the skills for resolving conflicts constructively.
4. Promoting the development of moral character.

CREATING A COOPERATIVE CONTEXT: ESTABLISHING A COMMUNITY AND SOCIAL INTERDEPENDENCE

The first key component of social and emotional learning is to create a cooperative context for instruction and life within the school. Social and emotional learning is inherently social. It most effectively occurs in a cooperative context in which individuals share common goals (i.e., positive goal interdependence), have a common fate (i.e., what happens to one member will happen to all members), and share a common culture. This context is often described as a *learning community* in which members share common goals. The school community is made up of the faculty and staff, the students, their parents, members of the neighborhood, and other stakeholders in the school, such as district administrators, government officials, college admission officers, and future employers. Within membership in the community, individuals fulfill their *need to belong* (i.e., need to form and maintain lasting, positive, and significant interpersonal relationships) (Baumeister & Leary, 1995) and need for *reference groups* (i.e., groups people identify with, compare their values and attitudes to, and use as a means for evaluating those values and attitudes) (Newcomb, 1943).

The heart of learning communities is *positive interdependence* (i.e., cooperation), which exists when individuals work together to achieve mutual goals (Deutsch, 1962; D. W. Johnson & R. Johnson, 1989, 2005a). It may be contrasted with *negative interdependence* (i.e., competition), which exists when individuals work against each other to achieve a goal that only one or a few may attain, and *social independence* (i.e., individualistic efforts), where the outcomes of each person are unaffected by others' actions. Structuring situations cooperatively results in individuals promoting each other's success, structuring situations competitively results in individuals opposing each other's success, and structuring situations individualistically results in no interaction among individuals. These interaction patterns affect numerous variables, which may be subsumed within the three broad and interrelated outcomes: effort to achieve, interpersonal relationships, and psychological health (D. W. Johnson & R. Johnson, 1989, 2005a).

Table 1.1 Meta-Analysis of Social Interdependence Studies: Mean Effect Size

Dependent Variable	Cooperative vs. Competitive	Cooperative vs. Individualistic	Competitive vs. Individualistic
Achievement	0.67	0.64	0.30
Interpersonal Attraction	0.67	0.60	0.08
Social Support	0.62	0.70	-0.13
Self-Esteem	0.58	0.44	-0.23
Time-On-Task	0.76	1.17	0.64
Attitudes toward Task	0.57	0.42	0.15
Quality of Reasoning	0.93	0.97	0.13
Perspective-Taking	0.61	0.44	-0.13
High Quality Studies			
Achievement	0.88	0.61	0.07
Interpersonal Attraction	0.82	0.62	0.27
Social Support	0.83	0.72	-0.13
Self-Esteem	0.67	0.45	-0.25

Source: Johnson, D. W., & Johnson, R. (1989). *Cooperation and competition: Theory and research.* Edina, MN: Interaction Book Company. Reprinted with permission.

THE POWER OF COOPERATION

Effort to Achieve

From table 1.1 it may be seen that cooperation promoted considerably greater effort to achieve than did competitive or individualistic efforts (effect sizes = 0.67 and 0.64 respectively). Effort exerted to achieve includes such variables as achievement and productivity, long-term retention, generation of new ideas and solutions, intrinsic motivation, achievement motivation, continuing motivation, and greater transfer of what is learned within one situation to another. Cooperators tended to spend more time on task than did competitors (effect size = 0.76) or students working individualistically (effect size = 1.17). Cooperation tended to promote more frequent use of higher level reasoning strategies than did competitive (effect size = 0.93) or individualistic (effect size = 0.97) efforts. Cooperation also tended to promote more accurate perspective taking than did competitive (effect size = 0.61) or individualistic (effect size = 0.44) efforts. Cooperative experiences, compared with competitive and individualistic ones, have been found to promote more positive attitudes toward the task and the experience of working on it (effect-sizes = 0.57 and 0.42 respectively).

Interpersonal Relationships

From table 1.1 it may be seen that cooperation generally promoted greater interpersonal attraction among individuals than did competitive or individualistic efforts (effect sizes = 0.67 and 0.60 respectively). Cooperative experiences also tended to promote greater social support from peers and from superiors (i.e., teachers) than did competitive (effect-size = 0.62) or individualistic (effect-size = 0.70) efforts.

Psychological Health

Psychological health is the ability to develop and maintain relationships in which cooperative action effectively takes place (D. W. Johnson & R. Johnson, 1989). We have conducted a series of studies relating cooperative, competitive, and individualistic efforts and attitudes to various indices of psychological health. The samples studied included middle-class junior high students, middle-class high school seniors, high-school age juvenile prisoners, adult prisoners, Olympic ice-hockey players, adult step-couples, and Chinese business personnel. The diversity of the samples studied and the variety of measures of psychological health provide considerable generalizability of the results of the studies. A strong relationship was found between cooperativeness and psychological health, a mixed relationship has been found with competitiveness and psychological health, and a strong relationship has been found between an individualistic orientation and psychological pathology.

One aspect of psychological health is the engagement in prosocial behavior and the avoidance of antisocial behavior. Cooperative experiences tend to increase the frequency with which participants engage in prosocial behaviors (D. W. Johnson & R. Johnson, 2008a). Choi, Johnson, and Johnson (submitted for publication), in a study involving 217 fourth- and fifth-grade students, found that both cooperative learning experiences and cooperative predispositions predicted the frequency with which the students engaged in prosocial behavior. Competitiveness and individualism, on the other hand, did not predict prosocial behavior. The opposite of prosocial behavior is antisocial behavior. One form of antisocial behavior is harm-intended aggression (i.e., bullying). The more cooperative the student, the less likely the student was to engage in harm-intended aggression. The more competitive the student, the more frequently the student engaged in harm-intended aggression.

Interpersonal and Small Group Skills

Every cooperative learning lesson is also a lesson in social skills. The research indicates that cooperative experiences lead to more frequent and more competent use of social skills than do competitive or individualistic experiences (D. W. Johnson & R. Johnson, 1989, 2008a). The studies focused on socially isolated and withdrawn students, emotionally disturbed adolescents, and regular students. Cooperation promotes more frequent, effective, and accurate communication than do competitive and individualistic situations.

Basic Elements of Cooperation

These outcomes tend to result only when cooperation is effectively structured to contain five basic elements (D. W. Johnson & R. Johnson, 1989, 1999, 2005a). First, there must be a strong sense of *positive interdependence*, so individuals believe they are linked with others so they cannot succeed unless the others do. Positive interdependence may be structured through mutual goals, joint rewards, divided resources, complementary roles, and a shared identity. Second, each collaborator must be *individually accountable* to do his or her fair share of the work. Third, collaborators must have the opportunity to *promote each other's success* by helping, assisting, supporting, encouraging, and praising each other's efforts to achieve. Fourth, working together cooperatively requires *interpersonal and small group skills*, such as leadership, decision-making, trust-building, communication, and conflict-management skills. Finally, cooperative groups must engage in *group processing*, which exists when group members discuss how well they are achieving their goals and maintaining effective working relationships.

Levels of Interdependence

Positive interdependence should be structured at all levels of the school: learning group, classroom, interclass, school, school-parent, and school-neighborhood. The learning group level is known as cooperative learning.

Cooperative learning is the instructional use of small groups so that students work together to maximize their own and each other's learning (Johnson, Johnson, & Holubec, 2008). Any assignment in any curriculum for any age student can be done cooperatively. There are three types of cooperative learning—formal, informal, and cooperative base groups. *Formal cooperative learning* consists of students working together, for one class period to several weeks, to achieve shared learning goals and complete jointly specific tasks and assignments. *Informal cooperative learning* consists of having students work together to achieve a joint learning goal in temporary, ad hoc groups that last from a few minutes to one class period. *Cooperative base groups* are long-term, heterogeneous cooperative learning groups with stable membership whose primary responsibilities are to provide support, encouragement, and assistance to make academic progress and develop cognitively and socially in healthy ways as well as holding each other accountable for striving to learn.

Positive interdependence may be extended to the classroom as a whole. Class goals may be established, class rewards or celebrations may be created, class roles may be structured, class processing may take place in class meetings, and a class identity may be created through a class name, slogan, flag, or song. Interclass interdependence may be established through organizing a set of classes into a neighborhood or school within a school, classes such as science and math may be integrated, and students of different ages may be involved as cross-class reading buddies. School level positive interdependence (D. W. Johnson & R. Johnson, 1994) may be established through a school mission statement, faculty and staff teaching teams and study groups, school task forces to solve school problems, and ad hoc decision-making groups during faculty meetings to involve all staff members in important school decisions. School-parent interdependence may be established through involving parents in strategic planning, producing a school newsletter, publishing the school yearbook, volunteering in classes, helping conduct special projects, and serving on all school committees or the site council. Finally, school-neighborhood interdependence may be created by eliciting local merchants to give a discount to students who have a card verifying that in the last grading period they achieved a "B" average or above. In return, classes could do neighborhood service projects, cleaning up a park or mowing the yards of elderly residents.

Promoting Positive Relationships

The second key component of social and emotional learning is promoting positive, caring, and supportive relationships among students and between students and faculty. People in all cultures are motivated to form relationships and join groups and to resist the dissolution of those relationships (Gardner, Pickett, & Brewer, 2000). The degree of emotional bonding that exists among students has a profound effect on students' social and emotional learning. There are two ways to discuss the importance of positive peer relationships—what is gained by being involved in such relationships and what are the consequences of being disconnected and alienated from peers.

Benefits of Positive Peer Relationships

Children, adolescents, and young adults need supportive and caring friends. Friends give a person a developmental advantage. The infinite benefits of interpersonal relationships cannot all be listed here. Only a few will be discussed. Relationships are the key to (a) physical health; (b) psychological health; (c) personal identity; (d) social, cognitive, and moral development; (e) coping with stress and adversity; (f) meaning and quality of life; (g) self-actualization; and (h) career success (D. W. Johnson, 2009; D. W. Johnson & F. Johnson, 2009; D. W. Johnson & R. Johnson, 1989).

Positive, supportive relationships are related to living longer lives, being ill less often, experiencing less severe illnesses, and recovering from illness and injury faster and more completely (e.g., Bowlby, 1969; Hartup & Stevens, 1997; Menec, 2003; Reis & Collins, 2004; Uchino, Uno, & Holt-Lunstad, 1999). People who are connected with others live longer than isolated people do in every age and ethnic/racial group and across all diseases. People who lack social and community ties tend to be twice as likely to die from any cause as were people who have such relationships.

Positive, supportive relationships are related to psychological health (e.g., Baumeister & Leary, 1995; Gardner, Gabriel, & Dickman, 2000; Johnson & Norem-Hebeisen, 1977; Rigby, 2000; Rubin, Bukowski, & Parker, 1998). People who, for one reason or another, are unable to establish acceptable relationships, tend to develop considerable anxiety, depression, frustration, and alienation. Positive, supportive relationships are related to psychological adjustment, lack of neuroticism and psychopathology, lack of psychological distress, self-reliance and autonomy, a coherent and integrated self-identity, higher self-esteem, increased general happiness, and coping effectively with stressful situations. Constructive interpersonal relationships, therefore, are both preventive and reparative.

Positive and supportive relationships provide the caring, information, resources, and feedback people need to cope with stress (e.g., D. W. Johnson & R. Johnson, 1989, 2005a; Reis & Collins, 2004). It is during major life transitions that stress tends to be highest and social support may be most needed. Positive relationships decrease the number and severity of stressful events in a person's life. They reduce anxiety and help appraise the nature of the stress and the person's ability to deal with it constructively. Discussions with supportive peers help people perceive the meaning of the stressful event, regain mastery over their lives, and enhance their self-esteem (e.g., Antonucci, Lansford, & Akiyama, 2001; Chappell & Badger, 1989). Discussions with supportive peers have helped addicted individuals, the bereaved, and all sorts of other individuals experiencing adversity, challenges, and stress (D. W. Johnson & F. Johnson, 2009).

Healthy social, cognitive, and moral development are based on positive and caring relationships in which individuals share and validate their perceptions of reality. According to Piaget (1950), Kohlberg (1969), and Vygotsky (1962), reality is socially constructed within relationships. As individuals strive to make sense of the world and determine what is real and what is illusory, they depend on other people to validate their perceptions and impressions. People cannot tell what is fair or unfair, good or bad, or beautiful or ugly without checking their perceptions and opinions with the perceptions and opinions of others. In order to make sense of the world, individuals need to share their perceptions and reactions with other people and find out whether or not other people perceive and react similarly.

Relationships have an important impact on a person's identity (i.e., self-definition of who they are as a person). People tend to see themselves as others see them. People develop personal relationships in which others get to know them and give them feedback on how they are perceived. From the reflections of others, people develop a clear and accurate picture of themselves. When others view an individual as a worthwhile, valuable person, the person tends to view himself or herself similarly. In addition, in their relationships individuals identify with others and adopt social roles such as "student" or "engineer" that become part of their self-identity.

The quality of your life is indicated by the answers to two questions: "What makes my life meaningful?" and "What makes my life happy?" When a national sample of people was asked, "What is it that makes your life meaningful?" almost all respondents said, "friends, parents, siblings, spouses, lovers, children, and feeling loved and wanted by others" (Diener & Seligman, 2002). When the same sample was asked, "What makes your life happy?" the most common answer was "intimate relationships." In a number of national surveys (Harter, Schmidt, & Hayes, 2003) most people considered it very important to have "a happy marriage, a good family, and good friends." Less importance was given to work, housing, beliefs, and financial security. There is no simple recipe for producing happiness, but the research indicates that for almost everyone a necessary ingredient is some kind of satisfying, close, personal, intimate relationship.

Finally, positive relationships with peers are related to academic achievement (Roseth, Johnson, & Johnson, 2008). The quality of students' relationships with peers has been found to be related to classroom grades, standardized test scores, and IQ.

Consequences of Alienation from Peers

Students who do not have friends are at risk (D. W. Johnson & R. Johnson, 1989, 2008a; Roseth, Johnson, & Johnson, 2008). Rejection by the normal peer group due to antisocial behavior, as well as inappropriate aggressive behavior, are positively correlated. Rejected children tend to be deficient in peer group entry, perception of peer group norms, response to provocation, and interpretation of prosocial interactions. Difficulties in peer relationships, such as having fewer friends, less contact with peers, less stable friendships over time, and less mature understanding of the reciprocities and intimacies involved in friendships, are related to being referred to child guidance clinics. Peer rejection is also related to academic difficulties.

Virtual Relationships

Positive relationships used to be limited primarily to the people nearby with whom individuals would directly interact. Not all relationships today, however, are face-to-face. The online world allows individuals to build relationships with people all over the world (D. W. Johnson & R. Johnson, 2008b). *Online relationships* have two major features: visual anonymity and limited channel (i.e., text only) communication. Websites such as "Facebook" and "My Space" specialize in helping people form and nurture online relationships. While online relationships can be very powerful, they lack physical presence, social context, and everyday interaction and experiences.

TEACHING STUDENTS SOCIAL SKILLS

The third key component of social and emotional learning is to teach students the interpersonal and small group skills they need to interact effectively with other people (D. W. Johnson, 2009; D. W. Johnson & F. Johnson, 2009). They include such skills as communication, trust building, leadership, decision-making, goal setting, social influence skills, and especially conflict resolution skills. Three of the areas in which social skills are highly important are (a) cognitive and social development, (b) career success, and (c) general well being.

Being socially skilled gives students a developmental advantage. The development of social competencies are inseparably related and form the foundation for academic success and peer acceptance and socially appropriate behavior. A student's social relationships play a powerful role in adjustment and success in school (Hawkins, Smith, & Catalano, 2001). They also enable individuals to form positive relationships characterized by peer acceptance and socially appropriate behavior and fewer problem behaviors. Social skills have been found to be related positively to academic outcomes (Bloodworth, Weissberg, Zins, & Walberg, 2001). Better social skills correlated with students' greater time-on-task, higher achievement scores, and better grades.

Being socially skilled is related to success in career settings (D. W. Johnson, 2009; D. W. Johnson & F. Johnson, 2009). One of the most well established social science principles is that people working together to achieve mutual goals are far more productive than are the same number of people working in isolation (D. W. Johnson & R. Johnson, 1989). Almost without exception, any meaningful task requires the efforts of more than one individual. Curing cancer, building a skyscraper, bringing a product to market, funding a new company, all require the efforts of many different people working together. While technical competencies are needed, career success may be primarily dependent on interpersonal competencies. The heart of most jobs, especially higher-paying, more interesting jobs, is leading others, getting others to cooperate, coping with complex power and influence issues, and helping solve people's problems in working with each other.

To do so one needs the interpersonal skills to motivate others to achieve goals, negotiate and mediate, get decisions implemented, exercise authority, and develop credibility. A national survey found that employers value five types of skills: communication, responsibility, interpersonal, initiative, and decision-making. The Center for Public Resources (1982) published a nationwide survey of businesses, labor unions, and educational institutions that found that 90 percent of the people fired from their jobs were fired for poor job attitudes, poor interpersonal relationships, inappropriate behavior, and inappropriate dress. Correspondingly, a recent survey found that the most frequent reason for people quitting their job is that their boss or supervisor lacked interpersonal skills.

Being socially skilled promotes students' general well being. The quality of individuals' social skills is related to the quality of their family life; their abilities to develop and maintain friendships; their enjoyment of leisure time activities that involve other people (such as team sports); and their ability to learn new skills and competencies and acquire knowledge, frames of reference, attitudes, and values from family, peers, friends, colleagues, and teachers. Two of the most important social and emotional competencies are interpersonal effectiveness and actualizing one's potential (D. W. Johnson, 2009; D. W. Johnson & F. Johnson, 2009). *Interpersonal effectiveness* is the degree to which the consequences of a person's behavior in interacting with others match the person's intentions. A person's interpersonal effectiveness largely determines the quality and course of his or her life. *Self-actualization* is the drive to actualize potential and take joy and a sense of fulfillment from being all that a person can be. Self-actualization is based on being aware of abilities and talents, applying them appropriately in a variety of situations, and celebrating their successful application. Being a student needs to include being committed to developing one's personal resources and abilities.

Conflict Resolution

Two of the most important sets of social skills that students need to master are skills involved in resolving conflicts of interests and those involving constructive controversies (D. W. Johnson & R. Johnson, 2005b, 2007). When managed constructively, conflicts can increase (a) individuals' energy, curiosity, and motivation; (b) achievement, retention, insight, creativity, problem-solving, and synthesis; (c) healthy cognitive and social development; (d) clarification of one's own and others' identity, commitments, and values; (e) quality of relationships; and (f) social and emotional learning. Managing conflicts constructively depends on (a) clear procedures for managing conflicts, (b) individuals being skilled in the use of the procedures and value using them, and (c) norms and values encouraging and supporting the use of the procedures. Faculty and staff need to teach students, and learn themselves, three procedures for managing conflicts: academic controversy, problem-solving (i.e., integrative negotiation), and peer mediation procedures.

Conflict Resolution Training

Conflicts may be based on individuals' differing interests within a situation. *Conflicts of interests* exist when the actions of one person attempting to maximize his or her wants and benefits prevents, blocks, or interferes with another person maximizing his or her wants and benefits (Deutsch, 1973). Conflicts of interests are resolved through negotiation and mediation. There are two ways to negotiate: *distributive* or *win-lose* (where one person benefits only if the opponent agrees to make a concession) and *integrative* or problem solving (where disputants work together to create an agreement that benefits everyone involved). In ongoing relationships, distributive negotiations result in destructive outcomes and integrative leads to constructive outcomes. The "Teaching Students to Be Peacemakers Program" began in the 1960s (D. W. Johnson & R. Johnson, 2005b) to teach students how to engage in problem-solving negotiations and mediate their schoolmates' conflicts. The steps in using problem-solving negotiations are:

1. Describing what you want, including using good communication skills and defining the conflict as a small and specific mutual problem.
2. Describing how you feel, including understanding how one feels and communicating it openly and clearly.
3. Describing the reasons for your wants and feelings, including expressing cooperative intentions, listening carefully, separating interests from positions, and differentiating before trying to integrate the two sets of interests.
4. Taking the other's perspective and summarizing your understanding of what the other person wants, how the other person feels, and the reasons underlying both, including being able to see the problem from both perspectives simultaneously.
5. Inventing three optional plans to resolve the conflict that maximize joint benefits and take both perspectives and sets of interests into account.
6. Choosing one and formalizing the agreement with a handshake, including making the agreement fair to all disputants, maximizing joint benefits, strengthening disputants' ability to work together cooperatively, and strengthening disputants' ability to resolve conflicts constructively in the future.

When students are unable to negotiate a resolution to their conflict, they may request help from a mediator. A *mediator* is a neutral person who helps two or more people resolve their conflict, usually by negotiating an integrative agreement. What the mediator does consists of the four steps of (D. W. Johnson & R. Johnson, 2005b):

1. Ending hostilities: The mediator must ensure that the hostile encounter is ended and the disputants have cooled off sufficiently to engage in rational problem-solving.
2. Ensuring disputants are committed to the mediation process: The mediator ensures that disputants are committed to the mediation process and are ready to negotiate in good faith. The mediator then introduces the process of mediation and sets the ground rules that (a) mediation is voluntary; (b) the mediator is neutral; (c) each person will have the chance to state his or her view of the conflict without interruption; and (d) each person agrees to solve the problem with no name calling or interrupting, being as honest as possible, abiding by any agreement made, and keeping anything said in mediation confidential.
3. Helping disputants successfully negotiate with each other: The mediator carefully takes disputants through the problem-solving negotiation steps and ensures that each disputant does each step competently.
4. Formalizing the agreement: The mediator solidifies the agreement into a contract and becomes "the keeper of the contract" by checking periodically with the disputants to make sure the agreement is working. If it is not, then the four steps of mediation begin again.

Each day the teacher selects two class members to serve as official mediators. Any conflicts students cannot resolve themselves are referred to the mediators. The mediators wear official T-shirts, patrol the playground and lunchroom, and are available to mediate any conflicts that occur in the classroom or school. The role of mediator is rotated so that all students in the class or school serve as mediators an equal amount of time. Initially, students mediate in pairs. This ensures that shy or nonverbal students get the same amount of experience as more extroverted and verbally fluent students.

If peer mediation fails, the teacher mediates the conflict. If teacher mediation fails, the teacher arbitrates by deciding who is right and who is wrong. If that fails, the principal mediates the conflict. If that fails, the principal arbitrates. Teaching all students to mediate properly results in a school-wide discipline program where students are empowered to regulate and control their own and their classmates' actions. Teachers and administrators are then free to spend more time and energy on instruction.

Sixteen studies have been conducted on the effectiveness of the Peacemaker Program in eight different schools in two different countries

Table 1.2 Meta-Analysis of Mean Peacemaker Studies: Mean Effect Sizes

Dependent Variable	Mean	Standard Deviation	Number of Effects
Academic Achievement	0.88	0.09	5
Academic Retention	0.70	0.31	4
Learned Procedure	2.25	1.98	13
Learned Procedure—Retention	3.34	4.16	9
Applied Procedure	2.16	1.31	4
Application—Retention	0.46	0.16	3
Strategy Constructiveness	1.60	1.70	21
Constructiveness—Retention	1.10	0.53	10
Strategy Two—Concerns	1.10	0.46	5
Two-Concerns—Retention	0.45	0.20	2
Integrative Negotiation	0.98	0.36	5
Positive Attitude	1.07	0.25	5
Negative Attitude	-0.61	0.37	2
Quality of Solutions	0.73	0	1

Source: Johnson, D. W., & Johnson, R. (2005). *Teaching students to be peacemakers* (4th ed.). Edina, MN: Interaction Book Company. Reprinted with permission.

(D. W. Johnson & R. Johnson, 1996a, 2005b). Students involved were from kindergarten through ninth grades. The studies were conducted in rural, suburban, and urban settings. The benefits of teaching students the problem-solving negotiation and the peer mediation procedures are as follow (see table 1.2).

First, students and faculty tended to develop a shared understanding of how conflicts should be managed and a common vocabulary to discuss conflicts. Second, students tended to learn the negotiation and mediation procedures (effect size = 2.25), retained their knowledge throughout the school year and into the following year (effect size = 3.34), applied the procedures to their and other people's conflicts (effect size = 2.16), transferred the procedures to non-classroom settings such as the playground and lunchroom, transferred the procedures to nonschool settings such as the home, and engaged in problem-solving rather than win-lose negotiations. Third, when students were involved in conflicts, trained students used more constructive strategies (effect size = 1.60) such as integrative negotiations (effect size = 0.98) than did untrained students. Fourth, students' attitudes toward conflict had to become more positive (effect size = 1.07). Students learned to view conflicts as potentially positive and faculty and parents viewed the conflict training as constructive and helpful. Fifth, students tended to resolve their conflicts without the involvement of faculty and administrators. The number of discipline problems teachers had to deal with decreased by about 60 percent and referrals to administrators dropped about 90 percent. Sixth, the conflict resolution procedures tended to enhance the basic values of the classroom and school. Seventh, students generally liked to engage in the procedures. Finally, when integrated into academic units, the conflict resolution training tended to increase academic achievement and long-term retention of the academic material (effect sizes = 0.88 and 0.70 respectively). Academic units, especially in subject areas such as literature and history, provided a setting to understand conflicts, practice how to resolve them, and use them to gain insight into the material being studied.

Constructive Controversy

A *controversy* exists when one person's ideas, opinions, information, theories, or conclusions are incompatible with those of another and the two seek to reach an agreement (D. W. Johnson & R. Johnson, 2007). Controversies are resolved by engaging in what Aristotle called *deliberate discourse* (i.e., the discussion of the advantages and disadvantages of proposed actions) aimed at synthesizing novel solutions (i.e., creative problem-solving).

Teaching students how to engage in the controversy process begins with randomly assigning students to heterogeneous cooperative learning groups of four members (D. W. Johnson & R. Johnson, 1979, 1989, 2007). The groups are given an issue on which to write a report and pass a test. Each cooperative group is divided into two pairs. One pair is given the con-position on the issue and the other pair is given the pro-position. Each pair is given the instructional materials needed to define their position and point them toward supporting information. The cooperative goal of reaching a consensus on the issue (i.e., by synthesizing the best reasoning from both sides) and writing a quality group report is highlighted. Students then (a) research, learn, and prepare the best case possible for their assigned position; (b) present the best case for their assigned position to ensure it gets a fair and complete hearing; (c) engage in an open discussion in which there is spirited disagreement as students freely exchange information and ideas while arguing forcefully and persuasively for their position, critically analyzing and refuting the opposing position, and rebutting attacks on their position and presenting counter arguments; (d) reverse perspectives and present the best case for the opposing position; and (e) drop all advocacy and find a synthesis on which all members can agree by summarizing the best evidence and reasoning from both sides and integrating it into a joint position that is new and unique, writing a group report, and processing how well the group functioned and celebrating the group's success and the hard work.

From table 1.3 it may be seen that the research (D. W. Johnson & R. Johnson, 1979, 1989, 2007) indicates that intellectual conflicts create higher achievement, characterized by longer retention, critical thinking, greater creativity, than concurrence seeking (effect size = 0.68), debate (effect size = 0.40), or individualistic efforts (effect size = 0.87). Students who participated

Table 1.3 Meta-Analysis of Academic Controversy Studies: Mean Effect Sizes

Dependent Variable	Controversy/ Concurrence Seeking	Controversy/ Debate	Controversy/ Individualistic Efforts
Achievement	0.68	0.40	0.87
Cognitive Reasoning	0.62	1.35	0.90
Perspective Taking	0.91	0.22	0.86
Motivation	0.75	0.45	0.71
Attitudes toward Task	0.58	0.81	0.64
Interpersonal Attraction	0.24	0.72	0.81
Social Support	0.32	0.92	1.52
Self-Esteem	0.39	0.51	0.85

Source: Johnson, D. W., & Johnson, R. (2007). *Creative controversy: Intellectual challenge in the classroom* (4th ed.). Edina, MN: Interaction Book Company. Reprinted with permission.

in academic controversies ended up using more higher-level reasoning and metacognitive thought more frequently than students participating in concurrence seeking (effect size = 0.62), debate (effect size = 1.35), or individualistic efforts (effect size = 0.90). In addition, students in academic controversies (a) more accurately took the other's perspective than did students participating in concurrence seeking (effect size = 0.91), debate (effect size = 0.22), or individualistic efforts (effect size = 0.86); (b) had greater continuing motivation to learn than students participating in concurrence seeking (effect size = 0.75), debate (effect size = 0.45), or individualistic efforts (effect size = 0.71); (c) developed more positive attitudes toward learning than students participating in concurrence seeking (effect size = 0.58), debate (effect size = 0.81), or individualistic efforts (effect size = 0.64); (d) developed more positive interpersonal relationships than did students participating in concurrence seeking (effect size = 0.24), debate (effect size = 0.72), or individualistic efforts (effect size = 0.81); (e) experienced greater social support than did students participating in concurrence seeking (effect size = 0.32), debate (effect size = 0.92), or individualistic efforts (effect size = 1.52); and (f) developed higher self-esteem than did students participating in concurrence seeking (effect size = 0.39), debate (effect size = 0.51), or individualistic efforts (effect size = 0.85). Engaging in a controversy can also be fun, enjoyable, and exciting.

PROMOTING THE DEVELOPMENT OF MORAL CHARACTER

The fourth key component of social and emotional learning is to promote the development of moral character (D. W. Johnson & R. Johnson, 2008a). Moral character depends on internalizing moral characteristics such as (a) frequent prosocial actions, (b) accurate perspective taking, and (c) moral *identity*.

Prosocial behaviors are actions that benefit other people by helping, supporting, encouraging their goal accomplishment or well being. There are benefits to being prosocial. Prosocial children tend to build positive relationships with peers (Asher & Rose, 1997) and, compared with schoolmates, are intrinsically motivated to build relationships with classmates, believe they are involved in positive relationships, value relationships, and enjoy positive well-being (Hawley, Little, & Pasupathi, 2002). Engaging in prosocial behavior influences how a person thinks of himself or herself (i.e., moral-identity). Midlarsky and Nemeroff (1995), for example, found that the self-esteem and self-view of people who had rescued Jews during the Holocaust were still being elevated fifty years later by the help they provided. Elementary school students who privately agreed to give up their recess time to work for hospitalized children saw themselves as more altruistic immediately and a month later (Cialdini, Eisenberg, Shell, & McCreath, 1987). Prosocial behavior tends both to enhance and verify individuals' self-definitions.

The opposite of prosocial behavior is antisocial behavior. One form of antisocial behavior is harm-intended aggression (i.e., bullying). Bullies tend to alienate their peers and experience diminished well-being (Asher & Rose, 1997) and tend to experience more loneliness, sadness, and anxiety than most students (Hawley, Little, & Pasupathi, 2002). Just as there are benefits for engaging in prosocial behavior, there are costs for engaging in antisocial behaviors such as harm-intended aggression.

The more frequent and accurate individuals' perspective taking and the lower their egocentrism, the better their moral character tends to be (D. W. Johnson & R. Johnson, 2008a). The opposite of perspective taking is egocentrism. Accurate perspective taking enhances individuals' ability to respond to others' needs with empathy, compassion, and support.

Moral identity involves seeing oneself as a moral person, with character, who acts with integrity. A moral orientation adds an "ought to," obligatory, quality to identity. Identity in a cooperative context defines the person as part of a community that shares a joint identity. Their promotive interaction tends to reflect egalitarianism (i.e., a belief in the equal worth of all members even though there may be differences in authority and status) and is characterized by mutual respect. Identity in a competitive context, on the other hand, defines a person as a separate individual striving to win either by outperforming others or preventing them from outperforming him or her. Thus, a competitor may have a moral identity involving the virtues of inequality, being a winner, and disdaining losers.

Moral Orientation

There are value systems that are inherently taught just by being in a cooperative, competitive, or individualistic situation (D. W. Johnson & R.

Johnson, 1994, 1996b, 2000, 2008a). The moral orientation in a cooperative situation focuses on self-respect, mutual respect, and equality (Deutsch, 1985) (see table 1.4). All group members are viewed as having equal value and as being equally deserving of respect, justice, and equality, even though there may be differences in authority and status. This egalitarianism implies a definition of injustice as inequalities that are not to the benefit of all (Rawls, 1971). Participants have a mutual responsibility to work for their own success and the success of all groupmates. Success results from joint efforts. Not only are members pleased about their own success, but they take pride and pleasure in groupmates' success and well-being. Other people are viewed as potential allies and facilitators of one's success. One's efforts contribute not only to one's own well-being but also to the success and well-being of collaborators and the general welfare. One's personal identity includes a group identity that fosters loyalty. The worth of each member, including oneself, is based upon one's membership in the human community; there is a basic and unconditional self-acceptance and acceptance of others. Members respect each other and themselves as unique individuals and appreciate the diverse resources members contribute to the group's efforts. Because completing the task contributes to other's well-being and the general welfare, the task is intrinsically motivating. Members feel a sense of responsibility to do their fair share of the work to complete the group's task and persevere in doing so, even when it is difficult to do so. Perspective-taking is ongoing and accurate, resulting in empathy and compassion for other members. Aggression toward other group members is seen as inappropriate. An obligation is felt to respond with help, support, and encouragement when a groupmate is in need. Members are committed to the long-term well-being of the group (i.e., the common good), and view promoting the success of others as a natural way of life.

The moral orientation in competitive situations is based on inequality and the win-lose struggle to determine who will have superior and who will have inferior outcomes (Deutsch, 1985; D. W. Johnson & R. Johnson, 1989). Competition teaches the necessity of prevailing over others to get more of something than anyone else. Success depends on outperforming the other participants and preventing anyone else from outperforming one. Other participants are viewed as rivals and threats to one's success. Engaging in competitive efforts inherently teaches that the natural way of life involves depriving others of the fruits of winning and opposing and obstructing the success of others. A person's value is contingent upon the relative success of his or her efforts; winners have value, losers do not. Thus, winners are envied and losers are disdained. One's own worth is also contingent, going up when one wins and going down when one loses. The task, such as learning, is just a means to winning, not of value in and of itself (e.g., highly competitive students when placed in a cooperative learning group

Table 1.4 Values Promoted by Positive and Negative Interdependence

	Oppositional Interaction	Promotive Interaction
Success	Outperforming Others	Shared, Joint Efforts
Other People	Rivals, Threats to Own Success	Allies, Potential Facilitators
Own Efforts	Deprive Others, Cause Their Failure	Facilitate, Contribute to Well-Being
Worth	Contingent on Winning	Basic Acceptance of Self and Others
Task	Extrinsic, Means to Winning	Intrinsic
Perspective Taking	None or Strategic	Empathy, Compassion
Aggression	Appropriate	Inappropriate
Justice	Equity	Equality, Need

have been quoted as saying, "If no one wins or loses, what is the point?"). Competitors either do not take the perspectives of others or do so in a strategic way to plan how to defeat them. Aggressing against others in order to win is viewed as appropriate, often necessary, and often admirable. An equity view of justice prevails—those who perform the highest should get the most rewards (i.e., losers are undeserving of rewards). Thus, competition is associated with less generosity, less willingness to take other people's perspectives, less inclination to trust others, greater aggression toward others, and less willingness to communicate accurately (Deutsch, 1962; D. W. Johnson & R. Johnson, 1989, 2005a, 2008a).

The moral orientation in individualistic situations is based on strict self-interest. In individualistic situations everyone is a separate individual whose success results from one's own efforts only. Interacting with others, either in a caring or an aggressive way, is inappropriate. The plight of others is to be ignored. One's own success is viewed as important; it is unimportant whether others are successful or unsuccessful. A person's worth depends on meeting criteria set by authority figures, such as teachers. The task is a means for achieving rewards. Thus, engaging in individualistic efforts inherently teaches individuals to focus on their own goals and view other peoples' success or failure as irrelevant and something to be ignored.

CLASSROOM APPLICATIONS

In order to achieve these goals, actual procedures need to be implemented in the classroom. First, schools must implement cooperative learning throughout all grade levels; doing so will ensure that the school is a learning community (Johnson, Johnson, & Holubec, 2008). Once a cooperative context is established, students should be taught how to resolve their conflicts of interests with classmates and faculty through integrative negotiations and peer mediation (D. W. Johnson & R. Johnson, 2005b). These conflicts need to be resolved justly, so that all members believe that justice prevails and they have been treated fairly. In addition, the constructive controversy procedure should be used to ensure that students disagree and challenge each other's thinking and come to a consensus based on their best reasoned judgment (D. W. Johnson & R. Johnson, 2007).

CONCLUSIONS AND RECOMMENDATIONS

Historically, social and emotional learning is the most important responsibility of schools. In the past several decades, however, an essentialist emphasis on basic cognitive knowledge and skills has dominated schools. It is based on seeing cognitive and social-emotional learning as a dichotomy resulting in teachers having to choose one or the other. This view is misleading, as cognitive and social emotional learning are actually two parts of a whole that cannot be separated from each other. The essentialist view of school, furthermore, neglects the fact that many courses were created to achieve social and emotional goals. Schools have to achieve some social and emotional goals, such as ensuring children and adolescents can fulfill the role responsibilities of being a student, before cognitive goals can be achieved; and there are adult responsibilities, such as citizenship and healthy living that can only be fulfilled if schools achieve social and emotional goals.

In order for effective social and emotional learning to exist in schools, certain conditions must be established. Schools first must establish positive interdependence in learning groups, classrooms, and the school as a whole. Positive relationships need to be developed among students and between students and faculty. Social skills must be taught to students, especially the skills involved in constructive conflict resolution. Good moral character must be induced. In order to achieve these goals, schools must implement cooperative learning throughout all grade levels (doing so will ensure that the school is a learning community), teach students how to resolve their conflicts of interests with classmates and faculty through integrative negotiations and peer mediation, and use the constructive controversy procedure to ensure students disagree and challenge each other's thinking.

REFERENCES

Antonucci, T. C., Lansford, J. E., & Akiyama, H. (2001). Impact of positive and negative aspects of marital relationships and friendships on wellbeing of older adults. *Applied Developmental Science, 5*(2), 68–75.

Asher, S., & Rose, A. (1997). Promoting children's social-emotional adjustment with peers. In P. Salovey & D. Shuyter (Eds.), *Emotional development and emotional intelligence: Educational implications* (pp. 196–203). New York: Basic Books.

Baumeister, R., & Leary, M. (1995). The need to belong: Desire for interpersonal attachment as a fundamental human motivation. *Psychological Bulletin, 117,* 497–529.

Bloodworth, M. R., Weissberg, R. P., Zins, J. E., & Walberg, H. J. (2001). Implications of social and emotional research for education: Evidence linking social skills and academic outcomes. *CEIC Review, 10*(6), 4–5.

Bowlby, J. (1969). *Attachment and loss* (Vol. 1). London: Hogarth Press.

Boyer, E. (1987). *College: The undergraduate experience in America.* New York: Harper & Row.

Campbell, J. (1965). The children's crusader: Colonel Francis W. Parker. Unpublished doctoral dissertation, Teachers College, Columbia University.

Center for Public Resources. (1982). *Basic skills in the U.S. workforce.* Washington, DC.

Chappell, N. L., & Badger, M. (1989). Social isolation and well being. *Journal of Gerontolology, 44*(5), 169–176.

Choi, J., Johnson, D. W., & Johnson, R. T. (submitted for publication). *Relationship among cooperative learning experiences, social interdependence, children's aggression, victimization, and prosocial behaviors.* Minneapolis: University of Minnesota, Cooperative Learning Center Research Report.

Cialdini, R. B., Eisenberg, N., Shell, R., & McCreath, H. (1987). Commitments to help by children: Effects on subsequent prosocial self-attributions. *British Journal of Social Psychology, 26,* 237–245.

Comer, J. P. (2004). *Leave no child behind: Preparing today's youth for tomorrow's world.* New Haven, CT: Yale University Press.

Diener, E., & Seligman, M. E. (2002). Very happy people. *Psychological Science, 13*(1), 81–84.

Deutsch, M. (1962). Cooperation and trust: Some theoretical notes. In M. Jones (Ed.), *Nebraska symposium on motivation* (pp. 275–319). Lincoln: University of Nebraska Press.

Deutsch, M. (1973). *The resolution of conflict.* New Haven, CT: Yale University Press.

Deutsch, M. (1985). *Distributive justice: A social psychological perspective.* New Haven, CT: Yale University Press.

Dewey, J. (1924). *The school and society.* Chicago: University of Chicago Press.

Elias, M. J. (1997). *Promoting social and emotional learning: Guidelines for educators.* Washington, DC: Association for Supervision & Curriculum Development.

Fuhrman, S., & Lazerson, M. (Eds.). (2005). *The public schools.* Oxford: Oxford University Press.

Gardner, W., Gabriel, S., & Dickman, A. (2000). The psychophysiology of interpersonal processes. In J. Cacioppo, L. Tassinary, & G. Bertson (Eds.), *The handbook of psychophysiology* (2nd ed.) (pp. 643–664). Cambridge: Cambridge University Press.

Gardner, W., Pickett, C., & Brewer, M. (2000). Social exclusion and selective memory: How the need to belong influences memory for social events. *Personality and Social Psychology Bulletin, 26,* 486–496.

Harter, J., Schmidt, E., & Hayes, T. (2003). *Employee engagement, satisfaction, and business-unit-level outcomes: A Meta-analysis.* Princeton, NJ: Gallup Organization.

Hartup, W. W., & Stevens, N. (1997). Friendships and adaptation in the life course. *Psychological Bulletin, 121*(3), 355–370.

Hawkins, J. D., Smith, B. H., & Catalano, R. F. (2001). Social development and social and emotional learning: The Seattle social development project. *CEIC Review, 10*(6), 18–19.

Hawley, P., Little, T., & Pasupathi, M. (2002). Winning friends and influencing peers: Strategies of peer influence in late childhood. *International Journal of Behavioral Development, 26*(5), 466–474.

Jackson, P. (1968). *Life in classrooms.* New York: Holt, Rinehart & Winston.

Johnson, D. W. (1973). The affective side of the schooling experience. *Elementary School Journal, 73,* 306–313.

Johnson, D. W. (1974). Evaluating affective outcomes of schools. In H. Walberg (Ed.), *Evaluating school performance* (pp. 99–112). Berkeley, CA: McCutchan.

Johnson, D. W. (2009). *Reaching out: Interpersonal effectiveness and self-actualization* (10th ed.). Boston: Allyn & Bacon.

Johnson, D. W., & Johnson, F. (2009). *Joining together: Group theory and group skills* (10th ed.). Boston: Allyn & Bacon.

Johnson, D. W., & Johnson, R. (1979). Conflict in the classroom: Controversy and learning. *Review of Educational Research, 49,* 51–61.

Johnson, D. W., & Johnson, R. (1989). *Cooperation and competition: Theory and research.* Edina, MN: Interaction Book Company.

Johnson, D. W., & Johnson, R. (1994). *Leading the cooperative school* (2nd ed.). Edina, MN: Interaction Book Company.

Johnson, D. W., & Johnson, R. (1996a). Conflict resolution and peer mediation programs in elementary and secondary schools: A review of the research. *Review of Educational Research, 66*(4), 459–506.

Johnson, D. W., & Johnson, R. (1996b). Cooperative learning and traditional American values. *NASSP Bulletin, 80*(579), 11–18.

Johnson, D. W., & Johnson, R. (1999). *Learning together and alone: Cooperative, competitive, and individualistic learning.* Boston: Allyn & Bacon.

Johnson, D. W., & Johnson, R. (2000). Cooperative learning, values, and culturally plural classrooms. In M. Leicester, C. Modgill, & S. Modgil, (Eds.), *Values, the classroom, and cultural diversity* (pp. 15–28). London: Cassell PLC.

Johnson, D. W., & Johnson, R. (2005a). New developments in social interdependence theory. *Psychology Monographs, 131*(4), 285–358.

Johnson, D. W., & Johnson, R. (2005b). *Teaching students to be peacemakers* (4th ed.). Edina, MN: Interaction Book Company.

Johnson, D. W., & Johnson, R. (2007). *Creative controversy: Intellectual challenge in the classroom* (4th ed.). Edina, MN: Interaction Book Company.

Johnson, D. W., & Johnson, R. (2008a). Social interdependence and moral character and moral education. In J. Nucci & D. Narvaez (Eds.), *Handbook of moral and character education* (pp. 204–229). New York: Routledge.

Johnson, D. W., & Johnson, R. (2008b). Cooperation and the use of technology. In J. M. Spector, M. D. Merrill, J. J. G. van Merrienboer, & M. P. Driscoll (Eds.).

Handbook of research on educational communications and technology (3rd ed., pp. 401–423). New York: Lawrence Erlbaum.

Johnson, D. W., Johnson, R., & Holubec, E. (2008). *Cooperation in the classroom* (7th ed.). Edina, MN: Interaction Book Company.

Johnson, D. W., & Norem-Hebeisen, A. (1977). Attitudes toward interdependence among persons and psychological health. *Psychological Reports, 40,* 843–850.

Kohlberg, L. (1969). Stage and sequence: The cognitive-developmental approach to socialization. In D. A. Goslin (Ed.), *Handbook of socialization theory and research* (pp. 347–480). Chicago: Rand McNally.

Menec, V. (2003). The relationship between everyday activities and successful aging: A 6-year longitudinal study. *Journal of Gerontology, 588*(2), 574–582.

Midlarsky, E., & Nemeroff, R. (1995, July). Heroes of the Holocaust: Predictors of their well-being in later life. Paper presented at the American Psychological Society meetings, New York.

Newcomb, T. (1943). *Personality and social change.* New York: Dryden.

Payton, J., Wardlaw, D., Graczyk, P., Bloodworth, M., Tompsett, C., & Weissberg, R. (2000). Social and emotional learning: A framework for promoting mental health and reducing risk behaviors in children and youth. *Journal of School Health, 70,* 179–185.

Piaget, J. (1950). *The psychology of intelligence.* New York: Harcourt Brace Jovanovich.

Rawls, J. (1971). *A theory of justice.* Cambridge, MA: Harvard University Press.

Reis, H., & Collins, W. (2004). Relationships, human behavior, and psychological science. *Current Directions in Psychological Science, 13,* 233–237.

Rigby, K. (2000). Effects of peer victimization in schools and perceived social support on adolescent well-being. *Journal of Adolescence, 23,* 57–68.

Roseth, C. J., Johnson, D. W., & Johnson, R. T. (2008). The relationship between interpersonal relationships and achievement within cooperative, competitive, and individualistic conditions: A meta-analysis. *Psychological Bulletin, 134*(2), 223–246.

Rubin, K. H., Bukowski, W. M., & Parker, J. G. (1998). Peer interactions, relationships, and groups. In W. Damon & N. Eisenberg (Eds.), *Handbook of child psychology: Vol. 3: Social, emotional, and personality development* (5th ed., pp. 619–780). New York: Wiley.

Uchino, B., Uno, D., & Holt-Lunstad, J. (1999). Social support, physiological processes, and health. *Current Directions in Psychological Science, 8,* 145–148.

Vygotsky, L. (1962). *Thought and language.* Cambridge, MA: MIT Press.

Zins, J., Weissberg, R., Wang, M., & Walberg, H. (Eds.). (2004). *Building academic success on social and emotional learning: What does the research say?* New York: Teachers College Press.

I

TEACHER DISPOSITIONS AND TEACHER PREPARATION PROGRAMS

Nancy P. Gallavan and Patrice R. LeBlanc

Affective teacher education mindfully intertwines knowledge, skills, and dispositions or what teachers should know, do, and believe about teaching and learning while becoming a teacher. A teacher's understanding of affect and affective education is visible throughout the teacher's development of the curriculum, the design of the instruction, the alignment of the assessments, and construction of the learning community. Each teacher not only teaches about affect as essential aspects of the subject's content and skills, every teacher models and reinforces affect as the accepted outlooks and behaviors exhibited in the multitude of interactions teachers and students experience each day. Through their formal and informal interactions, teachers and students exchange ideas and express attitudes that reflect their individual characteristics and values.

Teacher candidates enter their teacher education programs bringing with them a wide range of personal characteristics based on their prior understanding and experiences that will manifest themselves in their pedagogical practices. Teacher educators are responsible for transforming the teaching candidate into a professional teacher who understands the importance and power of affective education and the role it plays in every aspect of the classroom. From previous research related to affective education, the three chapters presented in part I of this text provide insights to guide and support teacher preparation.

First in part I is chapter 2, written by Maria McKenna who offers a comprehensive look at dispositions and the accompanying responsibilities for teacher education faculty and their teacher candidates. McKenna proposes that teacher educators and teacher candidates construct practitioners' codes to guide their development, assessment, and manifestation of dispositions.

Then in chapter 3, prepared by Nancy P. Gallavan, Terrell M. Peace, and Regina M. Ryel Thomason, the authors examine teacher candidates' perceptions of teachers' professional dispositions. From their investigation with teacher candidates, Gallavan, Peace, and Thomason share the dispositions that candidates value as the most important. Their findings reveal that candidates value a balance of dispositions that correspond with the four Pathwise Domains, but the dispositions that they value most are concerned with establishing the environment and facilitating instruction.

Finally, in chapter 4, Cheryl J. Rike and L. Kathryn Sharp share a tool developed and used at the University of Memphis for assessing preservice teachers' dispositions. This chapter provides guidance for teacher educators to create an instrument and administer it with teacher candidates based on research conducted with personnel in human resources with the Memphis School District. This partnership illustrates the importance of teaching, modeling, and reinforcing dispositions with teacher candidates to start their careers with success.

The three chapters in part I provide an overview of dispositions in concept and practice that will benefit teacher educators in higher education. Additionally, they benefit the many partners in schools, including classroom teachers, school administrators, and school personnel responsible for professional development, who serve as teacher educators in their work as mentor teachers to teacher candidates and novice teachers.

2

Dispositions: Responsibilities of Teacher Educators and Teacher Candidates

Maria McKenna

ABSTRACT

The National Council for Accreditation of Teacher Education mandate to assess teacher candidates' dispositions is currently the center of much debate in teacher education. However, little attention has been paid to the roles and responsibilities that might guide teacher educators and teacher candidates regarding dispositional assessments. This chapter asserts that teacher education professionals must act with teacher development as their central focus when examining dispositions, which may demand a shift in current dispositional assessment practices. To this end, this paper defines two practitioners' codes, one for teacher educators and one for teacher candidates, surrounding the roles and responsibilities each has related to the development and evaluation of dispositions.

DISPOSITIONS: UNDERSTANDINGS AND RESPONSIBILITIES OF FACULTY AND STUDENTS

The requirement by the National Council for Accreditation of Teacher Education (NCATE) in 2000 that teacher education programs assess teacher candidates' dispositions for accreditation purposes has been met with mixed reactions over the past eight years. Confusion over the meaning of the term dispositions, the debate over how and with what tools to measure teacher candidate dispositions, and, more recently, a shift to unpacking the philosophical underpinnings and intent of the mandate have kept a small group of authors heavily immersed in the specifics of implementation, measurement, and validity of dispositional assessments (see Burant, Chubbuck, & Whipp, 2007; Damon, 2005, 2007; Diez, 2007; Maylone, 2002; McKnight, 2004; Raths, 2001). Simultaneously, teacher education programs have been busy trying to make sense of the dispositions debate, making for tedious work as programs try to keep up with the frequently changing definition as dictated by NCATE, while at the same time also developing or acquiring the measurement tools as a program to fulfill that mandate (Lang & Wilkerson, 2007; NCATE, 2007a; Wasicsko, 2004; Wayda & Lund, 2005).

Initially, it appears, the call to assess dispositions led to a scramble by many teacher educators to fulfill the requirement without widespread or rigorous explorations of why or how to do so in the first place. Teacher educators were responding quickly to the new expectation, many of whom were under the pressure of reaccreditation. Checklists, scales, and rubrics of varying complexity were implemented in many teacher education programs, perhaps with some debate and disagreement on the particulars, but with the ultimate goal for many programs to have an assessment tool in place right away (Helm, 2006a, 2006b; Lang & Wilkerson, 2007; Wasicsko, 2004). This practical reaction of teacher education programs seems only natural and understandable given the high stakes accompanying the new mandate. Teacher educators in many schools and departments, already stretched thin with departmental obligations and duties, added dispositional assessments to their lists of tasks to complete without additional pay or time added to their days.

SHIFTING FOCUS

To NCATE's credit, since the introduction of this mandate in 2000, the organization has made clear that their rationale for assessing teacher candidates' dispositions was not just about accountability for teacher suitability or preparedness. NCATE has refined what they mean by the term disposition and encouraged institutions to reflect on how to operationalize their own individualized understandings (Benninga et al., 2008; NCATE, 2007b). Additionally, to this end, in 2007 the American Association of Colleges of Teacher Education (AACTE) convened the Task Force on Teacher Education as a Moral Community (TEAMC), which was charged with unpacking the disposition debate and working toward a common and clearer understanding of why and how dispositions play into teacher education. The charge given to TEAMC to clarify and relate dispositions to the NCATE accreditation framework seems to be a direct result of two phenomena: confusion emanating from teacher educators as they revisited their teacher education programs to address the mandate and a call from the field for a deeper examination of the rationale and meaning behind assessing dispositions (Levine, 2007).

Encouragingly, the present tide in teacher education accreditation appears to have turned away from simply fulfilling the mandate to assess dispositions to a thoughtful discourse in which more and more teacher educators are participating and contributing to the definition and role of dispositions in teacher education. Over the past two years, the increasing number of presentations, papers, forums, and discussion groups surrounding dispositions at the annual conferences of both the Association of Teacher Educators and AACTE is indicative of this shift. In actuality, over the past two years, the topic of teacher candidates' dispositions seems to have become a regular staple of teacher education discourse, as indicated by more than one national education publication. In fact, the *Journal of Teacher Education* (2007) and the *Journal of Educational Controversy* (2007) both recently published issues dedicated solely to dispositions. Moreover, this shift is seen with programs examining teacher competency, not just in terms of content area knowledge or pedagogical skill, but also with dispositions in mind.

MISSING VOICE

Despite all of the conversations, one notable voice missing from the debate on understanding the place of dispositional assessment in teacher education is the teacher candidates' perspectives. This oversight was recently noted at a presentation by two former teacher candidates at the 2008 AACTE Annual Conference in New Orleans, Louisiana (Lamberth & Opalinski, 2008). The former teacher candidates noted in their presentation that, while ultimately grateful for the focus on dispositions in their respective programs, there was little help provided for understanding what was acceptable and what was not acceptable in the learning processes for understanding and exploring teacher dispositions. Both presenters also highlighted the concern they and their fellow teacher candidates had as they went through their programs regarding how to reconcile the differences between the types of dispositions they believed were preferable in classrooms and the dispositions demonstrated by teachers, who were acting in ways sometimes antithetical to their understandings. Similarly, these former candidates both recalled finding themselves in practicum classroom situations where, at times, their reactions to the students with whom they were interacting were less than ideal. These dispositions discrepancies occurred despite the teacher candidates' cognitive understanding of dispositions. Additionally, little time or attention was given to processing those discrepancies (Lamberth & Opalinski, 2008). Moreover, these teacher candidates often had difficulty with the dispositions terminology, dispositions assessments, and the challenges that dispositions assessments can pose to their personal belief systems and practices. Lamberth and Opalinski's sharing of the difficulties they experienced reconciling the discrepancies between what they were learning about ideal teaching behaviors, actual practices, and their personal histories or experiences provides valuable information for teacher educators.

At the core of each teacher education program is the common goal of developing each teacher candidate into a capable classroom practitioner, and, while it is true that the professionals associated with each teacher education institution can have a wholly unique way of integrating, assessing, and reflecting upon teacher candidates' dispositions, some common parameters for implementing dispositions assessment could prove incredibly useful. To this end, a closer examination of teacher candidates' perspectives is warranted as a means to honor the learning process associated with the development of dispositions. Lamberth and Opalinski's (2008) personal accounts of the struggle that they endured as teacher candidates remind education faculty to focus on that core goal of teacher development.

ENHANCING THE INTEGRATION OF DISPOSITIONS IN TEACHER EDUCATION PROGRAMS

By design, when teacher candidates enter into their teacher education programs, the assumption is not that they already know the pedagogy or content needed to teach but that they learn and hone the pedagogy and content while advancing through their programs. Additionally, the opportunity to practice their new learning in practical situations is afforded teacher candidates. The same process must hold true for teacher candidates as they understand, develop, and refine dispositions. Teacher educators must develop a variety of ways to integrate dispositions into their programs, providing opportunities for teacher candidates' development and assessment of dispositions with reflection.

Practitioner codes are one way to enhance disposition integration into teacher education programs. These codes define the roles and responsibilities teacher educators and teacher candidates have related to the development and assessment of dispositions. By developing a teacher educator and teacher candidate code, the process of dispositional development and assessment is framed. For example, the teacher educators' code identifies roles and responsibilities related to assessment of candidates' dispositions. It also allows teacher educators the latitude to move beyond simply assessing dispositions to integrating dispositional awareness and growth into coursework and practicum reflections. Furthermore, the teacher candidates' code helps to make expectations clearer for candidates, specifically their obligations for understanding, reflecting, and acknowledging their own dispositions. Therefore, these practitioners' codes help ensure that teacher candidates are afforded opportunities for discussion, reflection, remediation, and growth of their dispositions, including how dispositions manifest themselves in actual classroom situations by teacher educators and classroom teachers. Finally, these codes solidify the important assertion made by NCATE that assessment of dispositions does not become a sorting exercise or exclusionary mechanism but an additional facet of teacher preparation worthy of the attention and time of teacher educators (NCATE, 2007b).

Taking recent published research on dispositions in teacher education into account (see Borko, Liston, & Whitcomb, 2007; Damon, 2007; Diez, 2007; Garmon, 2005; Mullin, 2003; Murray, 2007), potential practitioners' codes related to the development and assessment of teacher candidates' dispositions are presented here for consideration. However, the existing literature in this field does not go far enough in creating actionable ideas for both candidates and faculty related to the successful and complete integration of the dispositional assessment mandate into teacher education programs. By creating the practitioners' codes related to dispositions, it is the hope of the author that all teacher education programs consider adopting or creating and subsequently using similar codes as a step in the process of addressing dispositions in teacher education.

Teacher Educators' Code

The teacher educators' code relating to dispositions begins by noting core beliefs that need to be held in order for individual teacher candidates' dispositions to be respected and acknowledged. The code also ensures that there is not one singular form or measure of dispositions that all candidates must conform to in order to become a successful teacher. In addition, the code for teacher educators begins with the examination of core understandings of the ontological nature of dispositions and moves on to guidelines for practices relative to that understanding. Finally, the code for teacher educators acknowledges both the role of faculty members in the development of dispositions and, perhaps more importantly, reflection on that development.

As teacher educators dedicated to developing teacher candidates' dispositions that are conducive and effective for classroom teaching, teacher educators should:

1. Recognize that educating children is a moral endeavor, implying a belief in the right of all individuals to learn and participate in schooling.
2. Recall that dispositional assessments cannot wholly characterize any individual's entire disposition.
3. Note that teacher candidates come with individual stories; each story brings with it a diverse background and set of experiences that form the foundation for many individual's beliefs and actions.

4. Ensure that teacher candidates are introduced to the term and underlying meaning of teacher dispositions at an early point in their teacher education program.
5. Remember that dispositions, as exhibited by teacher candidates' behaviors in courses and practicum situations, are contextual.
6. Agree that dispositions of teacher candidates are evolving, dynamic, and must be measured by mentors, supervisors, and the candidates themselves with models and measurement tools that examine growth over time.
7. Assert that teacher candidates have a right and should be afforded time to reflect upon and question ideas, theories, assertions, and requirements of the teacher education program, including acquisition, application, appreciation, and assessment of dispositions.
8. Believe that teacher candidates need, and should be afforded, a variety of diverse experiences to use and contextualize dispositions.
9. Trust that most teacher candidates can grow in their beliefs and understandings of various dispositions.
10. Accept as true that teacher candidates have the right to leave a teacher education program as a result of a growing awareness of their unsuitability for the teaching profession based on what they learn about their dispositions, and teacher educators have the right to ask a candidate to leave.

Teacher Candidates' Code

Concurrently, in order for to fulfill the notion of dispositions as one of the three core aspects of teacher candidates' growth, teacher candidates should be asked to adopt or write a teacher candidate's code in relation to dispositions. Incorporating Lamberth and Opalinski's (2008) sentiments, a teacher candidate's code might include the following.

As a teacher candidate I recognize that:

1. My beliefs and values about individuals, groups, and/or educational ideas may be challenged in this teacher education program.
2. My dispositions, particularly related to education, are evolving.
3. My understanding of teacher dispositions and the ability to demonstrate that those dispositions influence my actions as a teacher are an integral part of my teacher preparation program.
4. My obligation related to the development of dispositions conducive to becoming a successful teacher also includes consistently reflecting on the theory, ideas, and dispositions that I am encouraged to develop.
5. My commitment to consistently working on applying teaching theory and understandings of my own dispositions to my teaching practice is essential to becoming a competent practitioner.

Practitioners' Code Development in Teacher Education Programs

As a practical measure, teacher educators should examine how to best develop the codes of conduct for their programs. Ideally, teacher educators should begin with a review of teacher candidates' dispositions development and assessment in their programs, and, together with teacher candidates, develop codes that are applicable to their unique instructional programs and processes. Teacher candidates' participation in the development of codes of conduct would assure that students are informed about the mandate to assess dispositions. Moreover, with candidate participation, the development of the codes would provide a built-in opportunity to explore the meaning of dispositions, dispositions unique to teacher education, and teacher candidates' own belief systems. In addition, these codes provide parameters for an area of teacher education that is arguably one of the most subjective in the field.

If as NCATE asserts that dispositions are as fundamental to teacher preparation as knowledge and skills, then they need to be addressed early and often in teacher education programs (NCATE, 2007b). The development of practitioners' codes provides an opportunity to begin disposition development. For example, the teacher candidates' code could be developed in a beginning level teacher education course. The ubiquitous, initial, personal philosophy of education paper that teacher candidates write early on in most programs could be postponed, instead having the candidates reflect on their personal dispositions and how those might change or need to be addressed within their educational career. Teacher candidates could then be asked to connect their code to their philosophy of education. Taken together, both the teacher educators' and teacher candidates' codes provide additional opportunities to explore and discuss the meanings of the term disposition in the unique context of teacher education. It is likely that this investigation may become even more fruitful and successful when teacher educators and teacher candidates create their own practitioner codes specific to their institutions and needs.

CONCLUSION

Together, both the teacher educators' and the teacher candidates' codes provide a frame for the process of dispositional development and assessment. They supply opportunities to explore and discuss the meaning of the term disposition in the context of teacher education. Creating these codes allows some assurances that the development and assessment of dispositions feature the development of teacher candidates, as opposed to the establishment of a screening mechanism or the construction of a factory model for creating teachers. Through participatory collaboration, teacher educators and teacher candidates can help lead the field of teacher education in a positive direction. As the desired knowledge, skills, and dispositions focus on reflective, human-centered practices of teaching, teacher candidates acquire insights that will benefit their work with PK–12 learners.

APPLICATION ACTIVITIES

Try the following activities to help you develop practitioners' codes.

For teacher educators:

1. With a colleague, review how teacher candidates' dispositions are developed and assessed in your program.
2. Draft a teacher educators' code that suits your program. Share it with other teacher educators for feedback.
3. Identify ways that teacher candidates' develop their own codes in the course of their program.

For teacher candidates:

1. With another teacher candidate, review and discuss the teacher candidates' dispositions proffered by your program. Identify which of these dispositions you possess.
2. Write your own teacher candidate code. Share it with another teacher candidate for feedback.

REFERENCES

Benninga, J., Diez, M., Dottin, E., Fieman-Nemser, S., Murrell, P., & Sockett, H. (2008, February). Making professional conduct in education more intelligent: Using knowledge and skills to enhance moral sensibilities (dispositions). Working paper presented at the annual meeting of the American Association of Colleges for Teacher Education, New Orleans, LA.

Borko, H., Liston, D., & Whitcomb, J. (2007). Apples and fishes: The debate over dispositions in teacher education. *Journal of Teacher Education, 58*(5), 359–364.

Borko, H., Liston, D., O'Dell, S., & Whitcomb, J. (Eds.). (2007). Developing dispositions: Professional ethic or political indoctrination? *Journal of Teacher Education, 58*(5).

Burant, T., Chubbuck, S., & Whipp, J. (2007). Reclaiming the moral in the dispositions debate. *Journal of Teacher Education*, *58*(5), 397–411.

Damon, W. (2005). *Forward: Personality test: the dispositional dispute in teacher preparation today, and what to do about it.* Thomas B. Fordham Foundation & Institute. (ERIC Document Reproduction Services No. ED489100).

Damon, W. (2007). Dispositions and teacher assessment: The need for a more rigorous definition. *Journal of Teacher Education, 58*(5), 365–369.

Diez, M. (2007). Looking back and moving forward: Three tensions in the teacher dispositions discourse. *Journal of Teacher Education, 58*(5), 388–396.

Garmon, M. A. (2005). Six key factors for changing pre-service teachers' attitudes/beliefs about diversity. *Educational Studies, 38*(3), 275–286.

Helm, C. (2006a). The assessment of teacher dispositions. *Clearing House: A Journal of Educational Strategies, Issues, and Ideas, 79*(6), 237–239.

Helm, C. (2006b). Teacher dispositions as predictors of good teaching. *Clearing House: A Journal of Educational Strategies, Issues, and Ideas, 79*(3), 117–118.

Kasprisin, L. (Ed.) (2007). *Journal of Educational Controversy, 2*(2).

Lamberth, K., & Opalinski, H. (2008, February). Innovations for teachers—how dispositions in teacher education affect our practice as classroom teachers. Roundtable presentation at the annual meeting of the American Association of Colleges for Teacher Education, New Orleans, LA.

Lang, W., & Wilkerson, J. (2007). *Assessing teacher dispositions.* Thousand Oaks, CA: Corwin Press.

Levine, A. (2007, March 2). Dispositions: An attempt to define teacher. *Teachers College Record Online.* Retrieved from www.tcrecord.org/Content.asp?ContentID=13708.

Maylone, N. (2002). *Identifying desirable pre-service teacher dispositions: An intractable problem?* (ERIC Document Reproduction Services No. ED463258).

McKnight, D. (2004). An inquiry of NCATE's move into virtue ethics by way of dispositions (Is this what Aristotle meant?). *Journal of the American Educational Studies Association, 35*(3), 212–230.

Mullin, D. (2003). *Developing a framework for the assessment of teacher candidate dispositions* (ERIC Document Reproduction Services No. ED479255).

Murray, F. (2007). Disposition a superfluous construct in teacher education. *Journal of Teacher Education, 58*(5), 381–387.

National Council for Accreditation of Teacher Education (NCATE). (2007a, October). Retrieved from www.ncate.org.

National Council for Accreditation of Teacher Education (NCATE). (2007b, December). *NCATE issues call for action; Defines professional dispositions as used in teacher education: NCATE News.* Retrieved from www.ncate.org/public/102407.asp?ch=148.

Raths, J. (2001). *Teachers' beliefs and teaching beliefs* (ERIC Document Reproduction Services No. ED452999).

Wasicsko, M. (2004). The 20-Minute hiring assessment: How to ensure you're hiring the best by gauging educator dispositions. *School Administrator, 61*(9), 40–42.

Wayda, V., & Lund, J. (2005). Assessing dispositions: An unresolved challenge in teacher education. *Journal of Physical Education, Recreation, and Dance, 76*(1), 34.

3

Examining Teacher Candidates' Perceptions of Teachers' Professional Dispositions

Nancy P. Gallavan, Terrell M. Peace, and Regina M. Ryel Thomason

ABSTRACT

Clear expectations frame teachers' content, pedagogical, and professional knowledge and skills; however, expectations framing teachers' professional dispositions, or affect, remain unclear. Research conducted with 224 candidates reveals that when rating 17 professional dispositions, candidates rate respectful, reliable, responsible, and honest as the four most important dispositions for teachers in general. However, candidates rank passionate, compassionate, fair, and flexible as the four most important dispositions for themselves individually. Analyses show that each list has one disposition that corresponds with each of four teaching goals aligned with the Pathwise Observation System. Asking candidates about dispositions demonstrates that candidates want to express voice, exact choice, and experience ownership or social agency in their own development, producing important implications for teacher educators and programs.

Throughout their teacher education programs, most teacher candidates are immersed in a variety of strategically designed university courses paired with a series of developmentally appropriate field experiences. Regardless of the institution's location, size, affiliation, and financial support, the program configurations and candidate expectations appear to be similar, especially at institutions accredited by the National Council for the Accreditation of Teacher Education (NCATE).

In general, teacher candidates are guided in fulfilling four overarching goals: (1) Planning the Curriculum and Community; (2) Monitoring the

Environment and Climate; (3) Facilitating the Instruction and Assessment; and (4) Reflecting on Outcomes and Practices (Danielson, 2007) to ensure effective learning, teaching, and schooling (Giovannelli, 2003). To accomplish these goals contributing to one's success and satisfaction, candidates must acquire content knowledge, pedagogical content knowledge and skills, professional content knowledge and skills, and, ultimately, professional teacher dispositions, or affect, necessary to help all students learn (NCATE, 2002).

LITERATURE REVIEW

Much research has been reported delineating content knowledge and pedagogical skills suitable to teaching in general, germane to teaching specific academic disciplines, and applicable to teaching particular groups and individual types of students (Gardner, 1993; Shulman, 1987; Vygotsky, 1986). Research not only informs and supports the development of a conceptual framework and curricular foundations for accredited teacher preparation programs and their courses, findings guide the assortment of standardized tests that institutions and states mandate for teacher candidates to pass prior to beginning their classroom internships and teaching careers as well as to maintain licensure.

Fewer guidelines have been published regarding teachers' professional dispositions. NCATE standards describe target dispositions as "classroom behaviors that create caring and supporting learning environments and encourage self-directed learning by all students" (NCATE, 2002, p. 58). NCATE standards also state that "teacher candidates will be able to recognize when their own professional dispositions may need to be adjusted and can develop plans to do so" (p. 58). More research is needed to identify teachers' professional dispositions (Balzano & Murray, 2003; Schussler, 2006), the roles that dispositions play in teacher education (Johnson & Reiman, 2007; Mullin, 2003), and how to assess dispositions (Harrison, Smithey, McAffee, & Weiner, 2006; Wayda & Lund, 2005).

Consequently, many professional education units have crafted lists of desired personality characteristics or individual dispositions that prospective teacher candidates must address when initially applying to their teacher education programs (Reising & Helm, 2006) and, subsequently, accepted candidates must demonstrate throughout their programs. To graduate, candidates are required to provide evidence of progress in their papers, projects, presentations, practica, and portfolios (Cudahy, Finnan, Jaruszewicz, & McCarty, 2002) with the most essential evidence of professionalism documented during the candidates' field experiences, that is, practica and internships (Hughes, 2007).

Acquiring, applying, and appreciating teachers' professional dispositions consume much time and effort in teacher education (Cudahy et al., 2002). However, teacher candidates rarely have been involved in identifying the desired professional dispositions, leaving them without voice, choice, and a sense of social agency or ownership in their own preparation standards and career expectations. Too often dispositions may seem like expectations that teacher education impose on the candidates.

Identifying teachers' professional dispositions raises three major concerns. Teacher educators and candidates tend to be (a) unsure as to what teachers' professional dispositions are (Damon, 2007), (b) unclear as to how important specific selected dispositions are to the teacher candidates themselves (Talbert-Johnson, 2006), and (c) uncertain as to how each of the specific selected dispositions relates to teaching efficacy (Yeh, 2006). Many units have constructed one list of candidates' knowledge that measures cognitive competence, a second list of candidates' skills that measures psychomotor proficiency, and a third list of candidates' dispositions related to affective acquisition that measures qualities of effective teachers (Stronge, 2002). The lists for cognitive competence, a.k.a., knowledge, and psychomotor proficiency, a.k.a., skills, tend to be well-defined and look much the same at all institutions; generally the lists are understood readily by teacher candidates and teacher educators. Evidence of understanding and application is produced easily.

However, the lists related to affective acquisition are less consistent among institutions, less clear to candidates and educators, and less easy for candidates to produce evidence to verify their understanding and application. Lists of affects or dispositions tend to be vague with few concrete descriptions as reinforced by findings reported by Walling and Fender (2007). In their research, Walling and Fender analyzed commonalities among institutions' lists of teachers' affect or dispositions. Their findings show that dispositions can be grouped into seven broad classifications: (a) communication, (b) diversity, (c) interpersonal skills, (d) lifelong learning, (e) personality traits, (f) professionalism, and (g) teaching skills. However, a unifying list of specific descriptors accompanying these broad classifications has not been adopted among teacher education institutions.

Currently more than 30 U.S. states (Strangis, Pringle, & Knopf, 2006) use the Pathwise Observation System (Danielson, 2007) to guide candidate preparation and teacher licensure. The Pathwise Observation System presents a protocol consisting of four domains that guide teacher candidates and teacher educators through the entire process through the goals of (1) preparation, (2) environment, (3) instruction, and (4) professionalism (see appendix 3A). Each of the four domains encompasses criteria for which teacher candidates must provide evidence of mastery during their course work, from their field experiences, and in their individual growth and development. The structure of the Pathwise Observation System emphasizes target knowledge and skills yet only implies desired dispositions.

RESEARCH QUESTIONS

Since identification of teacher's professional dispositions tends to differ among institutions, many professional educational units continue to update and revise their lists of teachers' dispositions. The lists tend to be authored almost exclusively by teacher educators and imposed onto the teacher candidates void of their voice, choice, or ownership, also known as social agency (Bandura, 1989). Without teacher candidates' participation in the identification process, candidates may be less likely to understand the meaning of dispositions, the purposes for acquiring them, and the benefits of applying them throughout their teaching. Based on this foundation, research was formulated to explore two questions with teacher candidates.

Question 1: What teachers' professional dispositions do you value (Carroll, 2005) for all teachers in general?

Question 2: As a future teacher, how important is each disposition to you individually and holistically (Korthagen, 2004) especially when compared and contrasted with other dispositions?

METHODOLOGY

Design

To address the two research questions, a written survey was administered as a nonexperimental research design (Babbie, 1995) to collect data from teacher candidates.

Participants

Participants included 224 teacher candidates enrolled in 5 different types of teacher education programs. For this research, a teacher candidate is a college or university student enrolled in a teacher education program. The participants included

(a) Twenty-nine teacher candidates enrolled in a new nontraditional undergraduate teacher education program located at a large state-supported community college operating in partnership with a large state-supported research-based university;
(b) Sixty-nine teacher candidates enrolled in an established traditional four-year undergraduate program located at a medium-sized state-supported teaching university;

(c) Forty-seven teacher candidates enrolled in an established traditional four-year undergraduate program located at a small private faith-based teaching university;
(d) Twenty-seven teacher candidates enrolled in a new nontraditional graduate teacher education program focused on one cohort of teachers at a charter school located at a large state-supported community college working in partnership with a large state-supported research-based university; and
(e) Fifty-two teacher candidates enrolled in a new nontraditional graduate teacher education program located at a medium-sized state-supported teaching university.

Teacher candidates were located at three different types of institutions to provide data from diverse age groups, personal backgrounds, and geographic locations. The candidates for this research were selected as they were enrolled in one of the required curriculum courses in each institution's teacher education program.

Data Sources

Survey Instrument

A review of the literature on teachers' professional dispositions (Balzano & Murray, 2003; Johnson & Reiman, 2007; Reising & Helm, 2006) and the websites for university teacher education programs, that is, Boise State University, Northern Illinois University, University of Kentucky, among others, revealed similar lists of desired teachers' professional dispositions. The researchers grouped similar dispositions into four major categories aligned with the Pathwise domains (Danielson, 2007; Educational Testing Service, 2002; Ryan & Alcock, 2002): (1) planning curriculum and community, (2) monitoring the environment and climate, (3) facilitating instruction and assessment, and (4) reflecting on outcomes and practices. Reliability of survey was ascertained by conducting a pilot study of the survey with teacher candidates (N=49) enrolled in the introductory courses one semester prior to the data collection to determine consistency in reporting data and ease with completing the protocol.

From each of the four categories, four dispositions were identified by the researchers as relevant descriptors resulting in 16 dispositions (see table 3.1). Researchers determined that the disposition of *professional* could have been included with each category, so the word professional was added to the overall list totaling 17 teachers' professional dispositions.

Survey Tasks

The 17 dispositions were arranged in alphabetical order on a survey designed for candidates to complete two tasks (see appendix 3B). The first

Table 3.1 Four Categories of Teachers' Professional Dispositions Aligned with Four Domains of Pathwise; Dispositions Selected by Researchers

Category 1, Domain A: Planning Curriculum and Community
1. committed to planning
2. flexible
3. reliable
4. willing to collaborate

Category 2, Domain B: Monitoring Environment and Climate
1. compassionate
2. friendly
3. responsible
4. sensitive

Category 3, Domain C: Facilitating Instruction and Assessment
1. inclusive
2. passionate
3. purposeful
4. respectful

Category 4, Domain D: Reflecting on Outcomes and Practices
1. decisive
2. fair
3. honest
4. reflective

Plus the disposition:
professional

Note: Professional dispositions are listed in alphabetical order in each category.

task asked candidates to rate each disposition as "extremely important," "somewhat important," or "not important." The candidates' responses provided data related to the first research question, probing the values that candidates place on various dispositions about teachers in general. Candidates also were invited, but not required, to report and rate three additional perceived teachers' professional dispositions giving candidates an opportunity to express voice (Wasicsko, 2002).

The second task asked candidates to reexamine the list of 17 dispositions and to rank them from 1 to 17, with 1 being "the most important," and 17 being "the least important." This task provided data related to the second research question, seeking clarity of importance to the candidates themselves as individuals. Ranking the dispositions required candidates to prioritize the dispositions, even if they had rated all or most of the dispositions as extremely important, and gave the candidates an opportunity to exact choice.

At the end of the survey, candidates provided identifying information related to four demographic items that included the candidate's gender, age group, progress in the teacher education program, and the type of program in which the candidate is enrolled. These data helped the researchers to analyze the data and report the findings connecting teachers' professional dispositions with both their chronological maturation and career plans.

Follow-up Research

Once the researchers determined that the disposition professional fit into all four of their categories, the researchers needed to collect additional descriptive data from the candidates, again giving candidates voice and ownership in the process. To achieve this goal, two participating groups totaling 99 of the teacher candidates in this study were given a note card and asked to define the disposition *professional* in one word or phrase.

Procedures

Survey Instrument

The survey was administered to each of the five groups of teacher candidates during the first month of the semester prior to initiation of any course instruction or in-class activities concentrating specifically on teachers' professional dispositions. The intent was to collect data not influenced by the course content or the course instructor. The survey required about 10 minutes for teacher candidates to complete.

Follow-up research

Due to the predominance of the disposition professional, additional research collecting descriptions of professional was conducted two weeks following the administration of the initial survey. This data collection required about five minutes for teacher candidates to complete by writing a descriptive word or phrase on a note card.

Data Analysis

Separate spreadsheets were constructed to record the candidates' ratings, rankings, additional dispositions, and demographics. Frequency counts and percentages were calculated for each set of collected data.

RESULTS AND DISCUSSION

Survey Instrument Data

A total of 227 surveys were administered with a 99 percent response rate; only 3 of the 227 surveys were unusable due to the candidates not completing the survey according to the directions. Since survey data were collected during class time, teacher candidates were available, compliant, and interested in the topic.

Four pieces of demographic data were collected describing the candidates: gender, age group, desired teaching level, and year in program (see table 3.2). Approximately two-thirds or 68 percent of the candidates were female and approximately one-third or 32 percent were male. Approximately two-thirds or 67 percent of the candidates were in the youngest age group (18–22); 17 percent were in the next age group (23–29). Only 6 percent were in the 30–39 age group, 7 percent were in the 40–49 age group, and 3 percent were in the 50 and older age group. The distributions of genders and age groups were anticipated.

Distribution of candidates within their teacher education programs was divided into fourths: 26 percent early to mid-program; 26 percent next to last year; 11 percent last year; 11 percent fifth year; 26 percent nontraditional programs. This distribution also was expected and desired to add depth and richness to the data.

The demographic data revealed that 45 percent of the candidates plan to teach pre-K to 4th grade, 18 percent plan to teach 5th to 8th grade, 31 percent plan to teach 9th to 12th grade, and 6 percent plan to teach a subject that covers pre-K to 12th grade. These data resemble the data that describe candidates enrolled in each of the five programs at the three institutions involved in this research.

In part 1 of the survey, candidates rated each of the items as "extremely important," "somewhat important," or "not important." Data in table 3.3 report the ratings of the dispositions in alphabetic order as printed on the survey (see table 3.3).

Table 3.2 Teacher Candidate Demographics

Gender	female		male							
	n	%	n	%						
	152	68%	72	32%						
Age Group	18–22		23–29		30–39		40–49		50–59+	
	n	%	n	%	n	%	n	%	n	%
	151	67%	38	17%	13	6%	15	7%	7	3%
Year in Program	early to mid		next to last year		last year		fifth year		nontraditional	
	n	%	n	%	n	%	n	%	n	%
	58	26%	58	26%	25	11%	25	11%	58	26%
Desired Teaching Level			preK–4		5–8		9–12		preK–12	
			n	%	n	%	n	%	n	%
			100	45%	40	18%	69	31%	13	6%

Table 3.3 Candidates' Ratings of Teachers' Professional Dispositions

	Extremely Important		Somewhat Important		Not Important	
Disposition	Teacher Candidates (N=224)					
	n	%	n	%	n	%
1. committed to planning	157	70%	60	27%	7	3%
2. compassionate	181	81%	38	17%	2	1%
3. decisive	125	56%	97	43%	2	1%
4. fair	75	78%	47	21%	2	1%
5. flexible	177	79%	45	20%	2	1%
6. friendly	157	70%	65	29%	2	1%
7. honest	206	92%	18	8%	0	0%
8. inclusive	130	58%	91	40%	5	2%
9. passionate	184	82%	41	18%	2	1%
10. professional	179	80%	43	19%	2	1%
11. purposeful	159	71%	63	28%	2	1%
12. reflective	100	45%	117	52%	7	3%
13. reliable	211	94%	13	6%	0	0%
14. respectful	213	95%	9	4%	2	1%
15. responsible	208	93%	16	7%	0	0%
16. sensitive	110	49%	105	47%	9	4%
17. willing to collaborate	143	65%	79	35%	2	1%

Included in part 1 of the survey was the request for teacher candidates to contribute as many as three additional teachers' professional dispositions. A total of 15 different dispositions were added across 69 surveys. Table 3.4 shows the 15 dispositions listed in order of frequency reported. These data capture the voices of the teacher candidates, allowing them to share their perceptions of desired dispositions and giving them ownership or social agency through participation in the identification process.

In part 2 of the survey, candidates ranked the 17 dispositions listed on the survey. Data in table 3.5 show the dispositions with the percentages of candidates ranking each item according to its degree of importance ranked 1 and aggregated by combining reported rankings of 1, 2, 3, 4, and 5 (see table 3.5).

Follow-up Research

During data gathering and class conversations, teacher candidates repeatedly questioned and discussed the meaning of the disposition professional. To help craft a practical meaning for teacher candidates, additional research was conducted asking two groups of the candidates involved in the research (N=99) to describe the disposition of professional in writing as shown in table 3.6. These data also illustrate the need to provide candidates agency and to give them voice.

Table 3.4 Candidates' Additional Teachers' Professional Dispositions

Dispositions (N=69)	Optional entries from Teacher Candidates	
	n	%
1. content knowledge	10	15%
2. organization	9	13%
3. enthusiasm	8	12%
4. communication	7	10%
5. role modeling	6	7%
6. availability	5	7%
7. care	4	6%
8. understanding	4	6%
9. approachability	3	4%
10. helpfulness	3	4%
11. thinking before speaking or acting	3	4%
12. engaging in class activities and discussions	2	2%
13. relevance	2	2%
14. cultural literacy	2	2%
15. intuition	1	1%

Table 3.5 Candidates' Rankings as Most Important Teachers' Professional Dispositions

Dispositions	Teacher Candidates (N=224)		
	Ranked 1		Combined Rankings (1, 2, 3, 4, 5)
	n	%	n
1. committed to planning	11	5%	84
2. compassionate	22	10%	91
3. decisive	3	1%	31
4. fair	18	8%	97
5. flexible	11	5%	91
6. friendly	11	5%	71
7. honest	13	6%	84
8. inclusive	2	1%	23
9. passionate	61	27%	104
10. professional	34	15%	116
11. purposeful	5	2%	39
12. reflective	0	0%	20
13. reliable	9	4%	87
14. respectful	10	4%	100
15. responsible	9	4%	97
16. sensitive	3	1%	17
17. willing to collaborate	3	1%	23

Findings

Analyses show that each of the four dispositions rated as "extremely important" by most of the candidates correspond to each of the four categories, each of which aligns with the four Pathwise domains shown in table 3.7.

Table 3.6 Candidates' Descriptions of the Disposition "Professional"

Dispositions	Follow-up Teacher Candidates (N=224)	
	n	%
1. integrity	19	8%
2. in-depth content knowledge	18	8%
3. communication skills	15	6%
4. enthusiasm and satisfaction	14	6%
5. genuine care for students and families	14	6%
6. organization	14	6%
7. preparation for classroom	12	6%
8. contemporary knowledge and attitude	10	4%
9. creativity and innovation	9	4%
10. listening skills	9	4%
11. reasonable expectations	8	4%
12. resourcefulness	8	4%
13. self-confidence	8	4%
14. self-starting	8	4%
15. appropriate dress	6	3%
16. appropriate humor	6	3%
17. boundaries	5	2%
18. confidentiality	5	2%
19. patience	5	2%
20. manners and kindness	4	2%
21. role modeling	4	2%
22. tact and diplomacy	4	2%
23. intuition	3	1%
24. openness to new ideas and changes	3	1%
25. participation in school governance/programs	3	1%
26. standard English	3	1%
27. preparation for meetings	2	1%
28. punctuality	2	1%
29. sense of equity and social justice	2	1%
30. understanding systems and protocol	1	1%

Table 3.7 Candidates' Highest Ratings of Teachers' Professional Dispositions Corresponding with Categories* Teacher Candidates (N=224)

Dispositions	Category	n	%
1. respectful	C3	213	95%
2. reliable	C1	211	94%
3. responsible	C2	208	93%
4. honest	C4	206	92%

*Categories: C1 = Planning the Curriculum and Community, C2 = Monitoring the Environment and Climate, C3 = Facilitating Instruction and Assessment, C4 = Reflecting on Outcomes and Practices

Table 3.8 Candidates' Highest Rankings of Teachers' Professional Dispositions Corresponding with Categories* Teacher Candidates (N=224)

Disposition	Category	n	%
1. passionate	C3	61	27%
2. compassionate	C2	22	10%
3. fair	C4	18	8%
4. flexible	C1	11	5%

*Categories: C1 = Planning the Curriculum and Community, C2 = Monitoring the Environment and Climate, C3 = Facilitating Instruction and Assessment, C4 = Reflecting on Outcomes and Practices

Table 3.9 Candidates' Highest-Ranking (Combined Rankings 1, 2, 3, 4, and 5) Dispositions Corresponding with Categories* Teacher Candidates (N=224)

Disposition	Category	n
1. passionate	C3	104
2. respectful	C3	100
3. responsible	C2	97
4. compassionate	C2	91

*Categories: C1 = Planning the Curriculum and Community, C2 = Monitoring the Environment and Climate, C3 = Facilitating Instruction and Assessment, C4 = Reflecting on Outcomes and Practices

Further analyses show that each of the four dispositions ranked as "extremely important" by most candidates also corresponds to one of the four categories as shown in table 3.8. Data in tables 3.7 and 3.8 confirm that candidates' perceptions of teachers' professional dispositions are balanced across all four categories and across all four Pathwise domains.

However, when combining the top five rankings of the dispositions, the teacher candidates prioritized the dispositions as connecting with categories 2 and 3 only, indicating the candidates' immediate concerns concentrate on their interactions within the classroom shown in table 3.9. These data show that candidates are more aware and focused on categories 2, Facilitating Instruction and Assessment, and 3, Monitoring the Environment and Climate, rather than categories 1, Planning the Curriculum and Community, and 4, Reflecting on Outcomes and Practices. Candidate awareness and insight may be limited due to their years of education and experience.

The lowest ratings and the lowest combined rankings of the dispositions corresponding to different categories are shown in tables 3.10 and 3.11. Data in these tables demonstrate that candidates need additional opportunities to advance their knowledge and skills related to collaborating, teaching all learners, being sensitive, and reflecting. These data correspond to the categories 1, Planning Curriculum and Community, and 4, Reflecting on Outcomes and Practices, rather than categories 2, Facilitating Instruction and Assessment, and 3, Monitoring Environment and Climate, as the data revealed in table 3.9.

Analyses of the candidates' descriptions of the disposition professional shown in table 3.12 reveal that each response corresponds with one of the four categories, each of which aligns to one of the four Pathwise domains. These data demonstrate that candidates identify professionalism as a balance of the four categories.

Data in tables 3.7 through 3.12 show that, in general, teacher candidates value professional dispositions that correspond to all four categories. Yet,

Table 3.10 Candidates' Lowest-Rated Dispositions Corresponding with Categories* Teacher Candidates (N=224)

Disposition	Category	n	%
14. inclusive	C3	130	58%
15. willing to collaborate	C1	126	56%
16. reflective	C4	110	49%
17. sensitive	C2	100	45%

*Categories: C1 = Planning the Curriculum and Community, C2= Monitoring the Environment and Climate, C3= Facilitating Instruction and Assessment, C4= Reflecting on Outcomes and Practices

Table 3.11 Candidates' Lowest-Ranked Dispositions (Combined Rankings 1, 2, 3, 4, 5) Corresponding with Categories* Teacher Candidates (N=224)

Disposition	Category	n
14. inclusive	C3	25
15. willing to collaborate	C1	23
16. reflective	C4	20
17. sensitive	C2	17

*Categories: C1 = Planning the Curriculum and Community, C2 = Monitoring the Environment and Climate, C3 = Facilitating Instruction and Assessment, C4 = Reflecting on Outcomes and Practices

Table 3.12 Candidates' Highest-Ranked Descriptors of Dispositions Corresponding with Categories* Follow-up Teacher Candidates (N=52)

Disposition	Category	n	%
1. content knowledge	C3	10	15%
2. organization	C2	9	13%
3. enthusiasm	C1	8	12%
4. communication	C4	7	10%

*Categories: C1 = Planning the Curriculum and Community, C2 = Monitoring the Environment and Climate, C3 = Facilitating Instruction and Assessment, C4 = Reflecting on Outcomes and Practices

teacher candidates appear to be more knowledgeable of and attentive to dispositions connected with categories 2 and 3 illustrating their concentration on managing the classroom and teaching lesson plans. Candidates would benefit from additional course work, field experience, and practical application of categories 1 and 4 to become better-prepared professionals.

When analyzing the data, two additional discoveries became evident. First, responses from the teacher candidates enrolled in the beginning or middle parts of their teacher education programs tend to report lower ratings and rankings for the dispositions of willing to collaborate, sensitive, inclusive, and reflective. These results indicate that during the early and middle parts of their programs, candidates may not have been introduced to these dispositions, or the candidates do not fully understand or appreciate the holistic nature associated with being an effective teacher. Teacher educators should focus on developing these four specific dispositions through course content, field experiences, and practical application.

Second, responses from teacher candidates identifying themselves as nontraditional tend to rate most dispositions as extremely important and consistently ranked the four lowest-rated and ranked dispositions of willing to collaborate, sensitive, inclusive, and reflective much higher than candidates identifying themselves as traditional. These results indicate that teacher candidates who have earned university degrees and bring working experience to their studies more likely know, understand, and appreciate these four dispositions as relevant and meaningful to effective learning, teaching, and schooling.

SUMMARY

The findings from this research indicate that teacher candidates highly value a wide range of professional dispositions that will benefit them as they prepare for their teaching careers (Ryan & Alcock, 2002). The four dispositions rated most important show that candidates voice well-balanced outlooks that they possess about teaching in general. And the four dispositions that candidates ranked most important exact their well-balanced choices as individuals.

Likewise, the findings assist teacher educators as they design programs, develop courses, and designate field experiences for teacher candidates to better understand and refine their professional dispositions (Ritchhart & Perkins, 2000). By participating in conversations and opportunities to choose desired dispositions, candidates develop ownership, or social agency in their future careers. These findings, in turn, fortify school partnerships with classroom teachers and school administrators who mentor candidates into their new teaching careers (Hughes, 2007) by reporting the dispositions that teacher candidates need additional opportunities to acquire, apply, and appreciate.

IMPLICATIONS FOR TEACHER EDUCATORS

During the last two decades, teacher educators have focused on compliance with the standards set by the National Council for Accreditation of Teacher Education, evident, in part, by their teacher candidates' knowledge, skills, and dispositions. Many units have concentrated on seven types of teacher knowledge (Shulman, 1987), adopting frameworks that develop teachers as reflective decision-makers (Schön, 1987). Identifying required knowledge and skills have dominated development of teacher education programs and research in teacher education (NCATE, 2002).

More recently, an increased focus has shifted onto teachers' professional dispositions, primarily identifying the desired dispositions, and, more essentially, dispositions that are important to the candidates themselves. These two questions framed the research and findings, particularly in consideration of works of Palmer (1998) who advocates connecting the personal with the professional and pedagogical foundations, the research of Diez (2006) examining the climate and assessment related to dispositions, and the Resolution on Affective Education written by the Association of Teacher Educators (ATE) Commission on Affective Education (2006) framing teacher education.

The ATE Resolution on Affective Education (2006) emphasizes that affect encompasses knowledge, skills, and dispositions that should be aligned with national and state standards. Teachers' dispositions are evident at all levels of schooling and throughout society. Teachers' dispositions are reflective of the whole person as evident in the cognitive, psychomotor, and affective domains of learning and expression. And, teachers' dispositions play powerful roles in all formal and informal learning environments evident in the curriculum, instruction, and assessment.

Today's teacher candidates benefit greatly from information, guidance, and support related to becoming a teacher by developing their dispositions or affect in addition to the requisite content knowledge and pedagogical skills. With 30 states using the Pathwise Observation System, the findings of this research provide teacher educators with evidence that candidates benefit by participating in conversations related to dispositions. Candidates want a voice in identifying appropriate professional dispositions as teachers in general, a choice in selecting the professional dispositions that are most important to them individually, and an opportunity to participate in developing social agency or ownership in the self-identification of one's professional dispositions. When candidates are invited into the process, their understanding, application, and commitment to teachers' professional dispositions will become more important and evident, benefiting their students and themselves.

Moving forward in the 21st century and interacting with today's new teachers, the children of the millennium, teacher educators at both accredited universities and partnership schools must be aware of their candidates holistically. Candidates acquire affect through their memories of past teachers, their interactions with the methods instructors, and the modeling by classroom mentors (Gallavan, Putney, & Brantley, 2002). Drawing upon the generational perpetuation of practice (Gallavan, 2007) and the apprenticeship of observation (Lortie, 1975), candidates become effective professionals.

More research investigating teachers' professional dispositions is needed, particularly to research perceptions of school partners, including classroom teachers, school administrators, faculty developers, and curriculum specialists. School partners provide the mentoring, induction support, and professional development that both establish and sustain teachers' dispositions throughout their careers.

APPLICATION ACTIVITIES

1. List four dispositions that all teachers should understand, value, and exhibit. Give a rationale for each of your four dispositions.
2. Compare and contrast your list with lists generated by your colleagues, that is, teacher candidates, practicing teachers, school administrators, teacher educators, and so forth.
3. Connect the dispositions with the four categories of the Pathwise domains (see appendix 3A). Verify that your list promotes well-balanced teacher candidate preparation.
4. Identify the professional dispositions that you have acquired; identify the professional dispositions that you want to develop.
5. Discuss the nature and value of teachers' professional dispositions with a colleague, noting the strengths and weaknesses of prescribing an established list of teachers' dispositions for all teacher candidates to acquire and exhibit.

APPENDIX 3A: PATHWISE OBSERVATION SYSTEM PROTOCOL

Domain A: Planning and Preparation

A1. Demonstrates knowledge of students (age group, diversity, interests, heritage)

A2. Selects instructional goals appropriate for lesson and students

A3. Demonstrates knowledge of content by designing instruction that connects past, present, and future content
A4. Demonstrates knowledge of pedagogy by planning appropriate instructional methods and learning activities, using appropriate materials and resources
A5. Assesses student learning by planning assessments appropriate for students and aligned with learning goals

Domain B: Classroom Environment

B1. Creates an environment that promotes fairness
B2. Creates an environment of respect and rapport
B3. Communicates challenging learning expectations
B4. Establishes and maintains consistent standards of behavior
B5. Organizes physical space for maximum learning and safety

Domain C: Instruction

C1. Communicates learning goals and instructional procedures
C2. Makes content comprehensible to students (coherent structure, makes material relevant to students)
C3. Extends students thinking
C4. Monitors learning, provides feedback, and adjusts learning activities to meet the needs of all students
C5. Uses instructional time effectively
C6. Communicates clearly and accurately (in speaking and writing), encourages effective communication
C7. Integrates technology into instruction
C8. Impacts student learning as evidenced by formative and/or summative assessments

Domain D: Professional Responsibilities

D1. Reflects on teaching
D2. Demonstrates a sense of efficacy (assumes responsibility for student learning)
D3. Builds professional relationships
D4. Communicates with families and communities
D5. Maintains accurate records
D6. Grows and develops professionally (service, memberships, use of research)
D7. Professional demeanor (adheres to school policies, dresses and behaves in a professional manner)

Source: Adapted with permission from Danielson, 2007.

APPENDIX 3B: SURVEY ON TEACHERS' PROFESSIONAL DISPOSITIONS THAT TEACHER CANDIDATES' WANT FOR THEMSELVES

Today's teachers are expected to have specific knowledge, skills, and dispositions to be effective. Your entire teacher education program has been designed to equip you with a range of content, practices, and experiences to prepare you and to enhance your success in any classroom.

In this study, we are looking specifically at teachers' professional dispositions. We think of dispositions as personality characteristics related to your outlook and spirit. Although you may hear teacher educators and classroom mentors talk about desired dispositions in today's teachers, we want to know what dispositions you think are important dispositions to be an effective teacher.

This survey has three parts and should take you less than 10 minutes to complete.

In part I, we want you to rate each of the given dispositions as being "extremely important," "somewhat important," or "not important." We also invite you to add at least three dispositions and to rate them as being "extremely important," "somewhat important," or "not important."

In part II, we want you to review the entire list of dispositions and rank them from 1 to 17, with 1 being the most important and 17 being the least important. No two dispositions should be given equal ranking.

In part III, we want you to tell us a little bit about yourself. Please circle one response for each of the four items. Then return this survey to the individual who is administering it. Your responses will not be shared with your course professors, field supervisors, or classroom teachers/mentors.

Thank you in advance for sharing your thoughts about the professional dispositions you want in yourself to be an effective teacher. We greatly appreciate your time and responses!

Part I. Rate each disposition you want for yourself to be an effective teacher by marking only one of the three boxes to the right of the disposition. Please add three of your own dispositions in lines 18 to 20 below and rate them the same way as you rated dispositions 1 to 17.

Part II. Return to the survey and rank each disposition as the dispositions you want for yourself by writing the numbers 1 through 17 in the box in the far right column. 1 = the most important, 2 = the second most important, and so forth with 17 = the least important.

Dispositions	Part I.			Part II.
Effective teachers must show that they understand and value how to be:	RATE each item by marking an X in the one appropriate column.			RANK 1–17, 1 = the most important
	Extremely important	Somewhat important	Not important	
1. Committed to planning				
2. Compassionate				
3. Decisive				
4. Fair				
5. Flexible				
6. Friendly				
7. Honest				
8. Inclusive				
9. Passionate				
10. Professional				
11. Purposeful				
12. Reflective				
13. Reliable				
14. Respectful				
15. Responsible				
16. Sensitive				
17. Willing to collaborate				
Additional dispositions Effective teachers must show that they understand and value how to be:	RATE each item by marking an X in the one appropriate column.			
	Extremely important	Somewhat important	Not important	
18.				
19.				
20.				

Part III. Tell us a little about you. Circle one response for each item and answer 4:

1. What is your gender?
   male
   female
2. What is your age group?
   18–22
   23–29
   30–39
   40–49
   50–59+

3. What is your year in this college program?
   early to mid-program
   next to last year
   last year
   fifth year
   nontraditional

4. What is your desired teaching level (and subject)?
   preK–4
   5–8
   9–12
   preK–12
   Subject area(s):

REFERENCES

Association of Teacher Educators Commission on Affective Education. (2006). *Affective education position statement.* Retrieved from www.ate1.org/pubs/Affective _Educatio.cfm.

Babbie, E. R. (1995). *The practice of social research* (7th ed.). Belmont, CA: Wadsworth.

Balzano, B. A., & Murray, C. E. (2003). Do you know them when you see them? Teacher candidate dispositions. Paper presented at the Annual Meeting of the American Association of Colleges for Teacher Education, New Orleans, LA.

Bandura, A. (1989). Human agency in social cognitive theory. *American Psychologist, 44,* 1175–1184.

Carroll, D. (2005). Developing dispositions for teaching: Teacher education programs as moral communities of practice. *The New Educator, 1*(2), 81–100.

Cudahy, D., Finnan, C., Jaruszewicz, C., & McCarty, B. (2002). Seeing dispositions: Translating our shared values into observable behavior. Paper presented at the First Annual Symposium on Educator Dispositions, Richmond, KY.

Damon, W. (2007). Dispositions and teacher assessment: The need for a more rigorous definition. *Journal of Teacher Education, 58*(5), 365–369.

Danielson, C. (2007). *Enhancing professional practice: A framework for teaching* (2nd ed.). Alexandria, VA: Association for Supervision and Curriculum Development.

Diez, M. E. (2006). Assessing dispositions: Climate and questions. *The New Educator, 2*(1), 57–72.

Educational Testing Service. (2002). *Pathwise classroom observation system: Orientation guide.* Princeton, NJ: author.

Gallavan, N. P. (2007). Seven perceptions that influence novice teachers' efficacy and cultural competence. *Praxis: The Center for Multicultural Education, 2*(1), 1–22.

Gallavan, N. P., Putney, L. G., & Brantley, D. K. (2002). The influences of modeling: Elementary school preservice teachers rate their levels of competence and confidence for teaching social studies. *Social Studies and the Young Learner, 14*(3), 28–30.

Gardner, H. (1993). *Frames of mind* (Rev. ed.). New York: Basic Books.

Giovannelli, M. (2003). Relationship between reflective dispositions toward teaching and effective teaching. *Journal of Educational Research, 96*(5), 293–309.

Harrison, J., Smithey, G., McAffee, H., & Weiner, C. (2006). Assessing candidate disposition for admission into teacher education: Can just anyone teach? *Action in Teacher Education, 27*(4), 72–80.

Hughes, M. (2007). Revising a mentor teacher program: One division's journey. Paper presented at the annual meeting of the Association of Teacher Educators, San Diego, CA.

Johnson, L. E., & Reiman, A. J. (2007). Beginning teacher disposition: Examining the moral/ethical domain. *Teaching and Teacher Education, 23*(5), 676–687.

Korthagen, F. A. J. (2004). In search of the essence of a good teacher: Toward a more holistic approach in teacher education. *Teaching and Teacher Education, 20*(1), 77–97.

Lortie, E. (1975). *Schoolteacher: A sociological study*. London: University of Chicago Press.

Mullin, D. (2003). *Developing a framework for the assessment of teacher candidate dispositions*. East Lansing, MI: National Center for Research on Teacher Learning (ERIC Document Reproduction Service No. ED479255).

National Council for Accreditation of Teacher Education. (2002). *Professional standards for the accreditation of schools, colleges, and departments of education*. Washington, DC: author.

Palmer, P. (1998). *The courage to teach: Exploring the inner landscape of a teacher's life*. San Francisco: Jossey-Bass.

Reising, B., & Helm, C. M. (2006, July/August). What's new in the assessment of teacher dispositions. *The Clearing House, 79*(6), 237–239.

Ritchhart, R., & Perkins, D. N. (2000). Life in the mindful classroom: Nurturing the disposition of mindfulness. *Journal of Social Issues, 56*(1), 27–47.

Ryan, P. M., & Alcock, M. A. (2002, Spring). Personal and interpersonal attributes in selecting teachers. *Action in Teacher Education, 24*(1), 58–67.

Schön, D. A. (1987). Educating the reflective practitioner. Paper presented at the annual meeting of the American Educational Research Association, Washington, DC.

Schussler, D. L. (2006). Defining dispositions: Wading through murky waters. *The Teacher Educator, 41*(4), 251–268.

Shulman, L. (1987). Knowledge and teaching: Foundations of the new reform. *Harvard Educational Review, 57*(1), 1–22.

Strangis, D. E., Pringle, R. M., & Knopf, H. T. (2006). Road map or roadblock? Science lesson planning and preservice teachers. *Action in Teacher Education, 28*(1), 73–84.

Stronge, J. H. (2002). *Qualities of effective teachers*. Alexandria, VA: Association for Supervision and Curriculum Development.

Talbert-Johnson, C. (2006). Preparing highly qualified teacher candidates for urban schools: The importance of dispositions. *Education and Urban Society, 39*(1), 147–160.

Vygotsky, L. (1986). *Thought and language*. Cambridge, MA: MIT Press.

Walling, B., & Fender, V. (2007). An analysis of defined disposition and assessment instruments from NCATE accredited institutions. Paper presented at the annual meeting of the Association of Teacher Educators, San Diego, CA.

Wasicsko, M. M. (2002). *Assessing educator dispositions: A perceptual psychological approach*. Retrieved from Eastern Kentucky University, Department of Education website www.education.eku.edu/Dean/DispositionsManual.pdf.

Wayda, V., & Lund, J. (2005). Assessing dispositions: An unresolved challenge in teacher education. *Journal of Physical Education, Recreation, and Dance, 76*(1), 34–41.

Yeh, Y. (2006). The interactive effects of personal traits and guided practices on preservice teachers' changes in personal teaching efficacy. *British Journal of Educational Technology, 37*(4), 513–526.

4

Developing and Assessing Teacher Candidates' Dispositions: A Beneficial Process for All

Cheryl J. Rike and L. Kathryn Sharp

ABSTRACT

Professional accreditation standards state that teacher candidates should be assessed on the knowledge, skills, and dispositions needed for them to become effective and reflective practitioners. This chapter describes the development and use of the Early Childhood Behavior and Disposition Checklist by the Early Childhood Program's faculty at the University of Memphis. The checklist provides information and a process for dispositions development in teacher candidates, while supporting and enhancing their self-assessment and reflective processes. Additionally, the checklist is used to help candidates envision themselves as effective professionals. The chapter also discusses the benefits for teacher candidates, the Early Childhood Program faculty, and the education profession that accrue from emphasis on disposition development and assessment. Application activities are included also.

Historically, teacher education has centered on preservice teachers, now known as teacher candidates, learning pedagogical knowledge and developing instructional skills designed to maximize PK–12th grade student achievement. One reason for this emphasis is that teachers with appropriate dispositions appear to more effectively motivate student learning (Evans, 2002). Other emphases stem from standards set by accreditation boards and professional organizations. The National Council for Accreditation of Teacher Education (NCATE), the Interstate New Teachers Assessment and Support Consortium (INTASC), and the Association of Childhood

Educators International have provided the primary emphasis on forming and assessing teacher candidates' dispositions in teacher education. In the area of Early Childhood Education, the National Association for the Education of Young Children (NAEYC) has developed standards specifically for teacher candidates planning to work with younger children. This emphasis, in turn, has resulted in Early Childhood college faculty around the country more carefully examining all aspects of their programs. The purpose of this chapter is to describe a disposition assessment plan developed by the Early Childhood Program at the University of Memphis that is working, beginning with a review of the current literature on dispositions.

LITERATURE REVIEW

Even though each of the organizations listed previously provides in-depth descriptions of desired behaviors based on acquired dispositions, one of the common problems encountered by college faculty and teacher candidates alike is that dispositions are rather elusive and hard to define—much less evaluate. For example, NCATE (2001) defines dispositions as:

> the values, commitments, and professional ethics that influence behaviors toward students, families, colleagues, and communities and affect student learning, motivation, and development as well as the educator's own professional growth. Dispositions are guided by beliefs and attitudes related to values such as caring, fairness, honesty, responsibility, and social justice. For example, they might include a belief that all students can learn, a vision of high and challenging standards, or a commitment to a safe and supportive learning environment (p. 53).

Assessing the qualities described by this definition is quite difficult because many dispositions can only be observed through behaviors and the choices that are made. It is difficult to evaluate beliefs, attitudes, and values; however, behaviors are obvious and can be monitored consistently. Furthermore, there are issues such as designing an assessment tool that works for the system as well as the individuals in the system. Since rating these qualities is highly subjective, consistency among raters is often a problem (Richardson & Onwuegbuzie, 2004).

Numerous researchers have attempted to more specifically define dispositions. Earlier studies attempted to identify the traits commonly held by effective teachers. Wong and Wong (1998) identified being lifelong learners and having high expectations for students as primary dispositions for effective teachers. Wenzlaff (1998) concurred regarding being lifelong learners and added being caring to the list. In 2000, Taylor and Wasicsko's research resulted in the following descriptors of appropriate teacher dispositions:

being democratic, enthusiastic, caring, flexible, creative, confident, and having high expectations for students. Thompson (2000) found sensitivity and understanding to be equally important. Wagner's (2001) findings added the descriptors of being thoughtful and responsible to the list.

Research by Evans (2002) found that appropriate dispositions enable teachers to initiate student learning. The dispositions identified by Evans included the following personality traits, attitudes, values, and beliefs: being caring, being creative, appearing confident, displaying a positive attitude, being approachable, responding, demonstrating reflectivity, and having high expectations for students. Evans and Nicholoson (2003) added the dispositions of being honest and trustworthy to this list.

In 2001, NCATE identified the following criteria as expected dispositions of teachers: being fair, caring, honest or trustworthy, and responsible. The National Board for Professional Teaching Standards (2002), in an independent study, identified those same dispositions and added the following as other descriptors: being thoughtful, curious, understanding, tolerant, lifelong learners, reflective, and having high expectations for students. Ryan and Alcock's (2002) study found being empathetic, responsible, and reflective are positive indicators of appropriate dispositions for teachers. Other researchers (Knobloch, 2002; Nowak-Fabrykowski & Caldwell, 2002) supported previous research, finding that being caring and having high expectations for students were extremely important characteristics.

In 2003, researchers confirmed some previously identified descriptors for effective dispositions for teachers and added some new ones. Suarez (2003) added empathy, sensitivity, and understanding. Major and Brock (2003) agreed with empathy and added having a positive attitude, while Evans and Nicolson (2003) stressed being thoughtful, cooperative, and responsible. Worley's (2003) findings agreed with the importance of being responsible, and Giovannelli (2003) confirmed the importance of being reflective and holding high expectations for students. More recent research by Erickson, Hyndman, and Wirtz, (2005) once again found factors such as the following personality traits, attitudes, values, and beliefs as important: being enthusiastic, caring, and lifelong learners. Wayda and Lund (2005) confirmed the importance of being thoughtful, honest or trustworthy, and responsible.

Lilian Katz (1993), when speaking on children's dispositions, described them as being "habits of the mind or tendencies to respond to certain situations in certain ways" (p. 2). She added that instruction and drill are not beneficial methods of teaching dispositions; dispositions must be modeled. Along with that modeling, learners must have opportunities to demonstrate the behaviors commensurate with specific dispositions. If one considers Katz's position in more global terms as developing learners' dispositions rather than just children's attitudes, one could say that college instructors are attempting to help teacher candidates develop specific, professional "habits of the mind" as well as tendencies "to respond to certain situations" in appropriate ways (Katz, p. 2). Therefore, following this logic clearly indicates that college instructors, particularly teacher educators, must model appropriate dispositions when teaching to and communicating with teacher candidates as well as providing them with opportunities to exhibit those dispositions in professional settings during practicum experiences.

The majority of researchers studying teacher dispositions agree that the best teachers are not only competent in their subject matter, but they also exhibit favorable dispositions. Many individuals, both in and outside of education, commonly attribute dispositions as a primary qualification of successful educators (Abernathy, 2002; Erickson, Hyndman, & Wirtz, 2005; Major & Brock, 2003; Taylor & Wasicsko, 2000; Wayda & Lund, 2005; Wenzlaff, 1998). The work of both Abernathy and Major and Brock suggest that teachers' beliefs and dispositions are essential in order for teachers to successfully improve educational outcomes for all students. According to Abernathy, an extremely important factor which may critically impact potential student achievement is the development of dispositions. Suarez (2003) concurred, stating that teachers' attitudes can have a positive or a negative effect on student learning.

To help prepare teacher candidates for successful careers, teacher education programs should strive to prepare effective teachers who can facilitate learning for all students and exhibit positive dispositions (Evans, 2002; Ginsberg & Whaley, 2003; Jackson, 2004; Major & Brock, 2003; Ryan & Alcock, 2002; Suarez, 2003; Taylor & Wasicsko, 2000). Educators recognize that student growth and achievement is largely dependent on the effectiveness of the teacher; it is also known that teacher effectiveness is greatly influenced by teacher dispositions (Burden & Byrd, 2007). While enrolled in teacher education programs, teacher candidates should be made aware of the expectations regarding dispositions (Wayda & Lund, 2005; Wenzlaff, 1998) as well as the means used to assess dispositions (Wayda & Lund, 2005). Awareness provides an opportunity for making necessary changes in one's professionalism in order to become a more effective educator. The research findings of Ryan and Alcock (2002) and Wayda and Lund (2005) predict that requiring an ongoing assessment of personal/interpersonal attributes for program retention will have a positive impact on teachers and the teaching profession, which will lead to improving the education of children.

While demonstrating appropriate dispositions is an important qualification for teachers, dispositions are difficult to assess (Erickson et al., 2005; Ginsberg & Whaley, 2003; Taylor & Wasicsko, 2000). Teacher educators are challenged in identifying consistent means to assess teacher candidates' dispositions (Ginsberg & Whaley, 2003; Taylor & Wasicsko, 2000; Wayda & Lund, 2005). Additionally, expecting consistent standards for assessment emphasizes the importance of incorporating dispositions as a part of the curriculum (Wayda & Lund, 2005). For some teacher educators, these dynamics have lead to the conclusion that teacher education programs should not only define specific dispositions, but they should also delineate those behaviors which exemplify the dispositions valued in order to have both consistent standards and the means for evaluating them.

In conclusion, a review of literature clearly demonstrates the important role that dispositions play in making education and educators more effective. There is a relationship between teacher effectiveness and teacher dispositions (Taylor & Wasicsko, 2000). Appropriate dispositions enable teachers to initiate student learning (Evans, 2002) and are essential for teachers to successfully improve educational outcomes for all students (Abernathy, 2002; Major & Brock, 2003). Even though it is a challenge to identify consistent norms by which to assess teacher candidates' dispositions (Ginsberg & Whaley, 2003; Taylor & Wasicsko, 2000; Wayda & Lund, 2005), having consistent standards for assessment emphasizes the importance of dispositions as a part of the curriculum (Wayda & Lund, 2005).

DEVELOPMENT OF THE EARLY CHILDHOOD BEHAVIOR AND DISPOSITION CHECKLIST

A review of the literature, research, reflection, and discussion of behaviors and dispositions displayed by teacher candidates led to the development of the Early Childhood Behavior and Disposition Checklist by the Early Childhood Program's faculty at the University of Memphis. This section of the chapter describes the development of the checklist, the pilot study of the checklist, and the implementation of the checklist in the Early Childhood Program.

Checklist Development

Naturally, the first priority for development of the checklist was to define a definition of the term disposition. It was determined the definition from NCATE (2001) would form the primary basis for the definition. In addition to forming that definition, Katz's (1993) beliefs regarding developing "habits of the mind" (p. 2) and appropriate reactions contributed to the faculty's construction of an overall definition. The resulting working definition of dispositions is the values, beliefs, and attitudes common to highly qualified educators as demonstrated by professional behaviors and ethical, reflective choices.

The faculty decided that, due to the many descriptions of appropriate dispositions as well as a plethora of research connecting appropriate dispositions with teacher effectiveness, another area of research would aid the development of this rating tool. This consideration led the faculty to a source of information that is often ignored: the people who hire teacher candidates and work with them for years. Therefore, a research project was designed to ask the group who employs the majority of the Early Childhood Program graduates, Memphis City School (MCS) Elementary Principals, about the dispositions and behaviors that are most valued in teachers.

The development of the Early Childhood Behavior and Dispositions Checklist occurred in four phases. During the first phase, the Early Childhood Program faculty considered behaviors and dispositions that are common to successful teachers as well as teacher candidates. Even though this area of professional development consists of a list of obvious behaviors that are easily assessed, such as taking class attendance, arriving at class on time, staying for the duration of the class, turning off cell phones, and so forth, these behaviors often present problems for many teacher candidates. The resulting section of the checklist was entitled "Classroom Behaviors."

Another area that candidates sometimes do not take seriously addresses their behaviors and commitment to their practicum assignments. The checklist section entitled "Practicum Behaviors," was designed to encourage candidates to plan and accomplish their practicum experiences in a professional manner, thus enabling them to reap the highest benefits from their experiences. A final consideration for these two sections of the checklist was that the faculty wanted candidates to develop two specific habits of professionals: responsibility and accountability. The faculty firmly believed those two habits form the basis of effective teaching.

In the second phase of checklist development, the faculty developed a list of dispositions that are less obvious and more difficult to assess. This section of the checklist was named "General Dispositions." The items selected for this list were based on the research literature, reflections, observations, and professional expertise of the Early Childhood Program's faculty. In addition, during this phase of development, the first author collaborated with the director of Early Childhood Education for MCS to identify general dispositions. The director was chosen to participate in this endeavor because of her commitment to improving early childhood education in MCS, a large urban district. The director provided insight regarding the system's needs, suggested adding some specific dispositions, helped distribute a survey of the elementary principals, and compiled the survey results. With the addition of the director's suggestions, the survey list of general dispositions totaled nine.

All 152 MCS elementary school principals were asked to rate the nine general dispositions of teachers that they felt were most important to being an effective teacher. Fifty-four elementary principals responded, yielding a survey response rate of 36 percent. Data analysis consisted of simple frequency counts. Since three of the dispositions tied for ranking, the final

Table 4.1 Responses from Survey of School Principals

1. Adjusts or revises lesson plans to meet student needs and/or changing circumstances
2. Has passion for teaching as a profession and demonstrates enthusiasm for working with children
3. Is committed to insuring that all students have the opportunity to achieve to the best of their potential
4. Demonstrates accountability for student learning and development
5. Treats all students fairly and equally while respecting individual differences and experiences
6. Works professionally with peers, parents, colleagues, and community agencies
7. Appreciates and values human diversity, showing respect for and sensitivity to individual students' varied perspectives, talents, and cultures, and adapts instruction/interactions accordingly
8. Realizes that learning is an ongoing process by committing to reflection, assessment, and self-assessment
9. Demonstrates commitment to the development of the whole child: cognitively, socially, emotionally, physically, and aesthetically
10. Persists in helping all children in becoming successful, life-long learners
11. Recognizes the value of intrinsic motivation to helping students develop the attitudes necessary for becoming life-long learners
12. Demonstrates integrity and honesty; meets ethical expectations

Source: Rike, C., & Sharp, L. K. (2008). Assessing pre-service teachers' dispositions: A critical dimension of professional preparation. *Childhood Education, Infancy through Early Adolescence, 84*(3), 150–153. Reprinted by permission of C. J. Rike and L. K. Sharp and the Association for Childhood Education International, 17904 Georgia Avenue, Suite 215, Olney, MD 20832. Copyright © 2008 by the Association.

general dispositions list consisted of 12 dispositions which are now part of the Early Childhood Behavior and Dispositions Checklist.

Checklist Pilot

During the 2005–2006 academic year, the Early Childhood Education Behavior and Disposition Checklist was piloted. Faculty members felt no need for training in using the assessment tool because they had been closely involved in the production of the instrument and knew the criteria. Also, faculty felt the behaviors and dispositions were straightforward and clearly apparent.

In the fall of 2005, all teacher candidates were given copies of the checklist accompanied by an in-depth explanation of how the checklist would be used. In an effort to provide consistency, one particular faculty member, the early childhood coordinator, explained the checklist to the students in every early childhood class. Specific behaviors that appropriately demonstrate dispositions were described, and the professional basis for acquiring the behaviors and dispositions were emphasized. Teacher candidates were encouraged to ask questions for clarification. They were made aware that all faculty members would be assessing dispositions and that everyone held the same expectations of all candidates. The coordinator further explained the procedures for using the checklist. Since the coordinator addressed every class, candidates were exposed to the criteria for the checklist several different times.

The final phase of the checklist development occurred at the end of the fall semester when the Early Childhood Program's faculty gathered to analyze the use of the checklist to compare and contrast the assessments. All faculty agreed that the checklist was clear and, although somewhat time consuming, certainly worth the effort involved. However, one faculty member discussed concerns regarding candidates using inappropriate communication skills both orally and in written work. Communication is particularly significant in early childhood education because the classroom teacher serves as a major language model for young children as they are learning language patterns and usage. Therefore, all faculty members agreed that a section entitled "Communication Skills" should be added to the checklist. This addition was made to the checklist, and it was again piloted in spring of 2006. No more modifications were deemed necessary, and the early childhood education faculty began to formally use the rating scale in the fall of 2006. Thus, the final form of the Early Childhood Education Behavior and Disposition Checklist is comprised of four parts: Class Behaviors, Practicum Behaviors, Communication Skills, and General Dispositions.

IMPLEMENTATION OF THE EARLY CHILDHOOD BEHAVIOR AND DISPOSITION CHECKLIST

For NCATE assessment purposes, all teacher candidates are rated at three separate times, in three different courses, taught by three different instructors in an effort to guard against rater bias. One assessment occurs in a course at the beginning of teacher candidates' professional preparation; another occurs in a course in the middle of their coursework; and the final assessment occurs during the last course that candidates complete prior to their internships. In addition to the three prescribed assessments, the checklist can also be used at any time there is a perceived problem with a teacher candidate that needs to be formally addressed. A complete copy of the Early Childhood Education Behavior and Disposition Checklist (Rike & Sharp, 2008b) can be found at the following website, coe.memphis.edu/icl/EarlyChildhoodFinalDisposition.htm.

Every effort is made among the faculty to consistently inform teacher candidates about teacher dispositions and behaviors. Therefore, at the beginning of each semester, one early childhood education faculty member (either the current or previous program coordinator) visits all early childhood classes and discusses dispositions, appropriate behaviors that demonstrate those dispositions, the checklist and its uses, and the procedures that will be followed. During the presentation, candidates receive copies of the checklist to use as a reference guide. Most candidates hear this "Disposition Presentation" several times each semester and many times during their teacher preparation experience. Teacher candidates are informed about the classes in which they will be assessed formally and are told that they can be assessed at any time if there is an indication of a problem with their behaviors. This process clearly defines the expectations for candidates and sets a positive tone for upcoming semesters.

Since all teacher candidates are informed individually and are provided copies of the checklist, they are well aware of the expectations held for them both at the university and in the schools. Most teacher candidates have found the checklist to be a welcome stepping-stone toward preparing for their future professional roles. Teacher candidates who are striving for excellence use the checklist as a tool to guide their reflection and improvement. Teacher candidates who are not quite as serious about their development and choose not to demonstrate expected behaviors and dispositions, soon learn there are standards that must be achieved. To insure consistency and fairness for all candidates, a procedure for using the checklist to modify inappropriate behaviors/dispositions has been developed (Rike & Sharp, 2008a).

Step 1: After the instructor has spoken with a candidate regarding a specific issue and no change has been noted, the instructor completes the checklist and discusses the specific problem with the candidate. The candidate provides a plan for changing the behavior(s) along with a timeline.

Step 2: The candidate either does or does not modify the behavior. If the candidate changes the behavior, there is no need for further intervention.

Step 3: If the candidate does not change the behavior, another checklist is completed and the candidate meets with the instructor and the early childhood coordinator. The discussion that takes place is direct and results in a renewed, instructor-designed plan for remediation accompanied by a reasonable timeline.

Step 4: After the previous steps have been followed, if there is still no obvious remediation, a recommendation is made by the early childhood coordinator to the director of the Teacher Education Program (TEP) that the candidate be dismissed from the Teacher Education Program (Rike & Sharp, p. 152).

At this point, the director follows the specific procedures designed by the College of Education for teacher candidate dismissal from TEP. Candidates may appeal the dismissal decision if they so choose. It is interesting to note that, to date, there have been only two candidates who have advanced to the dismissal level. In both cases, all appeals failed and the candidates were dismissed from TEP. One of the candidates appealed the decision to the president of the University of Memphis level, yet the dismissal remained. The failure of these appeals is due to exact documentation provided. In each instance, the faculty could state the exact times and dates candidates were informed of the expectations and procedures that were to be followed. Documentation also described efforts made to help candidates remedy the situation, remediation plans that were developed, results of conferences, and the results of those efforts. In the appeal process, careful documentation is a powerful tool.

BENEFITS OF DISPOSITION DEVELOPMENT AND ASSESSMENT

Early Childhood Program faculty at the University of Memphis have found the effects of consistently developing and assessing students' dispositions to be beneficial to the teacher candidates, the teacher education faculty, the teacher education program, and the teaching profession. This section of the chapter presents the benefits accrued.

Benefits for Teacher Candidates

Since the "Disposition Presentation" is repeated in every class each semester, information about behaviors and dispositions is delivered to all candidates multiple times throughout the teacher education program. Therefore, as teacher candidates begin their programs, they are made aware of the expectations held for them. Candidates are encouraged to self-assess and to determine their strengths and weaknesses repeatedly. As candidates progress through their programs, they constantly reflect on their own professional growth. They are supported in their endeavors with specific information and feedback from the Checklist. This process enormously benefits teacher candidates by helping them recognize growth and change over time. Since beginning use of the checklist, the Early Childhood Program's faculty has found it is possible to cultivate candidates' positive dispositions while decreasing the influence of more negative ones, as candidates continue on their journeys of becoming effective practitioners (Rike & Sharp, 2008a).

The following examples of the application of the checklist further illuminate its positive benefits. One candidate with high grades and an acceptable level of performance in the university classroom often twirled her hair while smacking chewing gum. This issue could be considered of no concern by some instructors; however, when viewed in light of how it would be perceived by both cooperating teachers in field placements and, even more importantly, by clinical observations and perspective employers during interviews, this behavior became an issue that needed to be addressed. Furthermore, this behavior served as an extremely negative model for the PK–12th grade students with whom the candidate was working. The behavior was pointed out to the candidate on the Checklist during a meeting held with the instructor. The candidate immediately began to change these unsightly, unconscious habits. Later, the candidate expressed gratitude for being alerted to the problem and helping her to alter her unprofessional mannerisms. She also indicated that through reflection she realized that her unconscious behaviors would have been a source of distraction for students and, therefore, negatively influence their learning. She further stated that these behaviors might be misinterpreted by administrators and parents. The feedback from this teacher candidate supported Evans's (2002) and Ryan and Alcock's (2002) emphasis on the reflective process.

Another teacher candidate was counseled for a lack of professional behavior regarding efforts to take responsibility for scheduling field experiences. She had scheduled her practicum hours during recess and lunch, thereby wasting a great amount of her practicum time. During her dispositions meeting, the candidate cried and indicated that she was embarrassed by what she had done. Since she had not chosen to actively work with children, additional field hours were added to her practicum. She returned to her field placement, which she had rescheduled at a time that allowed her to constantly work with children. Furthermore, she demonstrated higher quality work, displayed an interest in using her time wisely, and accepted feedback from the classroom teacher. This candidate was highly successful during the semester following the practicum incident and expressed that she was grateful for the specific feedback. She stated, "I needed this to work harder. It was hard to hear, but I needed to do better. I want to be a good teacher."

Another teacher candidate who had a similar experience in scheduling her practicum later said, "I just never realized how serious this whole thing was until I got this form. Then I really began to think about my career and what kind of teacher I wanted to become." Following the feedback, she became an outstanding intern and, subsequently, a successful practicing teacher. Later, in these two candidates' professional portfolios, both of them described in detail the reflection process that resulted from their disposition conferences. Further, the candidates related this process to their professional growth. Echoing Katz (1993), the candidates stated that reflection had become an unconscious habit. They also indicated in their self-assessments that they were becoming effective decision-makers (INTASC, 1992).

In addition to these specific examples, faculty have found that teacher candidates' attitudes, in general, have become more positive, and that candidates are more confident of their abilities to become effective teachers. These benefits are particularly evident when teacher candidates begin their internships. At the University of Memphis, a seminar class is held in conjunction with the internship. Fortunately, the same instructor has conducted the seminar for several years and has noted improvement in the confidence levels of interns during the internship, the ultimate test of their knowledge, skills, and dispositions. Prior to the emphasis on developing behaviors and dispositions, the internship seminar was often consumed by interns discussing feeling overwhelmed because they were working so hard. Much time was filled with teacher candidates complaining about their own students and their students' behaviors, and, ultimately, questioning their abilities to teach. Now, the general consensus is "I'm prepared. I can do this!" Candidates, through self-assessments and reflective statements, attribute their confidence to growth in teaching expertise and an understanding of the importance in developing professional dispositions (Burden & Byrd, 2007; Rike & Sharp, 2007; Taylor & Wasicsko, 2000).

During the piloting of the checklist and after beginning its use, the faculty asked interns to express their opinions regarding the work associated with dispositions during their classes and fieldwork. Interns overwhelmingly found the experiences to be positive, and many interns stated that they felt better prepared for their careers in teaching due to their attention to behaviors and dispositions (Rike & Sharp, 2007). For example, one intern wrote, "Being aware of my teaching dispositions has enabled me to focus more on the dispositions that need to be improved. It has also made me aware of not only the teacher I have become, but also the kind of person I have become in general. I am more aware of the type of person and teacher I would like to be." Another intern echoed these thoughts and specifically addressed the usefulness of the checklist. "Having the disposition sheet helped me to be more aware of what I need to accomplish and achieve in my professional experience. I was able to see areas that needed to be improved as well as what I have already achieved."

Benefits for the Early Childhood Program's Faculty

Creation of the Early Childhood Education Disposition and Behavior Checklist required the Early Childhood Program's faculty to seriously consider the types of teacher candidates being produced. The examination of factors affecting professionalism as well as those specific to working with young children resulted in the teacher education faculty reflecting on their own dispositions; faculty became more focused on developing reflective teacher candidates with appropriate behaviors. The process provided a growth opportunity for faculty which led to improved teaching and guidance for the teacher candidates and the continued development of the program. Furthermore, the process led to faculty becoming intensely aware of the importance of role modeling and the need to clearly demonstrate the dispositions that should be developed in teacher candidates.

The emphasis on developing appropriate dispositions has resulted in significant changes in curricula, course requirements, and expectations for teaching behaviors from the Early Childhood Program's faculty. For example, rather than delivering content revolving solely around knowledge and skills, professors are often leading discussions on making ethical choices. Indeed, the NAEYC's Code of Ethical Conduct (2005) is examined in depth, and candidates are given opportunities to discuss scenarios, or case studies, in which various choices are possible. Assignments for reflective papers have been revamped to require teacher candidates to examine their behaviors and dispositions in addition to their knowledge and skills. The result is the creation of a plan for professional growth stemming from their reflections. Instructors are becoming more specific and open when discussing their own beliefs and choices with candidates as they model the reflective process. In this way, faculty are not only modeling appropriate dispositions but also making sure that candidates recognize and understand that, even faculty and candidates who have years of experience in education still must be reflective, make ethical decisions, and examine their own biases and behaviors on a continuous basis. Much more emphasis has been placed on all aspects of professionalism.

The Early Childhood Program's reputation in the educational community in Memphis is becoming more prestigious. One factor attributed to the improvement is the consistent work being done with behaviors and dispositions. Practicing teachers welcome candidates into their classrooms for practicum experiences as well as internships. Placing candidates in schools each semester for field experiences necessitates communicating expectations with classroom teachers and school administrators. Since the program began conducting the disposition presentations and completing the checklist, fewer complaints about candidates have been received from teachers and administrators. Mentor teachers provide more positive feedback about their candidates' performance in their field experiences with statements about how professional the candidates are, how receptive candidates are to feedback, and that candidates are consistently prepared. Thus, addressing behaviors and dispositions with teacher candidates has truly strengthened the prestige of the teacher education program within the community.

Another benefit of the process for developing and assessing dispositions has been the added prestige of the Early Childhood Program within the department and college at the university. The program also has been strengthened by the faculty's obvious commitment to developing teacher candidates who demonstrate the knowledge, skills, and dispositions that lead to professional effectiveness. The Early Childhood Program has become well known for its development of professional educators. Other departments, as well as the Teacher Education Program, have applauded the faculty's abilities to help candidates who do not demonstrate appropriate behaviors and dispositions in making other career choices. Furthermore, the Early Childhood Behavior and Dispositions Checklist and implementation process has been used as a model for other areas in the department as they develop their own assessments tools and procedures.

The Early Childhood Program's faculty firmly believes the work on establishing the checklist has improved and strengthened the program at the University of Memphis. The program is stronger because the faculty is better able to help candidates evaluate and develop their own knowledge, skills, behaviors, and dispositions. One of the program's goals is to help candidates envision themselves as professionals. In order to accomplish this task, candidates must learn to assess themselves realistically as they develop their "habits of the mind" (Katz, 1993, p. 2). This ability allows candidates to eventually recognize how they have grown professionally and prepares them for a successful career. This recognition becomes quite evident when one reads a reflective comment made by an intern during the final semester. "I am thankful that I was held to the same set of professional standards that will be expected from me in the teaching field." Furthermore, this comment demonstrates how faculty are closing the gap, or the "disconnect" between the university classroom setting and the candidate's own future classroom.

Benefits to the Education Profession

Clearly describing and assessing dispositions has provided candidates with a concept of the type of professional they are expected to become. While early identification of problematic dispositions or behaviors is important, the candidates' abilities accompanied by their desire to engage in reflective practices and act on feedback are crucial to their continued professional growth. An overwhelming majority of teacher candidates will become quite successful; however, at the other end of the spectrum, faculty will find candidates who should not teach.

In these rare cases, the Early Childhood Behaviors and Dispositions Checklist provides solid documentation for the counseling process. Such was the case for a candidate who was dismissed from the program for multiple reasons. This candidate was often late or absent from class and the practicum experiences. The candidate did not follow guidelines regarding lesson planning or implementation, did not appropriately work with children, lied to the instructor, made up experiences describing working effectively with children when the candidate actually had not attended a single day of the practicum, and, in general, showed a lack of professionalism in all behaviors. Further, when counseled using the checklist, the candidate was unwilling to accept responsibility or ownership of the problems, which indicated an even greater problem. "Accepts responsibility for one's actions" is more than just a standard; it constitutes a major component in the process of becoming a professional educator. Obviously, the candidate did not value or care about becoming an effective teacher. By using the checklist in the prescribed manner, the Early Childhood Program faculty provided clear documentation that culminated in the dismissal of the candidate from the program. The documentation also provided concrete evidence of efforts made on the part of faculty to help the candidate remedy problems, while highlighting the teacher candidate's lack of commitment and professionalism throughout the entire appeal process. In essence, the checklist furnished the documentation needed to effectively allow the faculty to perform their duty as gatekeepers for the early childhood profession. Furthermore, the checklist provided evidence necessary for keeping someone who is ineffective and not committed to teaching from being able to negatively influence the lives of countless children.

CONCLUSION

When evaluating and attempting to shape human behaviors and dispositions, there is no exact model. It is unreasonable to search for a tool to completely assess all aspects of teaching. However, it is quite possible to create a relatively simple form of documentation that provides a standard for teacher candidates' performances as they work through their licensure programs. By naming the desired behaviors and dispositions and creating an objective form of documentation of their demonstration, teacher candidates can receive the guidance and support they will need to be successful as they enter the profession. This process has provided a road map for future educators as they, like all learners, are evaluated holistically with specific, tailored feedback and a plan of action for improvement in needed areas.

APPLICATION ACTIVITIES

Here are several activities that will help teacher educators develop and assess dispositions related to the profession.

1. Encourage teacher candidates to conduct a self-assessment using the Early Childhood Behavior and Disposition Checklist.
2. Consider using the completed checklist as a piece of evidence for the teacher candidate's professional portfolio.
3. Conduct a self-assessment using the Early Childhood Behavior and Disposition Checklist as a teacher educator.

4. Design a similar checklist relevant to your program as a framework or source for class conversations, journal topics, or reflective writing exercises.
5. Use the checklist designed in the previous activity as a source of documentation of teacher candidates' ongoing professional development and growth over time. This documentation can continue during internship and further into their teaching careers.

REFERENCES

Abernathy, T. V. (2002). Using a storybook prompt to uncover in-service and preservice teachers' dispositions toward struggling students. *The Teacher Educator, 38*(2), 78–98.

Burden, P. R., & Byrd, D. M. (2007). *Methods for effective teaching: Promoting K–12 student understanding* (4th ed.). Boston: Allyn and Bacon.

Erickson, P., Hyndman, J., & Wirtz, P. (2005). Why is the study of dispositions a necessary component of an effective teacher educator preparation program? *Essays in Education, 13*. Retrieved from www.usca.edu/essays/vol13spring2005.html.

Evans, J., & Nicholson, K. (2003). Building a community of learners: Manhattan College Elementary Education Program. *Teacher Education Quarterly, 30*(1), 137–150.

Evans, J. F. (2002). Effective teachers: An investigation from the perspectives of elementary school students. *Action in Teacher Education, 24*(3), 51–62.

Ginsberg, R., & Whaley, D. (2003). Admission and retention policies in teacher preparation programs: Legal and practical issues. *The Teacher Educator, 38*(3), 169–189.

Giovannelli, M. (2003). Relationship between reflective disposition toward teaching and effective teaching. *Journal of Educational Research, 96*(5), 293–309.

Interstate New Teacher Assessment and Support Consortium (INTASC). (1992). *Model standards for beginning teacher licensing, assessment and development: A resource for state dialogue*. Washington, DC: Council of Chief State School Officers.

Jackson, D. H. (2004). Nurturing future educators. *The Delta Kappa Gamma Bulletin, 70*(2), 15–17.

Katz, L. G. (1993). *Dispositions: Definitions and implications for early childhood practice*. Champaign, IL (ERIC Document Reproduction Service No. ED360104).

Knobloch, N. A. (2002). What is a qualified, competent and caring teacher? *The Agricultural Education Magazine, 75*(2), 22–30.

Major, E. M., & Brock, C. H. (2003). Fostering positive dispositions toward diversity: Dialogical explorations of a moral dilemma. *Teacher Education Quarterly, 30*(4), 7–26.

National Association for the Education of Young Children. (2005). *Code of ethical conduct and statement of commitment*. Retrieved from www.naeyc.org/about/positions/PSeth05.asp.

National Board for Professional Teaching Standards. (2002). *What teachers should know and be able to do*. Arlington, VA: author.

National Council for Accreditation of Teacher Education. (2001). *Professional standards for the accreditation of schools, colleges, and departments of education*. Washington, DC: author.

Nowak-Fabrykowski, K., & Caldwell, P. (2002). Developing a caring attitude in the early childhood pre-service teachers. *Education, 123*(2), 358–364.

Richardson, D., & Onwuegbuzie, A. J. (2004). Attitudes toward dispositions of teachers. *Academic Exchange Quarterly, 8*(3), 31–36.

Rike, C. J., & Sharp, L. K. (2007). Exit interviews and transcripts from teacher candidate interviews. Unpublished raw data.

Rike, C. J., & Sharp, L. K. (2008a). Assessing pre-service teachers' dispositions: A critical dimension of professional preparation. *Childhood Education, Infancy through Early Adolescence, 84*(3), 150–153.

Rike, C. J., & Sharp, L. K. (2008b). *Early childhood education behaviors and dispositions checklist form*. Retrieved from coe.memphis.edu/icl/EarlyChildhoodFinal Disposition.htm.

Ryan, P. M., & Alcock, M. A. (2002). Personal and interpersonal attributes in selecting teachers. *Action in Teacher Education, 24*(1), 58–67.

Suarez, D. (2003). The development of empathetic dispositions through global experiences. *Educational Horizons, 81*(4), 180–182.

Taylor, R., & Wasicsko, M. (2000). The dispositions to teach. Paper presented at the annual meeting of the Southeast Regional Association of Teacher Educators, Lexington, KY. Retrieved May 12, 2006 from 64.233.169.104/search?q=cache:uHstnSScWw8J:www.educatordispositions.org/dispositions/The%2520Dispositons%2520to%2520Teach.pdf+taylor+and+wasicsko,+the+disposition+to+teach&hl=en&ct=clnk&cd=2&gl=us.

Thompson, G. (2000). The real deal on bilingual education: Former language minority students discuss effective and ineffective instructional practices. *Educational Horizons, 78*(2), 128–138.

Wagner, T. (2001). Leadership for learning: An action theory of school change. *Phi Delta Kappan, 82*(5), 378–383.

Wayda, V., & Lund, J. (2005). Assessing dispositions: An unresolved challenge in teacher education. *Journal of Physical Education, Recreation, and Dance, 76*(1), 34–41.

Wenzlaff, T. L. (1998). Dispositions and portfolio development: Is there a connection? *Education, 118*(4), 564–572.

Worley, V. (2003). The teacher's place in the moral equation: In locos parentis. *Philosophy of Education Yearbook*. Champaign, IL: PES Publication Office.

Wong, H. K., & Wong, R. T. (1998). *The first days of school: How to be an effective teacher*. Sunnyvale, CA: Wong Publishing.

II

TEACHERS' PRACTICES AND PROFESSIONALISM

Nancy P. Gallavan and Patrice R. LeBlanc

Successful classroom teaching requires individuals who artfully establish safe and inviting learning environments where all students are engaged and actively participate in both the immediate and long-term learning processes that are standards-based, student-centered, and developmentally appropriate. This charge is complex and challenging; yet effective classroom teachers create this scene many times every day.

Although concerned with the content and processes associated with their grade levels and subject areas, these teachers recognize the importance of forming meaningful relationships with their students as an essential component for effective teaching and learning to occur. Teachers' dispositions and characteristics contribute significantly to building rewarding relationships. However, defining preferable dispositions and identifying specific characteristics is a complicated conversation that teacher educators and classroom teachers face, both to maintain a high quality of classroom teachers and for accreditation purposes.

Teacher educators and classroom teachers working with teacher candidates fully understand their roles and responsibilities in modeling desirable dispositions with the candidates and PK–12th grade students. As classroom teachers mentor teacher interns and novice teachers alike, classroom teachers accept the multifaceted tasks of guiding and supporting interns and novices as models to their own young learners.

Part II shares two chapters that address diverse perspectives and classroom practices associated with dispositions. In chapter 5, Richard D. Osguthorpe makes the case for teacher manner and morally good teaching. Osguthorpe presents a reconceputalization of the concept of teacher manner as an alternative to the focus on teachers' moral character and discusses the ramifications of this reconceptualization.

In chapter 6, Thomas E. Baker summarizes case studies of seven teacher candidate interns, each of whom connects and writes about one student in their classrooms during their internships. The interns share their discoveries and insights about their individual students that the interns then extrapolate to understanding PK–12th grade students at their prospective teaching age groups. The case studies reveal the importance of transforming the sense of hopelessness to hopefulness in both the PK–12th grade learners and the interns as they embark on their careers in teaching.

5

A Reconceptualization of Teacher Manner

Richard D. Osguthorpe

ABSTRACT

The putative relationship between the moral character of a teacher and the moral development of a student pervades the scholarship related to affective education. However, it is not clear how such a relationship exists, and this chapter assumes that a primary reason for its indeterminacy is the ambiguity of the concept of moral character. This chapter addresses this ambiguity and proposes a reconceptualization of the concept of teacher manner as a proxy for the moral character of a teacher. The purpose in doing so is to put these concepts in greater relief, provide a means for exploration into this relationship, and explore alternative connections between teacher manner and good teaching practice.

It has long been assumed that best practices for affective education in schools for the PK–12 community necessitate that teachers model high quality dispositions and moral character for their students. This fundamental assumption rests on the putative relationship between the moral character of a teacher and the moral development of a student. It is a relationship that is widely asserted in the scholarship on affective education, particularly in the seminal work related to the moral dimensions of teaching (Campbell, 1997, 2003; Fenstermacher, 1990; Goodlad, Soder, & Sirotnik, 1990; Hansen, 1998, 2001a, 2001b; Jackson, Boostrom, & Hansen, 1993; Noddings, 1992, 2002; Sockett, 1993; Strike, 1990; Strike & Soltis, 1992) and in the programmatic prescriptions of character education (see Berkowitz & Bier, 2005; Lickona & Davidson, 2005; Ryan &

Bohlin, 1999). And although the relationship is intuitively appealing, its use often lacks any attempts at either conceptual or empirical validation (see Halstead & Taylor, 2000; Solomon, Watson, & Battistich, 2001). It may very well be the case that teachers, via their moral character, have a strong influence on the moral development of their students. However, it may also be the case that the relationship is an indeterminate one or does not exist at all.

What is missing from the scholarship on affective education is an account that describes how to go about demonstrating whether or not a connection exists and just what that connection might be. This chapter is not, however, an attempt to empirically validate (or invalidate) this putative relationship. Instead, it asks prior questions and seeks conceptual clarity related to this relationship and its operationalization in future research and practice. Understanding and meaning are sought primarily through philosophical analysis (see Searle, 1996; Williams, 1996), and the objective of this chapter is to show that the concepts connected in this relationship are so vague and ambiguous as to render most claims of a relationship incomprehensible. This chapter focuses particularly on the ambiguities of the concept of moral character and proposes an alternative concept for examining the supposed relationship between the moral character of a teacher and the moral development of a student.

In the first part of the chapter, I clarify my use of the concept of moral character, and I examine two propositions that point to its inherent ambiguities and inconsistencies in use. In the second part, I explore the concept of teacher manner as a proxy for moral character and suggest that a proper understanding of teacher manner might give us a better grasp on the relationship between the moral character of a teacher and the moral development of a student—positioning the relationship in greater relief and demonstrating how the concept of manner may show promise for continued empirical study in affective education.

THE MORAL CHARACTER OF A TEACHER

There was a time in the first half of the 20th century that the study of moral character enjoyed a prominent place in both psychology and philosophy. In the preface to his work on the psychology of character, Roback (1927) suggests, "The subject of character or, in the wider sense, personality has within the last decade come to occupy the forefront of the psychological sciences" (p. ix). A primary goal of character studies during the early 1900s was to elaborate and clarify the term and its operationalization so that it could be used accurately in the new science of psychology. For example, Roback (1927) compiled a comprehensive text that addressed all aspects of the concept of character. In it, he suggests the text provides a clarity of concept that could greatly enhance future research and analysis. Roback's text, along with Hartshorne and May's (1928–1930) studies on the nature of character, and Allport's (1937) distinction between character and personality are but a few examples of seminal psychological work on the subject of character that set out to clarify its meaning and guide its use (see also Jones, 1955; Ligon, 1956; Peters, 1981). Despite these attempts to clarify meaning, character remains a conceptually slippery concept and does not lend itself well to empirical study. As Peck and Havighurst (1960) contend,

> There is perhaps no study of human behavior more fraught with risk of subjective bias and culture-bound prejudice than is the study of moral character. Yet in no aspect of life is objective knowledge and understanding more essential to human happiness. . . . Although much wise thought has been accorded the subject through several millennia, relatively little scientific research has yet been done. (p. v)

Indeed, when subjected to empirical study, character is a difficult concept to rid of bias and to pin down and make explicit, as Roback's voluminous work attests.

However, when a person speaks of moral character, and often when it is the subject of study and research, little of this difficulty is present or accounted for in its use. The term raises few questions as to meaning. There seems to be a general understanding of character, and it can surely be used in a variety of contexts, but, despite the ease with which the term character is employed, it is not always clear what it means. Thus, if there are terms or concepts that are both easily understood and ambiguous, character appears to be one of them. The inconsistencies and ambiguities of the term character are made manifest in the following two propositions: (a) character is something that is both visible and invisible and (b) character is both changeable and unchangeable.

These propositions are but several that point toward the ambiguity of the concept of character, particularly in the more recent philosophical and psychological literature cited previously. There are surely others, but these have particular salience for affective education and the relationship that is believed to exist between the moral character of teachers and the moral development of students. My intent is not to resolve all of the confusion that the term character presents. Instead, it is my intention that the discussion of these propositions, and the various meanings and uses of the term character, will illuminate the ways that the concept of moral character might cause confusion when discussing the moral character of a teacher and when conducting empirical research that connects it to the moral development of a student.

What Does It Mean to Observe Character?

Character is not a concrete entity; it cannot be seen. It resides, if it resides at all, somewhere inside each person—hidden from view. Both philosophers and psychologists have noted the abstractness of the phenomenon of character, resulting in various analyses of the term. Most of the analyses begin with an etymological description, pointing out that character is derived from the Greek term for engraving and means an enduring mark or lasting impression concerning what is distinct about a person. Although it is an enduring mark, it is not a visible mark. Indeed, character is an engraving, but an invisible one, and where it is engraved is anyone's guess—perhaps on the heart, soul, or mind? This reference to a mark is metaphorical, but it is certainly not clear what this metaphorical mark actually denotes. Whatever the case, it cannot be seen; it can only be inferred from situational action and reaction.

Character also seems to refer to some inner mechanism or some set of internal components that regulate our intentions and behaviors, particularly in the realm of moral matters. Despite this additional meaning and clarification, the concept of character is no more visible. For example, recalling a lecture by Allport in 1950, Coles (1986) offers a definition of character as "a moral center that [is], quite simply, there" (p. 137). He also quotes Kierkegaard to clarify the meaning of character: "Character is that which is engraved . . . but the sand and the sea have no character, and neither has abstract intelligence, for character is really inwardness" (Kierkegaard as cited in Coles, 1986, p. 154). Defining character in this way, as a moral center or inwardness, does little to render the concept visible. In fact, it may make it even more difficult to understand or pin down and even more abstract in nature.

That said, the difficulty in analyzing character is that it is described as something invisible, but the term is also used as if it is visible. Ryan and Bohlin (1999), for example, hold that character is not visible: "Character is one of those familiar words that often turns out to be difficult to pin down. Like all abstractions, you can't see character, you can't touch it; you can't taste it" (p. 5). However, they also contend that character can be discerned and perceived in others: "When we are around individuals who have the right stuff—that is, who have character—we know it" (p. 5). Character cannot be seen, but it can be perceived, discerned, and known. What does it mean, in this case, to perceive and discern? It would seem that to perceive and discern, in this case, is related to an ability to see certain behaviors when around these types of individuals.

Thus, character is apparently related to, perhaps sometimes conflated with, the behavior that stands in evidence of it. As Sabini and Silver (1982) point out, "Character belongs to a person, but not like his nose, his car, or even his height. It is shown by behavior, but behavior is evidence of character, not character itself; character endures over time, but it is not a thing" (p. 156).

It seems easy to make this distinction between character and evidence of character, but it is not altogether clear which one is being referenced when the term character is used. Likely, this confusion is the result of the abstract nature of the concept of character. It is relatively easy to describe what is meant by evidence of character, but describing character itself is a more difficult task—particularly when it is referred to as a moral center, inwardness, or the right stuff.

It is character's apparent connection to behavior that leads to ambiguity and inconsistency—it is not likely that there would be any clear conception of character without its behavioral manifestation. Put another way, behavior appears to be more than just evidence of character, it might be the only evidence of character. It is, possibly, the only glimpse of that inward mark or moral center. Phrased another way, evidence of character does not leave an enduring mark, it is the mark. For example, how would a child describe the character of a neighbor whom the child knew nothing about and whom the child had never met; perhaps the neighbor just moved into the apartment next door? Could the child say with any certainty that the neighbor is or is not honest, caring, just, or courageous? The answer to this question is likely no. The child would seemingly have to wait until there had been enough contact with the neighbor to draw even preliminary conclusions about the neighbor's character. In fact, it might be that only in cases of self-deception could people even suggest to themselves that they are honest without exhibiting honesty in their behavior. In other words, a person's character appears to be inextricably tied to behavioral evidence of character. For evidence of character precedes any engraving or mark. In the end, the evidence might just be the mark.

The interesting point here is that the connection between character and behavioral evidence of character is apparently so strong as to almost render the distinction between the two useless. If people are not described as honest without evidence that they have acted in an honest way on numerous occasions, then it would seem that the sum total of these honest acts is character. How many times must a person be honest or act honestly to be described as an honest person? Answers to this question will vary, but the question itself certainly implies that one act of honesty does not necessarily delineate one as an honest person, and that these acts do not necessarily leave a visible mark. Instead, these acts contribute to the making of a mark that is continually a work or engraving in progress.

In this way, there seems to be no character without evidence of character. Again, if asked to describe a person's character, then apparently only character traits for which there is adequate behavioral evidence are listed. When a person is described as courageous, the referent does not appear to be some invisible, inward mark or moral center; it is the instance that this person jumped into the path of an oncoming car to save a child, stood up to management in defense of fellow employees, and so on. Hence, it would seem that character is in some measure visible, even though what is claimed to be seen is perhaps not character itself, but merely evidence of it. More importantly, when questions arise regarding whether character can be observed, it seems that character might be better described as something that is event-determined rather than an enduring trait. In other words, character might be a more context-dependent phenomenon than it is a stable disposition.

The examination of what it means to observe character also provides an early indication of how difficult it is to establish a relationship between the moral character of a teacher and the moral development of a student—despite the ease with which researchers and practitioners employ these respective concepts and the subsequent temptation to presume a connection between them. However, if in fact character has this contextual aspect, it lacks the kind of stability and clarity that would allow researchers and practitioners to definitively say that the moral character of a teacher has a causally influential effect on the moral development of a student.

What Does It Mean to Change Character?

Ironically, another inconsistency in the way character is described is that it is spoken of in terms of both consistency and change. To speak of character as something that is consistent and unchanging hearkens back to the original meaning of the term as an engraving or enduring mark. Character, in this sense, refers to those distinctive traits that mark one as a person, that are consistent and enduring over time. The language of engraving leaves little room to equivocate—few words conjure up anything more permanent than that which is engraved. In their study of moral character, Peck and Havighurst (1960) describe a phenomenon that they call the "permanence of character structure" (p. 162) at every level of morality.

> There is no evidence to suggest any "predestination" in this phenomenon. From all that could be found, moral character is formed by the child's family experiences, not genetically inherent. However, by the age of ten—indeed, perhaps much earlier—whatever character the child has, he is likely to have for life, in most cases. (p. 162)

Peck and Havighurst also argue that it was difficult to find any additional forces outside of home and family that affected any type of change in character. Regardless of the empirical data in support of the claim that a child's character is permanent at the age of ten, the point here is that character is often described as an unchanging entity; as something that is permanently engraved.

When a person's character is described in this way, we often speak in a language of prediction (see Sabini & Silver, 1982). In other words, when we say that a person is compassionate, we imply that this person will act in a compassionate way in the future. Furthermore, if we do not qualify our prediction, by saying the person is usually or typically compassionate, then we seem to mean that this person is always—and will always be—compassionate. The predictive nature of character language emphasizes its unchangeable qualities. When we speak of character in this way, we are not merely suggesting that there is a possibility that a person will act in a certain way, we are saying that a person has acted this way in the past and, marked in such a way, will act this way in the future. When we refer to character we imply permanence via prediction.

However, despite this character language that implies permanence, when we speak of character we also speak of character change. For Goffman (1967), this inconsistency is simply the way we conceive of character.

> On the one hand, [character] refers to what is essential and unchanging about the individual—what is *characteristic* of him. On the other, it refers to attributes that can be generated and destroyed during fateful moments. . . . Thus a paradox. Character is both unchanging and changeable. And yet that is how we conceive of it. (p. 238, emphasis in original)

To illustrate, there are multiple ways that changeability is implied when speaking of character. These types of change—which I will refer to as wholesale, fateful, contextual, and out-of-character—shed light on the complexity of the term character. The first type of character change that we speak of, and perhaps the most common, refers to a wholesale change. When we speak of character change in this way we refer to a complete transformation—from some vice to its complimentary virtue or vice versa. For example, we speak of the mean-spirited and dishonest convicted felon who, after years in prison, reenters society as a changed person—kind and honest and perhaps even counsels troubled youth to emulate his transformation. We also speak of the friendly and compassionate person who, after several tragic life events, becomes bitter, closed, and uncaring. These wholesale changes of character refer to a complete reversal, from one extreme to the other.

The second type of character change refers to what might be called a fateful change. As mentioned previously, it is common to speak of character change that takes place in those critical moments that require a person to decide between virtue and vice. Whether or not these moments are necessarily fateful is debatable, but it is not unusual to speak of a person's character changing in this way. For example, Goffman (1967) describes how a person's character might change when put to the test under extraordinary circumstances.

> The principled behavior he manages to exhibit during ordinary occasions may break down. The quick consciousness of what his principles are costing him at the moment may cause his wonted decency to falter, and in the heat and haste of the moment, naked self-interest may obtrude. Or, contrariwise, the sudden high cost of correct behavior may serve only to confirm his principledness. (p. 216)

Goffman argues that the latter person is identified as strong, while the former is labeled as weak. This type of change may not be change in character at all—it might merely be an affirmation of character. However, when a person occupies that murky area between virtue and vice and decides a course of action in accordance with either, this decision is spoken of in terms of change, perhaps even fateful change.

The third type of character change refers to a contextual change. That is, a change in character based on the context of a situation or place. For example, it is possible to speak of hard-driving, uncaring bosses at work, who are real softies with their children and compassionate caregivers at home. Are said bosses uncaring or compassionate? Hard-driving or soft? When speaking of character without a change of context, it is normal to choose between traits, either they are uncaring or compassionate, based on behavioral evidence over time. However, with a change in context, it is typically acknowledged that a person can exhibit both virtue and corresponding vice—merely changing from one context to another.

The fourth type of character change refers to an out-of-character change. This type of change is perhaps the least drastic of the four. For example, when a brave person or a person who is considered to be brave does something cowardly for the first time, the cowardly behavior is brushed off as a lapse in character. This type of behavior is described as out-of-character for the offending person. If the person continues to act in a cowardly way, then the previous estimation of braveness might be revised, but the implication here is that a person's character can change, if but for a small moment, and then change back. This type of change is perhaps more aberration than change, but it is described nonetheless as change—albeit a temporary one.

To add even more complexity to these four types of character change, such change is often qualified by suggesting consistency. In other words, when these types of character change are discussed, it is implied that there was no real change at all. Wholesale change is qualified by suggesting that a person had it inside all along. Fateful change is qualified by implying that the action or behavior was merely a confirmation of deep down character. Contextual change is qualified by implying that the person's true character is closer to that exhibited in one context and that the behavior exhibited in the other context is merely an act or show. The final qualification of character is self-explanatory: out-of-character change is qualified by suggesting that the behavior was out-of-character—dismissing it as a lapse or slip-up. The point here is that there are multiple ways to speak of character change, but these ways are also moderated by suggesting or implying a permanence of character structure.

Thus, to speak of character typically entails some measure of equivocation, as character is described as both unchanging and changeable. Furthermore, there are multiple ways to detail character change, including wholesale, fateful, contextual, and out-of-character. Adding to this complexity is the suggestion of a middle ground to avoid equivocation and the qualification of what is meant by character change, perhaps exacerbating the equivocation. In other words, it is common to flip and flop and then flip back when speaking of a person's character, suggesting that perhaps any change was not really change after all. Whether or not character actually changes becomes secondary to the fact that the concept is not employed with enough precision to accurately determine an answer.

Summary

Inquiries into whether or not it is possible to observe character and whether or not it is possible to change character point to troubling vagueness and ambiguity in the way that the term character is employed. Such complexity gives rise to some difficult questions that bear heavily on a more nuanced understanding of the relationship that is believed to obtain between the moral character of a teacher and the moral development of a student. Several of these questions are mentioned here and examined in later sections.

In the first section, I showed that character is described as something that both can and cannot be seen. When character is described as something that cannot be seen, it is spoken of as something akin to a moral center, inwardness, or perhaps even the right stuff. When character is described as something that can be seen, it would be more precise to speak of evidence of character or behavioral manifestations of character. Thus, it might be possible to vicariously see character via some behavioral manifestation of it, but it is simply that—"evidence of character, not character itself" (Sabini & Silver, 1982, p. 156). Even if character can somehow be perceived or discerned through some additional sense, it seems that behavioral evidence of character is still the primary if not only determiner—as it seems implausible to suggest that a person's character could be inferred, knowing nothing about nor having met or spoken with said person. In this way, there is no character without evidence of character. But, if character cannot be seen, if it is only possible to see potential evidence of character, then how might researchers, for example, determine the effect that the moral character of a teacher has on the moral development of a student?

In the second section, I emphasized that character is described as both unchanging and changeable, and I described four types of character change. When character is described as unchanging, the original meaning of the term is implied—an enduring mark, lasting impression, or engraving. A language of prediction is employed, suggesting a permanence of character structure. When character is described as changeable, the reference is to wholesale, fateful, contextual, and out-of-character types of change. The term character can also denote a language of habit—suggesting it occupies the middle ground between changeable and unchanging—and references to change are often qualified. Thus, equivocation is often an inherent part of descriptions of character, in which character remains stable but is subject to change. Moreover, rules for what constitutes character change are arbitrary. For example, how many times must a person act out-of-character before such action becomes actual evidence of character?

Each of these hanging questions merits additional analysis. The important point here is that it is not always clear what the term character means. It is employed with ease in conversation, but it is used with little precision. It is simply a term that is both easily understood and ambiguous.

MANNER AS A PROXY FOR MORAL CHARACTER

The propositions presented in the previous sections reflect the ambiguities of the concept of moral character. Given these ambiguities and inconsistencies in use, is it prudent to conclude that the indeterminacy of the concept renders the relationship between the moral character of a teacher and the moral development of a student futile as an object of study? Such a conclusion seems hasty in light of the persistence and pervasiveness of this relationship in the affective education literature cited at the beginning of this chapter; it is an intuitively appealing relationship that has endured centuries of scholarship. What is needed are alternative ways to proceed with the study of this relationship and the relevance of teachers' moral character to their practice. Assuming that the moral character of teachers influences the way that they teach, different options are needed for examining that influence with regard for the complexities of the concept of moral character.

In these concluding sections, I explore one option by examining the concept of teacher manner. In the first section, I take a closer look at the concept itself and explore its evolution and different iterations. My purpose in this first section is to reveal the nuances of manner and identify some possible ambiguities. In the second section, I explore the ambiguities of manner in relation to the concept of moral character and propose a reconceptualization of manner that gives us a better grasp on the relationship between the moral character of a teacher and the moral development of a student. My purpose in this second section is to put the complexities of the relationship in greater relief and demonstrate how the concept of manner shows promise for empirical study.

The Evolution of the Concept of Manner

The roots of the concept of manner can be found in Fenstermacher's criticism of the nature of educational research in the 1970s. Although manner was not mentioned by name in this early work, his concern focused on how educational researchers presented their findings to teacher educators: "Generating knowledge, and getting people to use it appropriately and well, are two different activities. The former is an outcome of good research. The latter is an outcome of good education" (Fenstermacher, 1979, p. 180). Hence, according to his analysis, even though educational researchers may produce findings applicable to teacher education, these findings are often forced upon teacher educators and students in a way that does not respect their moral agency. As Fenstermacher suggests, the educational researchers who do account for moral agency are

> not interested in peddling findings to high bidders for their talents, be these rule makers, policy makers, or policy administrators. On the contrary, their primary and mutually held concern is for the education of teachers that is expressive and evocative of the education they hope teachers will provide for their students. (p. 182)

To be expressive and evocative of good education in this way is to display a manner of a certain kind.

Fenstermacher's (1979) analysis of the literature laid the foundation for the introduction of the term manner. In his exploration of research on teaching, Fenstermacher (1986) argues that presenting research findings to teachers in a certain way is just as important as the findings themselves: "manner is as much a part of the content to be conveyed to the student as the facts, theories, arguments, and insights of the subject being taught" (p. 47). To describe the substance of manner in this context, Fenstermacher points to an Aristotelian conception of virtue.

> Manner consists primarily of moral and intellectual virtues. . . . Of the moral virtues pertinent to education, one thinks immediately of fairness, respect, openness, and honesty—to name just a few. Of the intellectual virtues, humility, creativity, reflectivity, dispassionateness (at the proper place and time), and honesty come quickly to mind. (p. 47)

Under this notion of teaching, teachers ought to teach in a manner that conveys not only instructional content but also certain virtues. Underlying this notion is the suggestion that teacher educators should foster a certain kind of manner in preservice teachers, virtues that can subsequently be passed on to students. Drawing on an Aristotelian conception of moral development (Aristotle, trans. 2000) and the work of R. S. Peters and Gilbert Ryle (see Peters, 1972; Ryle, 1972), Fenstermacher (1986) suggests that these virtues are fostered by modeling them: "The manner of one who possesses these traits of character is learned by modeling, by being around persons who are like this, and by being encouraged to imitate these persons and adapt your actions to the demands of these traits" (p. 47).

Fenstermacher (1992) also argues that fostering the acquisition of character traits is not to be confused with fostering the acquisition of subject matter content. To distinguish the fostering of virtue from say the teaching of mathematics, he calls for a more expansive view of the concept of pedagogy. He argues that manner, along with method, is one of two constituent elements of a concept of pedagogy, which has historically relied only on methods of instruction to define its territory. In brief, Fenstermacher distinguishes method from manner by saying, "method is the general descriptive term that we give to a broad range of teaching behaviors whose purpose is to convey content" while "manner is the term that I apply to human action that exhibits the particular traits or dispositions of a person" (pp. 96–97).

To illustrate this difference, Fenstermacher (1992) points out that this distinction is closely connected to the question, "Can virtue be taught?" He inquires "whether teachers can employ manner to impart virtue in somewhat the same way they employ method to impart knowledge" (p. 99). This distinction first led Fenstermacher to conclude that virtue or traits of character are not taught or learned in the same way that subject matter is taught or learned. Instead, character traits and dispositions are caught or picked-up by being around persons who possess these same traits and express them in a certain kind of manner. Manner, in this sense, is productive of virtue and closely related, if not synonymous, to modeling.

> Manner that is productive of the intellectual virtues is manner that promotes a respect for evidence, a sense of tentativeness and willingness to suspend one's pet notions as the exploration proceeds, an appreciation of and regard for the canons of inquiry and the demands of truth telling, and an openness to alternative and competing ideas. Manner that is productive of the moral virtues is manner that encompasses such traits as compassion, fairness, tolerance, caring, and honesty. (Fenstermacher, 1992, p. 99)

The connection between manner and method then lies in the possibility that these virtues are often expressed in actions that are linked to "teaching behaviors whose purpose it is to convey content [subject matter]" (Fenstermacher, 1992, p. 96).

Thus, these early iterations of manner suggest a concept that is difficult to distinguish both from the concept of moral character and the concept of modeling. In summary, recall the earliest iteration of manner was closely connected to the concept of moral character, perhaps indistinguishable. As Fenstermacher (1986) states, "[Manner] consists of the moral and intellectual virtues" and "Manner is learned by modeling" (p. 47). Substituting "moral character" for manner in this instance would not change the meaning of either concept. If it is synonymous with moral character, then manner is subject to the same questions explored in the first section (i.e., Can we observe it? Can we change it?). However, subsequent iterations of manner revealed a more nuanced concept.

The next iteration of manner shifted the focus from the traits of moral character themselves to a way of passing on such traits, or modeling. For example, Fenstermacher (1992) suggests that "manner is . . . human action that exhibits the particular traits or dispositions of a person" (p. 96). He also goes on to say, "teachers can employ manner to impart virtue" and "manner . . . is productive of the moral virtues" (Fenstermacher, 1992, p. 99). The shift here is slight but, in doing so, the emphasis is placed on how a teacher conveys or expresses traits of moral character (i.e., virtue) as opposed to the embodiment of the traits themselves. The inconsistency of use raises a conundrum similar to those discussed in the section regarding moral character: is manner best defined as conduct expressive of a teacher's moral character or as a teacher's moral character itself? In other words, is manner a means of conveying something or is it something to be conveyed? Or can it be both? These inconsistencies will be addressed in the next section along with a reconceptualization of manner that puts the concept in greater relief.

Resolving the Ambiguities of Manner

The most recent iteration of manner resolves some of these inconsistencies by opening the possibility that manner is more closely connected to teachers' personae than it is to their actual moral character traits and dispositions, that which is supposedly engraved. In this sense, "manner . . . is conduct that expresses highly regarded moral and intellectual traits" (Fenstermacher, 2001, p. 649). Notice that the reference to moral and intellectual traits does not indicate that the person expressing them possesses these traits. In other words, manner is part of teachers' personae in such a way that they can, in their conduct, even their method, express traits of moral character that they do not possess, that are not necessarily engraved.

These iterations of manner reveal a concept that succumbs to some of the same criticisms levied in this chapter against the scholarship of affective education. However, these iterations also suggest ways to become pedagogically engaged with the expression of moral character (i.e., manner) that do not result in the same problems inherent in trying to render the actual moral character of a teacher a viable object of study. What has become apparent in the analysis presented here is that researchers and practitioners need a different way of speaking about the expression of virtue in teaching. The concept of moral character carries with it too much vagueness and inconsistency in use—although this inconsistency is rarely identified—rendering it difficult to establish a connection to the moral development of a student. The concept of manner, however, with its most recent focus on expression, allows us to avoid the complexities of trait language and focus on the manifestation or display of virtue rather than on the possession of virtue. It is this iteration of manner that holds promise for empirical study.

The distinction is subtle, but it is an important one for at least two reasons. First, it makes the virtues more visible and accessible to the researcher or teacher who wants to study their role in classrooms. For example, Fallona (1998, 2000) has shown how manner is made visible in the practice of teaching. However, she acknowledges that there are, at times, high levels of interpretation in such study because of the difficulties inherent in observing a teacher's character and connecting those observations to a teacher's self-assessment. Distinguishing teacher manner from actual or engraved character enables researchers to draw their own conclusions concerning what is being engraved without attending to many of the complexities involved in the information game that might otherwise be taking place. Put another way, the beauty or virtue is in the eye of the beholder, which still requires some level of interpretation of manner contingent on the researcher's perspective and context. However, it eliminates the need to make attributions of moral character. It also leaves open the question of how best to empirically study manner in teaching practice.

Second, this subtle distinction also helps extricate the concept of teacher manner from its assumed relationship to the moral development of students. That is, focusing on teachers' expressions of virtue—as opposed to their possession of virtue—shifts attention to the influence teacher manner has on a teacher's practice and away from its supposed impact on the moral development of students. Most of the implications that have been proffered for teacher manner attend exclusively to its role—in teacher education for example—of "promot[ing] the development of teachers who take seriously their moral charge to be models of conduct who instill the moral and intellectual virtues needed to live a good and happy life" (Fallona, 2000, p. 693; see also Fenstermacher, 2002; Miletta, 2004; Richardson & Fallona, 2001). For teacher educators, attending to manner as an element of teacher persona suggests taking up the manner of teacher candidates as a means of improving their future practice, not as a means of instilling moral character in their future students. In other words, it gets teacher educators out of the moral education business and back to the business of good teacher education; focusing on both manner and method as integral to good teaching (see Fenstermacher & Richardson, 2005).

It might be tempting to suggest that manner is merely method in disguise, but the temptation to conflate method and manner is likely due to conceiving manner as something that only has moral development as an outcome. When manner is conceived as the way that methods are employed, it is possible to see the distinctness and the interconnectedness of manner and method. For example, teachers can employ wait time responsibly or irresponsibly; grade fairly or unfairly; cue with kindness or unkindness. Such teachers do not necessarily embody these virtues or traits of moral character, but they are part of their teaching personae that they adopt in the classroom.

CONCLUSION

This chapter reexamines the ambiguities of a teacher's moral character by reexploring the concept of manner. It puts the complexities of manner in greater relief and demonstrates how manner shows promise for continued empirical study. These complexities are all variations on the ambiguities of moral character that were put forth in the first portion of the chapter and attended to in the subsequent analysis. However, where the ambiguities of moral character are difficult to resolve, the concept of manner provides us an opportunity to address these inconsistencies and proceed with the study of the different forms a relationship might take between manner and moral development and, perhaps more importantly, between manner and good teaching.

Such a study requires a reconceptualization of manner as a part of a teacher's persona, placing emphasis on the expression of moral character traits—that may or may not be engraved. By so doing, the concept of manner avoids some of the ambiguity and inconsistency that befalls the concept of moral character. This reconceptualization also shifts attention away from moral development and positions manner as an important component of pedagogy that is both distinct from and interconnected with a teacher's method. Conceived in this way, the concept of manner provides one option for proceeding with the study of what constitutes morally good teaching.

Thus, this analysis provides two important applications for future research: it sets forth a reconceptualization of teacher manner that provides a new basis for examining the moral character or manner of teachers, and it also provides teacher educators with a new rationale for attending to the moral character or manner of teacher candidates. The first move here is subtle but also important in that it extricates manner from the ambiguities of character and links it more closely to persona, which lends itself to researcher interpretation and inference. The second move, building off of the first, dismisses or brackets the putative connection between teacher manner and student moral development, and it focuses attention on the relationship between teacher manner and good teaching practice. The emphasis here is on teaching in a manner that is good, right, and virtuous.

APPLICATION ACTIVITIES

From this analysis of character and subsequent reconceptualization of manner, there are three interconnected application activities for researchers and practitioners alike. First, the limitations of the concept of moral character ought to be acknowledged in research and practice aimed at assessing teacher character, particularly its putative connection to the moral development of students. Second, teacher education programs should consider incorporating a conception of teacher dispositions that is akin to the reconceptualization of manner presented here, focusing on the virtuous ways that teacher candidates convey their content, and not solely on the supposed virtues that teacher candidates possess. Finally, research on affective and moral education ought to attend to constructing additional rationales for requiring teachers to be of good character, connecting what is good, right, and virtuous, with effective and responsible teaching.

REFERENCES

Allport, G. (1937). *Pattern and growth in personality*. New York: Holt, Rinehart, and Winston, Inc.

Aristotle. (2000). *Nicomachean ethics* (R. Crisp, Trans.). New York: Cambridge University Press.

Berkowitz, M. W., & Bier, M. C. (2005). *What works?* Washington, DC: Character Education Partnership.

Campbell, E. (1997). Connecting the ethics of teaching and moral education. *Journal of Teacher Education, 48*(4), 255–263.

Campbell, E. (2003). *The ethical teacher*. Philadelphia: Open University Press.

Coles, R. (1986). *The moral life of children*. Boston: Atlantic Monthly Press.

Fallona, C. (1998). Manner in teaching: A study in moral virtue. Unpublished doctoral dissertation, University of Arizona.

Fallona, C. (2000). Manner in teaching: A study in observing and interpreting teachers' moral virtues. *Teaching and Teacher Education, 16*(7), 681–695.

Fenstermacher, G. D. (1979). A philosophical consideration of recent research on teacher effectiveness. In L. S. Shulman (Ed.), *Review of research in education 6* (pp. 157–185). Itaska, IL: F. E. Peacock Publishers.

Fenstermacher, G. D. (1986). Philosophy of research on teaching: Three aspects. In M. C. Wittrock (Ed.), *Handbook of research on teaching* (3rd ed., pp. 37–49). New York: Macmillan.

Fenstermacher, G. D. (1990). Some moral considerations on teaching as a profession. In J. I. Goodlad, R. Soder, & K. Sirotnik (Eds.). *The moral dimensions of teaching* (pp. 130–151). San Francisco: Jossey-Bass.

Fenstermacher, G. D. (1992). The concepts of method and manner in teaching. In F. K. Oser, A. Dick, & J. Patry (Eds.), *Effective and responsible teaching: The new synthesis* (pp. 95–108). San Francisco: Jossey-Bass.

Fenstermacher, G. D. (2001). On the concept of manner and its visibility in teaching practice. *Journal of Curriculum Studies, 33*(6), 639–653.

Fenstermacher, G. D. (2002, April). Pedagogy in three dimensions: Method, style, and manner in classroom teaching. Unpublished paper presented at Teacher's College, Columbia University.

Fenstermacher, G. D., & Richardson, V. (2005). On making determinations of quality in teaching. *Teachers College Record, 107*(1), 186–213.

Goffman, E. (1967). *Interaction ritual: Essays in face-to-face behavior.* New York: Doubleday.

Goodlad, J. I., Soder, R., & Sirotnik, K. (1990). *The moral dimensions of teaching.* San Francisco: Jossey-Bass.

Halstead, J. M., & Taylor, M. J. (2000). Learning and teaching about values: A review of recent research. *Cambridge Journal of Education, 30*(2), 169–202.

Hansen, D. T. (1998). The moral is in the practice. *Teaching and Teacher Education, 14*(6), 643–655.

Hansen, D. T. (2001a). Teaching as a moral activity. In V. Richardson (Ed.), *Handbook of research on teaching* (4th ed., pp. 826–857). Washington, DC: American Educational Research Association.

Hansen, D. T. (2001b). *Exploring the moral heart of teaching: Toward a teacher's creed.* New York: Teachers College Press.

Hartshorne, H., & May, A. (1928–1930). *Studies in the nature of character: Vol. 1. Studies in deceit; Vol. 2. Studies in self-control; Vol. 3. Studies in the organization of character.* New York: Macmillan.

Jackson, P., Boostrom, R., & Hansen, D. (1993). *The moral life of schools.* San Francisco: Jossey-Bass.

Jones, E. (1955). *Sigmund Freud, life and works* (Vol. 2). London: Hogarth Press.

Lickona, T., & Davidson, M. (2005). *Smart and good high schools: Developing excellence and ethics for success in school, work, and beyond.* Cortland: Center for the 4th and 5th Rs, State University of New York College at Cortland.

Ligon, E. M. (1956). *Dimensions of character.* New York: Macmillan.

Miletta, A. (2004). Managing dilemmas: Uncovering moral and intellectual dimensions of classroom life. Unpublished doctoral dissertation, University of Michigan.

Noddings, N. (1992). *The challenge to care in schools: An alternative approach to education.* New York: Teachers College Press.

Noddings, N. (2002). *Educating moral people: A caring alternative to character education.* New York: Teachers College Press.

Peck, R. F., & Havighurst, R. J. (1960). *The psychology of character development.* New York: Wiley.

Peters, R. S. (1972). Education and human development. In R. F. Dearden, P. H. Hirst, & R. S. Peters (Eds.), *Education and the development of reason* (pp. 501–520). London: Routledge & Kegan Paul.

Peters, R. S. (1981). *Moral development and moral education.* London: George Allen & Unwin Ltd.

Richardson, V., & Fallona, C. (2001). Classroom management as method and manner. *Journal of Curriculum Studies, 33*(6), 705–728.

Roback, A. A. (1927). *The psychology of character*. London: Routledge & Kegan Paul.

Ryan, K., & Bohlin, K. (1999). *Building character in schools*. San Francisco: Jossey-Bass.

Ryle, G. (1972). Can virtue be taught? In R. F. Dearden, P. H. Hirst, & R. S. Peters (Eds.), *Education and the development of reason* (pp. 434–447). London: Routledge & Kegan Paul.

Sabini, J., & Silver, M. (1982). *Moralities of everyday life*. Oxford: Oxford University Press.

Searle, J. R. (1996). *Contemporary philosophy in the United States*. Oxford: Blackwell.

Sockett, H. (1993). *The moral base for teacher professionalism*. New York: Teachers College Press.

Solomon, D., Watson, M. & Battistich, V. (2001). Teaching and schooling effects on moral/prosocial development. In V. Richardson (Ed.) *The handbook on research and teaching* (pp. 566–603). Washington, DC: American Educational Research Association.

Strike, K. A. (1990). The legal and moral responsibility of teachers. In J. I. Goodlad, R. Soder, & K. Sirotnik (Eds.), *The moral dimensions of teaching* (pp. 188–223). San Francisco: Jossey-Bass.

Strike, K. A., & Soltis, J. (1992). *The ethics of teaching* (2nd ed.). New York: Teachers College Press.

Williams, B. (1996). Contemporary philosophy: A second look. In N. Bunnin & E. P. Tsui James (Eds.), *The Blackwell companion to philosophy* (pp. 23–34). Oxford: Blackwell.

6

Hope and Heart in Action: Case Studies of Teacher Interns Reaching Students

Thomas E. Baker

ABSTRACT

Teachers want positive relationships with students, but demands placed on teachers can create stress that can lead to hopelessness. The author supervised seven secondary teacher interns enrolled in a five-year teacher education program. Writing a case study about a challenging student was one of several assignments designed to help the interns become hopeful educators. Common themes ran through the case studies. Interns expressed faith that their students could succeed, made efforts to develop stronger personal relationships with students, thought of new ways to help their students, then put their plans into action. The author discusses how the program's curriculum and ethos lead teacher candidates to become hopeful teachers. Finally, the author suggests application activities.

This chapter presents and discusses the significance of "Case Studies of Hope and Heart" written by seven teacher candidate interns enrolled in a five-year master of arts in teaching program. Although the interns taught in a wide variety of middle and high schools in rural, urban, small city, and suburban settings, each of the interns encountered students who were struggling. Students' struggles stemmed from limited English proficiency, personal and family problems, extreme shyness, poor previous instruction, mistrust of teachers, drug use, excessive need for attention, and a mismatch between the required curriculum and the students' interests and learning styles. By listening to their students' voices, establishing personal relationships with their students, and innovating instruction designed specifically to reach their struggling students, the seven interns succeeded in providing a more equitable education for their students who faced difficulties as described in the case studies.

REVIEW OF THE LITERATURE

Hopeful Teachers

Teachers, especially novices, want to have positive personal relationships with each of their students, but, as Ayers (2006) notes, educational policies today can make students invisible or at least reduce them from people and personalities to scores and labels. Bunting (2006) asks, "Is there a way for teachers to build a personal niche in the uptight world of teaching to the dictates of others" (p. 76)? The accountability demands of No Child Left Behind (USDOE, 2001), which may seem at odds with what teachers learned in their preparation program, along with feelings of isolation and of being overwhelmed often cause stress in beginning teachers (Scherff, Ollis, & Rosencrans, 2006; Snow-Gerono & Franklin, 2006). That stress is compounded when they discover that they cannot merely focus on their students (Collingridge, 2008), but must "wear many hats in the school" (Garii, 2008, p. 81). Unresolved stress can lead to hopelessness, both for them and their learners.

Reflecting on the characteristics of a hopeful teacher, Sergiovanni (2004) distinguishes between teachers who "wish" all of their students will succeed but lack faith in them and have no action plan, and teachers who "hope" that their students will succeed, have faith that they can, ask themselves what they can do to help bring it about, and then put their plan into action. Meadows (2006) indicates that some teachers profess to believe that all children can learn, but because they lack hope, they water down expectations for struggling learners rather than providing them with appropriate academic challenge. Teachers who have hope, which Taulbert (2006) calls the Eighth Habit of Heart for educators, have a telic image of themselves and their students. They do not believe that they are inevitably stuck in present conditions. A belief in future possibilities for oneself and one's students is a hallmark of the hopeful teacher. "Without hope, we would have little use for tomorrow" (Goodlad, Mantle-Bromley, & Goodlad, 2004, p. 125).

Hope in adolescents is a validated psychological construct that functions as "a moderator in the relationship between stressful life events and adolescent well-being" (Valle, Huebner, & Suldo, 2006, p. 393). Hopeful teachers who establish trusting relationships with their students and are unafraid to try new approaches are far more likely to nurture hope in their students than teachers who lack hope, fear risk, and fail to develop personal relationships with students. Students of hopeful teachers, particularly struggling students, are more likely to feel that their teacher cares about them, listens to them, supports them, and suggests new ways for them to deal with challenges. Those students are also more likely to act on the teacher's suggestions.

Case Writing

Teacher educators have used case writing as a way for their students to reflect on and learn from their teaching experiences (Floyd & Bodur, 2005; Meadows, 2006; Shulman & Colbert, 1988; Shulman & Mesa-Baines, 1993). Case writing in teacher education often deals with instructional strategies, but Mathison and Pohan (2007) have described its use to foster reflective thinking about professional interactions with students, parents, colleagues, and administrators. In a longitudinal study of case writing in the Stanford Teacher Education Program, Hammerness, Darling-Hammond, and Shulman (2001) emphasized that a preservice teacher's case study should be "a case of something" (p. 2). The narratives discussed in this chapter are cases of something; they describe teacher interns' hopeful behavior in the face of challenges.

Learning through case study writing is, in a sense, learning through reflection, an idea that is not new. Dewey (1938/1963) emphasized the importance of learning through retrospective reflection. He said that we do not learn from our past experiences, but from what we make of those experiences. Schön (1987) studied practitioners' reflections in the midst of experience as they analyzed and responded to problems that arose. The case studies discussed in this chapter have elements of both Dewey's and Schön's notion of learning through reflection.

CONTEXT

The author supervised seven secondary teacher interns in a five-year teacher education program. The names of the interns, their students, and their mentor teachers have been changed to protect their identities. Five of the interns taught in public high schools and one taught in a public middle school. The seventh intern taught in a private high school whose mission is to have 100 percent of its graduates admitted to selective four-year colleges and universities. Three interns were white females, two were white males, one was a Hispanic female, and one was an Asian American female.

Writing a case study of "hope and heart" about their teaching experience was one of several assignments designed to help the interns develop as hopeful educators. By giving voice to both their challenges and their accomplishments in a case study, as well as through seminars, journals, and online discussions, the interns reflected on and affirmed what they had learned about their own growth as teachers. In the case studies they wrote, the seven intern teachers were asked to focus on their relationship with a challenging or struggling student, describing the problem, how they tried to help the student, and the outcome. The student they chose to write about may have been disruptive, may have been academically disengaged, may have had personal problems that impinged on class performance, may have lacked prerequisite knowledge and skills to succeed in class, or may have lacked confidence and displayed helplessness.

All candidates in the graduate phase of the five-year teacher education program at the college involved in this study have earned a bachelor of arts degree, have successfully completed three undergraduate education courses with supervised teaching experiences, and have met all requirements for admission to the graduate program, including teaching field requirements and the successful completion of three psychology courses. Education professors observe and confer several times with candidates during their early field experiences. On-campus learning activities in the undergraduate courses include reading assignment discussions, collaborative projects, individual writing assignments, student presentations, computer lab activities, and entries in reflective journals that professors read and respond to via e-mail.

Before beginning the full-time teaching internship in their final semester of their graduate year, candidates complete six graduate courses (the equivalent of 24 semester hours) that include advanced foundational courses, instructional methodology courses with field components, a research and assessment course, and for candidates seeking certification in grades 8–12, two graduate electives in their subject area. Interns may serve as teachers-of-record in their own classroom on a special permit issued by the state. Thus, the interns discussed in this chapter are both beginning teachers and graduate students enrolled in the final semester of their teacher education programs. Principals assign interns to mentors in their departments. Interns earn 3 course credits, the equivalent of 12 semester hours.

Every semester, two professors supervise a total of approximately 10 to 16 interns. One professor oversees the elementary school interns and the other oversees the secondary school interns. The professors observe the interns in their classrooms several times throughout the semester. Interns communicate with their group's professor and with each other weekly via Moodle discussion forums. (Moodle is an online course management system that offers interactive discussion boards among its many features.) Both the professor and the interns pose questions and topics. Interns respond to their peers' questions, offer support and suggestions for solving problems, and share ideas and practices that have worked well for them. Interns e-mail a reflection journal entry to their professor biweekly. In addition, interns read four articles of their choice related to designated themes and post their reviews on Moodle for their peers and the professor to read and share comments. Secondary interns meet with their supervising professor in a biweekly evening seminar on campus. All interns must return to campus for two all-day in-service sessions that deal with topics such as preparation for the state pedagogy exam, using educational technology, and teaching special needs students and students with limited ability in English in the regular classroom.

METHODS

In an orientation seminar held prior to the start of their internships, the author explained expectations and assignments, including the case study the interns would write and its purpose. Novice teachers sometimes feel hopeless when confronted with students whose needs they do not know how to meet (McCann & Johannessen, 2004). This assignment pushed the interns to analyze their interactions with a student who needed extra encouragement, to persist in trying new ways to help the student, and, at the end of the semester, to describe how the student had progressed and what the intern had learned from this exercise.

Near the end of the semester, interns wrote their case studies in the form of a three to four page typed paper that clearly described the following: the context in which the intern was teaching, a profile of the student they chose to write about including the student's particular difficulty or problem, the intern's analysis of the situation, the development and implementation of a plan to help the student, the results of the intern's efforts, and a reflection on what the intern learned from the case writing experience. Interns shared their case studies with their peers in the next to last seminar before submitting them. The case study writing assignment was distinct from the requirement to submit biweekly reflection journal entries, but some interns' entries occasionally discussed the student they eventually chose for their case study.

The author analyzed the case studies individually and as a group to identify instances that indicated the interns were becoming hopeful educators. Criteria for hopefulness were: (1) expressions of belief that the student could succeed and/or improve and that the intern could help him or her do so; (2) descriptions of efforts to develop a stronger personal relationship with the student; (3) evidence that the intern implanted a plan of action; (4) evidence of persistence; and (5) description of positive changes in the student's academic performance, behavior, or attitude.

It is important to note that in direct quotations from the case studies presented, the interns wrote in the first person when describing their own actions and thoughts and in the third person when referring to their students. The author wrote in the third person when summarizing and commenting on each case study, always trying to help "the audience to follow the 'story' that is being unveiled" (White, Woodfield, & Ritchie, 2003, p. 289).

THE INTERNS SPEAK

Ann's Case

Ann, a white female, taught French to ninth graders in a fairly affluent suburban school. She was alarmed to learn of the prevalence of drug use among her students. One of her students in particular caught her attention. Claire dressed in baggy, black clothes, used black make-up and nail polish, and wore Goth-style jewelry. It was widely rumored that she regularly used drugs. Sensing that Claire was isolated and troubled because others judged her negatively, Ann decided to initiate special efforts to communicate personally with her. In response, Claire asked if she could begin eating lunch with Ann and her mentor teacher. They agreed. As Ann and Claire got to know each other better, Ann discovered that despite Claire's off-putting appearance, she was actually "a kind, polite, respectful, imaginative, and extremely intelligent young lady."

One day during lunch, Claire confided that she had decided to get off drugs, and that she had been clean for two weeks. Ann was supportive and nonjudgmental, and continued to be available to talk with Claire. Although she still wore Goth attire, Claire's attitude and performance in class improved significantly. Claire continued to eat lunch with Ann and her mentor teacher, and they let her talk about issues of concern to her without "lecturing." Ann wrote, "I feel truly blessed to have played at least some small part in her recovery."

Jared's Case

Jared, a white male, taught Spanish I, Spanish II, and a Spanish class for native speakers in an older middle school in a city that has grown from a population of 30,000 to over 100,000 in the last dozen years. (Because of the small number of students in the class for native speakers, and also because of its unique challenges, Jared was given permission to write his case study about this class as a whole.) At first, Jared felt overwhelmed because some of his native Spanish-speaking students, or "heritage speakers," were literate in Spanish while some were not. However, instead of giving up, he became energized by the challenge. He made special efforts to get to know each student personally. He offered to tutor his students before and after school. They were surprised and delighted when Jared told them that he wanted to learn their colloquialisms. They believed that they spoke inferior Spanish.

Jared worked tirelessly and imaginatively to create engaging, effective new materials, learning aids, and activities. In his second of four observations spaced throughout the semester, and after Jared had begun to implement his new ideas, the author noticed that students in Jared's native-speaker class demonstrated more confidence in their responses, volunteered more frequently, were engaged more diligently in learning activities and assignments, and demonstrated increasing success in their responses. As Jared wrote in his case, he observed continuing improvement in this class throughout the semester. The initial atmosphere of uncertainty and resistance, he said, had been replaced by one of enthusiasm and mutual respect.

Matt's Case

Matt, a white male, taught high school speech in a city of 300,000 citizens situated between two larger cities. Danielle was the first in her family to apply to college. She had been raised by her single mother, who had died of cancer two years before. Danielle was angry and devastated when she was denied admission to the university that was her first choice and the only one to which she had applied. Matt wrote, "It hit me that here is a girl who wants to learn and wants to make something better of her life, but she did not get into the school of her choice. I am trying to renew her hope by showing her that this does not have to be a bad thing."

Matt offered to help Danielle write an appeal for a review of her application and also helped her with applications to two other institutions, meeting with her before and after school. At the time Matt wrote his case study, Danielle was awaiting word from the institutions, but Matt was hopeful. In his words,

> She became a stronger person who I have no doubt will succeed. I told her that there will be many times when you ask why something happened, but you can't dwell on the whys in life. You have to accept it and make the best of what you were dealt. Whatever happens, I told her, you will be successful. As I reflect on our interactions over the semester, I realize that Danielle taught me a lot about why I get up each morning to teach high school students. She taught me that I do it because I want to help them reach their goals. I want to make a difference in their lives because I know they will make a difference in mine.

Elena's Case

Elena, a Hispanic female, taught U.S. and world history in a small, rural district adjacent to a city of approximately 37,000 people. Elena wrote that she felt apprehensive and overwhelmed at first, despite her previous success in the teacher education program and in her history courses. "What if, after all my classes and other field experiences, it turns out that I am an incompetent teacher?" she remembered thinking. Elena sought ideas and support from Mrs. Caine, her mentor teacher, who gave Elena free access to her voluminous materials, made suggestions, and answered Elena's questions. Mrs. Caine often assured Elena that she was doing a fine job and would be an excellent teacher. Elena learned from her colleagues that Mrs. Caine did not give compliments lightly. With her confidence bolstered, Elena said that after she "took a step back and relaxed," she was able to enjoy teaching her students. She worked on getting to know them personally so she could better tailor lessons to accommodate varied learning styles. As a result, Elena wrote,

> Some of my challenging students became my favorites. Troy is a prime example, a sweet kid but not a great student. He can be bouncing off the walls or he can just sit there with his head on the desk. I know he has a difficult home life. He is generally a fun and warm person, but he struggles with his motivation in class. Troy has trouble paying attention and has a hard time with written assignments. When he feels frustrated, he acts helpless and gives up.

At first, Elena and Troy had some conflicts because she did not know how to help him. After getting to know him better, and seeking more information and suggestions from Mrs. Caine, Elena began to modify some of his assignments in respectful ways. She started to check his progress more frequently and to give him specific, supportive feedback on his performance. Periodically, Elena asked Troy how he felt he was progressing, which activities interested him, and with which ones he was struggling. On his own, Troy began to talk with Elena before and after school to discuss his performance in class. He even offered suggestions for learning activities for the entire class. "It is still a struggle to make sure he turns in his work," wrote Elena, "but Troy is someone I am happy to see every day."

Nicole's Case

Nicole, a white female, taught ninth grade English in a private K–12 school that had just moved to its new, multibuilding campus in a suburb of a large city. Both parents and the school's staff expected that every graduate of the upper school would be accepted to a four-year college, a daunting challenge. A large glass case in the main hall of the upper school displays seniors' acceptance letters and scholarship awards, many from highly respected colleges and universities around the nation.

One of Nicole's students, Grant, posed challenges at first. He made disruptive jokes, sought attention inappropriately, failed to complete assignments, and apparently was not studying the material the class was reading. After a few classroom incidents, Nicole spoke with Grant privately about his unacceptable performance. He admitted that he should improve his behavior and promised to do so. However, he also said that he felt frustrated by the content, Dickens's *Great Expectations*, which Nicole was teaching in a rather traditional fashion. He simply could not identify with the characters and the events in the novel.

While Grant's behavior and lack of effort could not be excused, Nicole reflected on the deeper reasons for them and contemplated ways to engage him and his classmates in the content with more enthusiasm. Nicole decided to scrap her plans for the next unit, wrap up *Great Expectations*, and begin the study of *Huckleberry Finn*. However, instead of introducing the novel with a lecture as she had previously done, she started with a website scavenger hunt, offering a free homework pass as a prize for the best job. Grant was galvanized into action. He stayed up late completing the assignment, and was so excited about it that he brought it to Nicole before school rather than wait until his English class began. Nicole was so impressed by his work that she asked him for advice on searching for websites. Amazed that a teacher would ask for his assistance, Grant gladly shared information and ideas. Through further conversations, Nicole was able to learn more about Grant as a person. His motivation and performance improved dramatically. Later in the *Huckleberry Finn* unit, small groups created board games based on the novel. Grant emerged as his group's leader. He also threw himself into creative writing assignments related to *Huckleberry Finn*. In Nicole's words,

> Through these different modalities, he was able to express his own unique voice and let others see him in a positive light. Besides using different learning modalities in assignments, I have been able to make a personal connection with Grant. By asking him about life outside of school (track meets, films), he could see that I was interested in him as a person. Without this personal connection, I do not think he would have attempted to change. Grant now enters the classroom with a huge smile on his face, which always brightens my day. He has made me strive to think of new and different ways to approach literature and my students as well.

Christie's Case

Christie, a white female, team-taught drama and theater arts in an older, diverse, one high school town of 24,000 citizens. The school has an ambitious theater program, putting on annual school productions and performing strongly in regional and state competitions. A few of the school's recent graduates went on to appear in films and regional theater.

Ben, a junior, impressed Christie as a hard-working, easy-going, respectful young man who loved theater, although he was shy and reserved by nature.

Christie learned that Ben had successfully played several character roles during his two and one-half years in theater classes, but he had never played the romantic lead. He auditioned for the lead in Morton Wishengrad's "The Rope Dancers," the play they had selected for the regional and state competition. Despite his innate shyness and lack of confidence, Christie and her colleague thought Ben was the right actor to play James, a hard-drinking, charming, Irish ruffian. At first Ben was elated, but panic soon set in. His role was absolutely crucial for the success of the play. Christie wondered if Ben could, in her words, "roughen and toughen up." Would he be able to convince the audience that his character was a womanizing Irish alcoholic who nevertheless loved his daughter deeply? One of his and Christie's greatest fears was whether or not he could be natural and believable when he kissed his costar.

As codirector, Christie went to work immediately to build Ben's confidence. She worked with him on the accent. After each rehearsal, she gave him numerous suggestions in a supportive way. As the rehearsals progressed, Christie was concerned that Ben's character was not coming alive fully, and his accent was more British than Irish. However, Christie kept coaching and encouraging him, never communicating doubts. Privately, she thought that it was a triumph merely for Ben to be attempting the role. If he did not win an acting award and if the play did not advance in competition, it would not be the end of the world.

After the final rehearsal, Ben was the last to leave the theater, telling Christie that he would stay to turn out the lights. The next day at the competition, Ben was so nervous that he spoke to no one, apparently oblivious to those around him. As Christie recounted in her case study, she gave him one last pep talk and a hug, telling him, "Have fun. The hard part is over. Now you are ready to introduce the audience to James and tell his story." After the curtain went up, shy, polite Ben, the boy who had struggled through rehearsals, had disappeared completely. James had taken over. When Christie ran back stage after the play, there were tears in her eyes and in Ben's. Not only did the play advance, but also Ben won the Best Actor Award for that round. As Christie reflected near the end of her case study,

> Ben showed us all something we had never seen before, his confidence. As a teacher, I knew that he had won more awards [than Best Actor] in his own mind. He had been able to put away his self-doubt. He learned to trust himself and his instincts. His award gave me hope for the system. Maybe the "little guy" can win every once in a while if he or she works hard. Ben told me afterwards that he knew he was going to win the award because he felt like a winner before he took the stage. He had come to believe in himself and in his directors. "You cast me for a reason, and I decided that I was going to meet the challenge."

Stephanie's Case

Stephanie, an Asian American female, taught Algebra II at an extremely large high school in a town with a population of 34,000 situated 16 miles from the center of a city of 1.3 million people. The student body is approximately 40 percent Hispanic and 40 percent African American. Stephanie started her internship in January, following a series of substitute teachers. The teacher who started the school year, an engineer by training who was seeking alternative certification, had been dismissed in October. Colleagues in her department told Stephanie many horror stories about the first teacher's ineffective instruction, lack of assessment, failure to use manipulatives and other instructional materials that remained unopened, and severe lack of management skills, to the point that students sometimes hurled golf balls across the room. Neither Stephanie nor the faculty in the teacher education program were informed of these problems in advance.

In her case study, Stephanie reflected on the significant challenges she had faced. She had to create a climate of order and mutual respect. She had to assess the deficiencies in her students' knowledge and help bring them up to speed so that they could meet the course's goals as well as pass the state test. She had to overcome the students' extremely negative attitudes toward their math class. They had come to view it as a lost cause, so they gave it neither effort nor respect. Most of all, Stephanie had to establish trust. Would she be able to persuade her students that she could offer them worthwhile instruction? Could she convince them that she would be there for them and not abandon them as their previous Algebra II teachers had done?

Stephanie described how she instituted new procedures, some of which worked but many of which were not effective. If one approach did not work, she tried something new. Stephanie did not expect an instant turn-around, but she knew that she must never give up hope. Beyond issues of discipline and management, Stephanie said, "I knew that I had to show them that I cared. I had to show them that I not only cared about them personally, but that I also cared about their instruction and their success in the class."

She began to give as much individual attention as possible to students during class, encouraging them to ask questions. Students were slow to respond at first, but eventually began to ask for clarification when they needed it. To establish more personal connections with students in her large, overcrowded classes, Stephanie offered to tutor students before and after school, and even during her conference period. Many students took Stephanie up on her offer, something that "greatly renewed my positive feelings about teaching and boosted my confidence in teaching." When some of those students told their friends who were not in Stephanie's classes to ask her to tutor them, she was glad to do so.

Stephanie cites one student in particular who "exemplifies the challenges and successes that I have had in this teaching experience." Shondra was both dependent and rejecting, often voicing hostile comments about the class. Lacking fundamental algebraic knowledge, she was easily frustrated and often gave up in despair. Shondra was angry if she did not get constant attention and help in class, but refused Stephanie's invitation to come for tutoring. Shondra's father demanded a conference with Stephanie to find out why she "refused to help" his daughter. Instead of becoming defensive, Stephanie wrote that she calmly explained the situation to the angry parent. Once he understood the situation, the father agreed that Shondra needed tutoring, and he made sure that she began right away. The tutoring went well, and Shondra grew in her ability to solve problems on her own. Instead of constantly asking for help with a problem, Shondra tried on her own first, and then asked if her solution was correct. As Stephanie reported in her case study, she was delighted to observe Shondra beginning to explain algebraic concepts to classmates when they became stumped.

DISCUSSION

Although their situations varied widely, all seven interns demonstrated that they were becoming hopeful educators. They showed hope and heart for their students both as learners and as persons. The author's analysis showed evidence in each case study of the five criteria described previously. The following themes that demonstrated hope ran through the case studies.

1. Each intern expressed faith both in the student's capacity to succeed and in the intern's ability to help the student.
2. Each intern made extra efforts to communicate with the student in order to develop a stronger personal relationship.
3. Rather than continuing to do the same things, each intern thought of new ways to help the student, put the new plan into action, and then reflected on the effects of their efforts.
4. Each intern reported using encouragement and authentic praise consistently.

Moreover, the interns were able to describe specific ways in which their students' attitudes or performance had improved as a result of their hopeful efforts. Ann invited communication with a student who was isolated by her drug use and the Goth style of dress she had adopted. Rather than ignoring her, the easy option, Ann demonstrated courage and caring by giving up free time to talk with Claire and to listen respectfully without trying to "fix" her. Ann's tacit hope for Claire's success helped Claire find hope within herself.

Although at first he felt discouraged and baffled by how best to teach his Spanish class of Spanish-speaking recent immigrants who differed widely in their level of literacy, Jared demonstrated heart and hope by putting his knowledge, experience, and creativity to work in forging a more responsive curriculum and making extra efforts to build personal relationships with each student in the small class. In response, the students took heart and became more engaged in learning.

Matt could have simply shaken his head in sympathy and referred Danielle to the school counselor, but he cared about this student who was fighting long odds to get a college education, and he believed that he could help her. Danielle felt discouraged and helpless because her first college application had been rejected. Matt helped her find hope and heart, not only with encouraging words, but also by taking time to critique her written appeal. He taught her that we must take action in order to realize our hopes.

Elena had hope that she could help Troy improve academically and behaviorally, despite his learning difficulties, learned helplessness, and occasional acting out caused by his frustration. She showed him that she cared about him by respectfully differentiating assignments, offering him frequent feedback and support, and listening to his suggestions for class activities. Troy responded with greater effort, more confidence, better behavior, and more communication with Elena.

Grant is the type of academically disengaged class clown that many teachers deal with by giving detentions, calling parents, and venting in the teachers' lounge, but Nicole hoped that Grant could become a productive, contributing class member. Rather than becoming defensive, Nicole looked at her teaching methods and curriculum objectively and decided to try innovative methods that might better meet Grant's needs. She also showed Grant that she cared about him by expressing interest in his extracurricular activities as well as by giving him a chance to showcase his computer savvy. As a result, his bored wisecracking was replaced with enthusiastic engagement.

Christie took a risk by casting Ben, a steady but shy student, in a demanding starring role because she believed he was ready to blossom. As he struggled in rehearsals, Christie was concerned, but she never conveyed her doubts to Ben. She focused on ways to nurture hope and heart in Ben through supportive feedback and encouragement. After his success, Ben told Christie that it was her belief in him that led him to believe he could meet the challenge.

Stephanie's teaching environment was probably the most challenging of all, yet she never gave up hope that she could win over her skeptical, poorly instructed students, even Shondra, one of her most hostile, helpless learners. Stephanie demonstrated the caring and the strength—the heart—to convince the students that she cared about them, that she believed they could learn the content, and that she would go to any lengths to help each student succeed.

CONCLUSION

By refusing to give up on the students, by making themselves available to the students, and by trying new ways to motivate and encourage them, the interns inspired their students to gain hope and confidence in themselves. The interns realized that if they were to help struggling students to overcome challenges or to become more productive class members, they had to convince students that they genuinely cared about them. That, in turn, required getting to know their students better, a task that takes extra effort. Their case studies indicate that the interns gave that effort willingly and wholeheartedly.

These interns also discovered that inspiring hope and heart in themselves as well as in their students takes persistence and time. The interns were not afraid to take risks that might or might not work the first time. They found new ways to connect to students if what they were doing was not working. The interns built trust by modeling trust. In Sergiovanni's (2004) terms, they put hope into action, they did not merely wish.

Can faculty in a teacher education program lead preservice teachers to develop hope and heart, as well as the ability to nurture it in their learners? It is possible. The small size of the program in which the interns were enrolled allows students and faculty members to get to know each other well, and for students to form bonds of support with each other. A series of progressively more responsible field experiences allows students in the program to work with the realities of teaching, both the challenges and the rewards. Through field experience seminars, postobservation conferences, reflection journal entries, writing case studies, and online discussion boards, candidates practice articulating and analyzing their teaching problems and successes, and they seek support from both faculty and peers.

All faculty members in the interns' teacher education program, whether new assistant professors or full professors with over 30 years of experience, observe students in the field. Because they know their students personally, academically, and as teacher candidates in field experiences, their advice and affirmations have specificity and more importantly, credibility. Generalities, abstract suggestions, and generic words of encouragement cannot build hope and heart in the novice teacher, no matter how warmly expressed.

Teaching teacher candidates how to write reflective journals and case studies in all field experiences may help them assess their growth as teachers and plan for future growth. Teacher education students also benefit from sharing their challenges, successes, and even their case studies with peers, both in seminars and via online discussions. Fundamentally, a teacher preparation program should have the depth, breadth, coherence, duration, and multiple supervised teaching experiences that allow its students to develop theoretical frameworks in which to analyze classroom events from various perspectives and to make informed professional decisions. They may then discover, as these seven interns did, that learning, both their students' and their own, takes time and commitment, hope and heart, but that the rewards are great.

The closing words of Stephanie's case study epitomize the ethos of the hopeful educator.

> From this experience, I have learned that nothing renews my hope and heart more than when a student says, "Oh, I get it now!" I believe this also renews the student's hope and heart. Success gives students the will to keep trying because we all like it when we succeed. In the future, I will always be on the lookout for "I get it moments," and I will keep those moments coming by always reminding the students that I am here to help them.

APPLICATION ACTIVITIES

The depth of feeling and thought and the evidence of growth as hopeful teachers found in the interns' case studies suggest that this is a learning activity worth keeping and refining. Although we should continue to encourage teacher interns and student teachers to seek advice from their education professors and mentor teachers, ultimately they must look within themselves to answer fundamental questions about their teaching challenges. How can I diagnose the causes of difficulty for this student or class? What might I do to make the situation better? Do I really believe that all my students can improve? Do I have the commitment, courage, and persistence to keep trying new ways to help a student? Am I a hopeful educator? This case writing assignment pushed the interns to answer these questions through purposeful reflection both on their relationship with a learner or small group of learners and on their efforts to better meet their learners' needs. The assignment also encouraged the interns to look beyond superficial solutions to deeper insights about the student and about themselves.

REFERENCES

Ayers, A. (2006). The hope and practice of teaching. *The Journal of Teacher Education, 57*(4), 269–277.

Bunting, C. (2006). Getting personal about teaching. *Phi Delta Kappan, 88*(1), 76–78.

Collingridge, D. (2008). Phenomenological insight on being hindered from fulfilling one's primary responsibility to educate students. *Alberta Journal of Educational Research, 54*(1), 112–123.

Dewey, J. (1938/1963). *Experience and education*. New York: Collier Books.

Floyd, D., & Bodur, Y. (2005). Using case study analysis and case writing to structure clinical experiences in a teacher education program. *The Educational Forum, 70*(1), 48–60.

Garii, B. (2008). A teacher's job doesn't only happen in the classroom: Preservice teachers, the classroom, and the school. *Action in Teacher Education, 30*(1), 81–92.

Goodlad, J., Mantle-Bromley, C., & Goodlad, S. (2004). *Education for everyone: Agenda for education in a democracy*. San Francisco: Jossey-Bass.

Hammerness, K., Darling-Hammond, L., & Shulman, L. (2001, April). Toward expert thinking: How case-writing contributes to the development of theory-based professional knowledge in student teachers. Paper presented at the Annual Meeting of the American Educational Research Association, Seattle, WA (ERIC Document Reproduction Service No. ED472392).

Mathison, C., & Pohan, C. (2007). Helping experienced and future teachers build professional interaction skills through the reading and writing of narratives. *Issues in Teacher Education, 16*(1), 61–73.

McCann, T., & Johannessen, L. (2004). Why do new teachers cry? *Clearing House, 77*(4), 138.

Meadows, E. (2006). Preparing teachers to be curious, open minded, and actively reflective: Dewey's ideas reconsidered. *Action in Teacher Education, 28*(2), 4–14.

Scherff, L., Ollis, J., & Rosencrans, L. (2006). Starting the journey together: A teacher and her "students" navigate their first semester in the secondary English classroom. *Issues in Teacher Education, 15*(2), 43–59.

Schön, D. (1987). *Educating the reflective practitioner*. San Francisco: Jossey-Bass.

Sergiovanni, T. (2004). Building a community of hope. *Educational Leadership, 61*(8), 33–38.

Shulman, J., & Colbert, J. (1988). *The intern teacher casebook*. San Francisco: Far West Laboratory for Educational Research and Development.

Shulman, J., & Mesa-Baines, A. (1993). *Diversity in the classroom: A casebook for teachers and teacher educators*. Mahwah, NJ: Lawrence Erlbaum.

Snow-Gerono, J., & Franklin, C. (2006). Mentor teachers share views on NCLB implementation. *Kappa Delta Pi Record, 43*(1), 20–24.

Taulbert, C. (2006). *Eight habits of the heart for educators: Building strong school communities through timeless values*. Thousand Oaks, CA: Corwin Press.

U.S. Department of Education (USDOE). (2001). *Executive summary of the no child left behind act*. Office of Elementary and Secondary Education. Retrieved from www.ed.gov/print/nclb/overview/intro/execsumm.html.

Valle, M., Huebner, E., & Suldo, S. (2006). An analysis of hope as a psychological strength. *Journal of School Psychology, 44*(5), 393–406.

White, C., Woodfield, K., & Ritchie, J. (2003). Reporting and presenting qualitative data. In J. Ritchie & J. Lewis (Eds.), *Qualitative research in practice: A guide for social science students and researchers* (pp. 287–320). London: Sage.

III

QUALITY AFFECTIVE EDUCATIONAL EXPERIENCES FOR PK–12

Nancy P. Gallavan and Patrice R. LeBlanc

Affective education encompasses many different teaching strategies, classroom approaches, and school programs. It includes efforts related to understanding and caring for oneself, interacting respectfully with others, critical thinking, decision-making, problem-solving, conflict resolution, violence prevention, abuse prevention, and so on. Schools encapsulate microcosms of society where students should feel safe and welcomed. As teachers prepare their students academically, teachers must also equip their students for productive citizenship and to become active, contributing members of their communities.

Questions surrounding the extent to which schools and educators can and should educate their young learners cognitively, physically, emotionally, and socially are addressed in part III. If schools educate the whole child, then affective education is embedded throughout the curriculum, instruction, assessments, community building, and classroom management modeled by every adult at the school, found in each classroom, and emanated throughout the building. Schools must offer sanctuaries that operate in unison with students, families, and society to educate the whole child.

Three chapters in part III share research findings related to affective education programs for classrooms and schools. In chapter 7, Donna J. Dockery provides an extensive background and description of various approaches that support affective education school programs. Dockery summarizes what works and the preparation required for classroom teachers to institute affective education programs in their classrooms.

In chapter 8, Candace H. Lacey, Patrice R. LeBlanc, and Nancy L. Maldonado report the findings from their research conducted at several elementary and middle schools related to the "Peace Works" conflict resolution program. The focus of the program is to reduce angry and aggressive behaviors and increase prosocial behaviors. Lacey, LeBlanc, and Maldonado describe the program, share their findings, and offer best practices for other educators to model and teach in their teacher education and PK–12th grade classrooms.

The third chapter in part III, chapter 9, offers an overview of the invitational education program authored by Gail E. Young and Alex J. Tripamer. Young and Tripamer are educators associated with an elementary school where invitational education served as the framework for opening their new school. The authors provide the details and benefits of this program for classroom teachers and school administrators to adopt in their own school settings.

Each chapter in part III encourages all educators and future educators to consider the possibilities for incorporating affective education as an integral part of the learning community, curriculum, and conduct. From the chapters in part III, educators should feel encouraged that guidance and support are readily available for educators to teach the whole child.

7

An Overview of Character Education and Recommendations for Implementation

Donna J. Dockery

ABSTRACT

Accompanying current emphasis on academic achievement as measured by high-stakes testing, schools are charged with promoting character development of all students. Character education is a rapidly growing movement encompassing a wide array of programs designed to promote caring, principled, and responsible students. Support for character education stems from the public, state, and federal governments, plus university schools of education. Challenges facing society and schools, such as decreased civility manifested as increased violence, bigotry, dishonesty, and intolerance, underscore the need to promote character development. Promising practices include service learning, classroom meetings, and student consultation. Effective programs focus on long-range, collaborative, and comprehensive implementation involving community members, families, and students. Recommendations for research directions and suggestions for schools of education are included.

SCHOOLS' RESPONSIBILITY IN CHARACTER EDUCATION DEVELOPMENT

Today's schools are charged with the daunting task of meeting the needs of all students they serve. In response to the high-stakes testing component of the No Child Left Behind Act (NCLB) (USDOE, 2001), many schools focus primarily on academics using curriculum standards, tutoring, and other instructional means for helping all students to pass standardized achievement tests (Clark & Amatea, 2004; Williams, 2000). It is important to note that NCLB also encourages instilling civic responsibility and competence in youth by developing and implementing character education programs in schools (USDOE).

Despite the NCLB inclusion of citizenship and character development, the tasks of preparing students to contribute to the society and the workforce while promoting character development are secondary to meeting academic standards as measured by state testing programs (Williams, 2000). Most classrooms, schools, districts, and states are narrowly focused on raising student test scores, rather than on developing the total student (Cohen, 2006). Developing the attitudes, skills, and behaviors needed for productive life and positive citizenship may be more difficult to address in schools than developing academics. Also, citizenship and character traits may be more challenging than academic achievement to measure empirically; however, positive character education outcomes remain important and valued aspects of effective schooling (Williams, 2000). A review of the literature indicates there is a variety of differing programs and strategies being implemented to promote positive character development; therefore, it is important to define what is meant by character education.

WHAT IS CHARACTER EDUCATION?

The mission of preparing students for success in life and work while encouraging them to become productive and positive citizens is not a new focus of education. Even in the early days of the American democracy, there was an expectation that citizens would participate in self-government and exemplify good character (Cohen, 2006). From the 1800s and the McGuffey Readers through the 1970s and Kohlberg's (1969) discussions of moral dilemmas, schools have always been involved in encouraging positive character development (Traiger, 1995). Over the years, this type of education has been labeled moral education, values education, affective education, civics, and citizenship education, in addition to character education which is the current term (Howard, Berkowitz, & Schaeffer, 2004). However, educators are confused about how best to define character education (Williams, 2000), and teacher educators agree that clearly defining character education is a priority (Jones, Ryan, & Bohlin, 1998).

Lickona (1993) suggests that character is a broad term that encompasses the cognitive, affective, and behavioral components of morality. Thus, knowledge, skills, and behaviors reflective of positive social development and ethical decision-making are some of the components of character education. Character education can also be defined by relational attributes using qualities such as civility, respect, and tolerance; by personal attributes such as self-discipline, perseverance, and effort; or by a combination of these virtues (Benninga, Berkowitz, Kuehn, & Smith, 2006). As described by Williams (2000), character education programming occurs whenever school faculty and staff make deliberate efforts to encourage caring, positive principles and responsibility in and among their students.

Character education may include a wide array of programs such as moral reasoning, life skills education, caring communities, health education, conflict resolution, peer mediation, ethics, and religious education (Howard et al., 2004). Programs may target specific issues such as bullying prevention and communication skills, or the programs may be more comprehensive in nature (Skaggs & Bodenhorn, 2006).

Cohen (2006) categorizes character education efforts in one of three approaches. The traditional approach emphasizes transmitting values and the concept of good behaviors; the caring approach focuses on developing caring relationships and includes relational and social-emotional themes in the curricula; and the developmental approach addresses decision-making, social action, and active participation by students (Cohen, 2006). The United States Department of Education (2008) defines character education as a broadly encompassing term that includes all efforts by schools, related social institutions, and parents to promote positive character development. Although these programs and efforts may be labeled using a variety of terms, character education has clear support from many constituents.

SUPPORT FOR CHARACTER EDUCATION

Currently there exists local, state, and federal support for character education, in addition to public and school interest in effective programs (Anderson, 2000; Cohen, 2006; Howard et al., 2004; Rose & Gallup, 2000; Wood & Roach, 1999). University schools of education and private organizations also advocate character education for children and adolescents (Cohen, 2006; Howard, 1993; Milson & Mehlig, 2002; Nielsen-Jones, Ryan, & Bohlin, 1999). Several contemporary educational developments, school and societal issues, and student concerns also support the need for effective character education in today's schools (Brandt & Wolfe, 1998; Britzman, 2005; Cohen, 2006; Kress & Elias, 2006; Pasi, 2001; Theberge & Karan, 2004; Welsh, 2000; Williams, 2000).

Support from the Public

Despite changes in terminology, the political climate, and current practices in schools, the Phi Delta Kappa/Gallup Polls of the Public's Attitudes toward the Public Schools have remained consistently positive regarding support for character education over the past 30 years (Cohen, 2006). A review of poll results clearly indicates the public's expectation that one primary mission of today's schools is preparing students to be productive citizens by helping them to obtain the skills needed to operate effectively in the world (Cohen, 2006). In the 2000 poll, respondents selected preparing people to become responsible citizens as the most important purpose of public schools (Rose & Gallup, 2000). In 2007, over two-thirds of respondents indicated that schools should be responsible for responding to affective concerns of students (Rose & Gallup, 2007). Survey responses reflect both local and national support for character education in schools and are noticeably positive, regardless of whether respondents had children enrolled in school or not (Rose & Gallup, 2000).

Support at the State Level

Although a majority of states advocate character education in schools, there is wide variation in programming policies, implementation, definitions, and funding for these educational initiatives (Howard et al., 2004). Of the 47 states and the District of Columbia that received federal character education grant funding for pilot programs by 2002, only 28 states had legislated character or citizenship education or service-learning (Cohen, 2006).

It is also important to note that the level of state support for character education programming varies, and that some state legislation simply encourages character education while some mandates character education (Howard et al., 2004). New York, for example, mandated character education in 2001. The policy, Education Law 801-a, requires instruction in civility, citizenship, and character education that must "ensure that the course of instruction in grades kindergarten through twelve includes a component on civility, citizenship and character education. Such component shall instruct students on the principles of honesty, tolerance, personal responsibility, respect for others, observance of laws and rules, courtesy, dignity and other traits which will enhance the quality of their experiences in, and contributions to, the community" (New York State Education Department, 2001, para. 2).

Maryland was the first state to mandate character education in the form of a required service learning component. Adopted in 1993, the resolution requires all students entering ninth grade to complete a service learning experience, but the mandate left the program design to individual school districts (Howard, 1993). Legislation requiring or encouraging the implementation of character education may or may not include funding from the state, which greatly impacts the actual implementation of character education programs in schools and communities (Howard et al., 2004).

Support at the National Level

At the national level, federally subsidized funds also support the development, implementation, and evaluation of character education programs (PAC, 2007). Initiated under the Clinton administration, by 2007 this competitive grant program provided funding for over 147 state and local agencies (PAC, 2007), and it encouraged states to initiate and formalize character education programming (Howard et al., 2004). Initially, the quality of implementation and evaluation of these pilot character education programs varied; later, funding supported both more rigorous evaluation and better quality programs (Howard et al., 2004).

Several national professional organizations including the National Education Association, the American School Counselor Association, the National Council for the Accreditation of Teacher Education, the American Association for Higher Education, and the Association for Supervision and Curriculum Development also support the importance of and need for preparing students to be successful in life through character education and similar initiatives (Cohen, 2006; Howard, 1993; Milson & Mehlig, 2002).

Support in Higher Education Schools of Education

A national survey of 600 deans of university schools of education demonstrated overwhelming support for teaching psychosocial skills and professional attributes needed to develop effective, productive citizens through PK–12 education (Nielsen-Jones et al., 1999). Although over 90 percent of the participants agreed with the need for character education in schools, less than 25 percent of the respondents thought that their teacher preparation programs had an appropriate emphasis on character education. A majority of respondents wanted to know more about best practices in character education; requested information on sample course syllabi, related books, and materials; and supported making character education a state requirement for teacher licensure (Nielsen-Jones et al., 1999). Despite this overwhelming support, few schools of education actively incorporate character education into their teacher preparation programs (Cohen, 2006).

Support from Current Developments in Education

Character education has been viewed as one of the most rapidly developing reform movements in education today (Williams, 2000). In addition to support from the public, state, and federal governments, schools of education, and national organizations, current developments in education also indicate that now is the time for a renewed emphasis on more effectively developing the psychosocial capital of our students (Cohen, 2006). Creating productive classroom environments, prekindergarten and school-readiness initiatives emphasizing social and emotional skills, and concerns about whether students have the abilities to solve complex and real-world problems, all support the need for effective character education in today's schools (Cohen, 2006).

Research regarding emotional intelligence and brain development provides additional support for encouraging character development in students (Cohen, 2006). It has been demonstrated that emotional intelligence is linked more strongly with success and satisfaction in life than academic success and IQ, and that skills related to emotional intelligence are highly valued in business and careers (Kress & Elias, 2006). Additionally, brain research suggests that learning is strongly connected with emotional states (Brandt & Wolfe, 1998), and that social and emotional capabilities can be developed in similar ways as fostering verbal and quantitative skills (Cohen, 2006). Increasing emotional intelligence as a way of preparing students for the future is a valuable component of character development.

Support from Current Issues in Schools

In the years following the shootings at Columbine High School in Littleton, Colorado, and other school shootings, concerns regarding school violence and student safety have come to the forefront (Welsh, 2000). These concerns resulted in the implementation of several character education initiatives to address school climate issues, promote healthy student interactions, and reduce harassment of students by peers (Pasi, 2001). According to the School Health Policies and Programs Study 2006, over 70 percent of states have adopted policies promoting positive school climates and more than 95 percent of schools have adopted bullying prevention policies (Jones, Fisher, Greene, Hertz, & Pritzl, 2007). Despite these policies, one in five of high school students worry a great deal about feeling safe at school (Metlife, 2002). Females (26 percent), low-income students (30 percent), and African American students (32 percent) are the most likely students to be most concerned about issues of school safety, according to the 2002 Metlife Survey of the American Teacher, which addressed student and teacher perceptions of school, home, and the community (Metlife, 2002).

In an effort to promote character education and school safety in support of decreasing school violence, educators must work toward building positive school climates (Edwards & Mullis, 2003). The authors note, however, that adopting policies of zero tolerance to aggressive acts by rigidly enforcing disciplinary codes and efforts for profiling school shooters only serve to further alienate students. Pasi (2001) concurs, explaining that although the popularity of adopting a law enforcement approach to addressing issues of school safety is understandable, an educational approach is preferable. Many school prevention efforts treat violent students as deviants while leaving the school climate intact in order to avoid taking responsibility for changes (Astor & Benbenishty, 2005). Efforts such as an increased police presence, locker and student searches, and metal detectors have not been proven effective in ensuring safe schools, although these measures may be appropriate in some situations (Hyman & Snook, 2000). Despite these findings, some state legislatures continue to focus primarily on crime prevention and punishment in their efforts to promote safe schools (Cohen, 2006).

Some schools have been assessing their school climates by surveying teachers, parents, and students; have initiated efforts to improve supervision of students; and have implemented programs to increase the character of all members of their school communities (Cohen, 2006). In response to concerns expressed on surveys, school personnel develop character education programming through bullying prevention, teaching conflict resolution skills, and providing peer mediation programs (Cohen, 2006). It is important for schools to emphasize the development of a positive school climate and to promote positive character development rather than limiting violence prevention efforts only to punitive measures (Edwards & Mullis, 2003).

Character education may also be used to prepare students to better manage school and societal concerns. Britzman (2005) notes that students face complex and challenging issues in today's schools including dishonesty and bigotry, in addition to decreased civility and civic responsibility. Teachers and parents agree that difficult societal issues, including the negative influence of the media, constant peer pressure, and an overall loss of civility in our communities, have negatively impacted our school environments (Theberge & Karan, 2004). In addition, concerns about the influence of the media with sensationalized messages regarding escalating violence, increased sexual activity, and a lack of tolerance pit families, schools, and communities in opposition to each other, with each one placing blame and assigning others the responsibility for preparing their students to be successful while resisting the media and peer messages regarding violence (Britzman, 2005; Lickona, 1993; Traiger, 1995). Due to changes in the schools and the larger society, educators face an increased responsibility to promote positive character in their students (Theberge & Karan, 2004).

Support from Student Issues

The 2002 Report Card on the Ethics of American Youth surveyed more than 12,000 students nationwide and revealed that almost three-fourths of all surveyed students admit to cheating on an exam within the year prior to the survey. Additionally, more than a third of all surveyed students admitted to stealing an item in the last year, with more than 40 percent stating they believed dishonesty was needed in order to get ahead in life (Britzman, 2005).

On a more positive note, 95 percent of the students surveyed indicated that being trustworthy is important (Britzman, 2005).

The 2002 Metlife Survey of the American Teacher surveyed over 2,300 middle and high school students regarding their schools, homes, and communities (Metlife, 2002). Less than a fifth of the students indicated that their schools successfully prepared students to get along with each other (17 percent) or to become good citizens (21 percent). Middle and junior high school students were more positive than high school students, as 13 percent of high school students believed their schools taught students to get along and only 10 percent of the high school students thought schools were effective in developing good citizens (Metlife, 2002). Results from both surveys support the need for effective character education programs in the schools to assist youth in making ethical decisions, getting along with peers, and developing appropriate citizenship skills.

In addition to needing help and direction with decision-making, today's students face challenges to their physical and emotional health. Suicide ideology, depression, abuse of alcohol and drugs, and sexual activity place the health of students in jeopardy. Educators are increasingly aware that students with these and similar significant social, emotional, or behavioral concerns need assistance to be successful in life (Cohen, 2006). Recent developments in drug and alcohol prevention efforts, sex education, health promotion, along with mental health and related initiatives provide additional rationales supporting the need for character education in schools (Cohen, 2006).

Evidence of Academic Achievement

Character education programs and related instructional strategies have been positively linked with student achievement, although much more of an emphasis has been placed on program implementation than upon rigorous research and evaluation of the results (Howard et al., 2004). Wang, Haertel, and Walberg (1994) reviewed 50 years of research and analyzed 11,000 statistical findings in an effort to determine the most significant influences on learning. Their meta-analysis indicates that several factors related to character education have a positive impact on academic achievement, such as classroom climate, positive social and behavioral attributes, and social interactions between teachers and students (Wang et al., 1994).

Benninga and his colleagues compared the extent of implementation of character education programs to academic achievement for 120 elementary schools in California over three years and also found a significant positive correlation between strong character education programs and academic achievement (Benninga et al., 2006). A further analysis of the most successful schools' character education programs revealed four indicators that were components of schools with both effective character education programs and high levels of student achievement. The four common attributes feature: (1) parents and teachers who model and encourage good character, (2) teachers and administrators who promote an environment of care and positive relationships, (3) quality opportunities for students to contribute positively to the school and community, and (4) facilities that ensure clean and safe physical environments (Benninga et al., 2006).

In another analysis, the What Works Clearinghouse (USDOE, 2007) identified 41 character education programs that attempt to promote character development by teaching students core values through specific activities and lessons. Although 14 different programs met the Clearinghouse's evidence standards, only three programs reported results related either to student achievement, such as standardized test scores, or to student persistence, such as attendance, retention, and graduation rates. One program demonstrated significantly positive effects on academic achievement and student behaviors, one had potentially positive effects in student achievement, and the third had no discernible effects (USDOE, 2007).

Several studies found that elementary school students who participated in personal and social skills training in classrooms and small groups demonstrated positive gains in reading and standardized test achievement scores, compared and contrasted with students who participated in classrooms that did not use affective curricular materials (Carns & Carns, 1991; Hadley, 1988; Lee, 1993). In a similar study revealing similar findings, Brigman, Webb, and Campbell (2007) evaluated Student Success Skills (SSS), a program of social and self-management skills combined with cognitive and metacognitive skills

In the study by Brigman and his colleagues (2007), elementary, middle, and high school counselors implemented the SSS curriculum with small groups as well as whole classes in grades five, six, eight, and nine. Significant increases were found in students' scores on the standardized state achievement tests in mathematics when compared and contrasted with the scores earned by a matched set of students who did not participate in the skill training classes or groups. Previous studies also found significant increases in reading achievement scores for students participating in the SSS program (Brigman & Campbell, 2003; Campbell & Brigman, 2005). Classroom teachers across participating urban, rural, and suburban schools reported similar significant increases in student behaviors associated with school success, although no control group data is available for comparison and contrast (Brigman & Campbell, 2003; Webb & Brigman, 2006; Webb, Brigman, & Campbell, 2005).

Promising new directions in promoting character education include educating both teachers and counselors to teach academic, social, and self-confidence skills through programs such as the SSS. Preliminary feedback indicates that instructing teachers and counselors about character education increases faculty and staff investment in utilizing program techniques, improves classroom climate, and generates increased results (Brigman et al., 2007). Providing supportive classroom climates and positive classroom management systems also have been linked to improved student learning (Wang et al., 1994). Academic achievement increases, problem behaviors decline, and classroom climate and relationships improve by teaching the skills related to character education (Cummings & Haverty, 1997; Dodd, 2000; Pasi, 2001).

It is also important to consider more than students' standardized test scores when assessing the impact of character education on student achievement. Zins, Bloodworth, Weissberg, and Walberg (2004) recommend investigating the relationship between character education programming and measures of school success to more accurately assess the effectiveness of character education initiatives. School success encompasses student attitudes such as motivation and responsibility; student behaviors such as attendance, study skills, and engagement; and student performance that includes grades and subject mastery, in addition to test scores (Zins et al., 2004). Use of the more broad measure of school success may provide further evidence of the connections between character education efforts and student achievement.

PROMISING COMPONENTS OF CHARACTER EDUCATION PROGRAMMING

As described previously, character education includes a wide array of programs, approaches, and principles that occur in schools whenever faculty and staff make deliberate efforts to develop caring, principled, and responsible students. Historically, many school districts and schools implemented character education programs that merely emphasized a characteristic of the week; however, effective character education includes more than posting lists of qualities associated with developing positive character (Cohen, 2006). Character education may include behavioral practice in the skills of communication, problem-solving, decision-making, and conflict resolution while fostering the development of positive citizens who are morally responsible, are self-disciplined, and share basic human values (Kress & Elias, 2006). Character education may incorporate citizenship, responsibility, and trustworthiness, as well as the moral and ethical values of respect, fairness, and caring. In addition, character education integrates behavioral, cognitive, and affective demonstration of these traits and skills (Williams, 2000).

Current trends in character education include focusing on similarities among people rather than emphasizing their differences; developing moral reasoning skills as well as promoting positive behaviors; addressing community as well as individual responsibilities; including affective, cognitive, and behavioral programming components; and emphasizing the importance of educators who serve as role models (Williams, 2000). Successful character education programs frequently incorporate several additional components, which are reviewed next.

Actualizing School Mission Statements

Although many school mission statements include preparing students for today's diverse world thorough positive citizenship and character development, most schools have not operationalized their mission or infused it throughout the total school program (Areglado, 2001). Skills related to character education have not always been translated into proven and effective practices in either the total school setting or in individual classrooms. Effective character education programming must include opportunities for students to practice the traits promoted in the school's mission (Martinson, 2003).

School-wide efforts in character education might include developing a school climate of care and a positive moral culture, offering service opportunities for all students that extend into the larger community, and developing partnerships with parents and community organizations in support of these efforts (Lickona, 1993). Lewis (1998) suggests that educators must model and exemplify the characteristics they expect their students to develop in every facet of school life, rather than simply implementing separate programs and classes to foster character development in isolation.

Developing positive character involves more than simply understanding and knowing the steps of decision-making, problem-solving, and conflict mediation; students benefit from opportunities to practice such skills in authentic settings (Edwards & Mullis, 2003). Lewis (1998) suggests that teacher advisory programs, classroom meetings, and collaborative student learning teams offer ideal avenues for developing social and supportive networks to provide students with the opportunities to practice social skills and positive behaviors in support of character development.

Using Service Learning

Seitsinger (2005) emphasizes the importance of providing service learning opportunities as a way that students can further incorporate the concepts of character education into their daily lives. Service learning, traditionally used in higher education, has expanded to PK–12 settings and provides students with opportunities to apply knowledge and skills learned in their classrooms in ways that benefit their communities through tutoring, peer mediation, and other service projects (Anderson, 2000). "This generous giving of time and energy back to the community encourages students to look beyond themselves. The end product of such a lesson will reinforce positive social behavior and develop essential citizenship skills" (Anderson, 2000, pp. 140–141).

In addition to promoting civic responsibility, service learning promotes academic, psychosocial, and career development skills (Stott & Jackson, 2005). Howard (1993) explains that students may gain confidence, learn about compassion and good citizenship, and develop a sense of justice through service learning activities and suggests that service may nurture students' nonacademic strengths and, thus, increase student motivation. In addition, developing service learning programs reflects the value that educators place on positive character development through active service to the larger community (Cohen, 2006). Effective service learning programs meet genuine community needs, are well integrated into the school's curricula, and provide ample opportunities for immediate processing and long range reflection (Cohen, 2006). The school climate should reflect the importance of these values and include parents and the community in the service learning process as a part of positive character development (Lickona, 1993).

Modeling and Enacting Skills of Character Education

It is imperative that students are provided with opportunities to practice the qualities and virtues of character education. Moral and ethical discussions should proceed to the level of real-world dilemmas, decision-making, and problem-solving (Martinson, 2003). Martinson (2003) emphasizes the importance of developing habits or repeatedly practicing a skill as an important way to positively impact moral and ethical development in youth. Teachers are encouraged to serve as caregivers and mentors; create democratic, moral, and cooperative classrooms; teach and practice moral reflection and conflict resolution; and use academic disciplines to discuss values and ethics (Lickona, 1993). Students should be involved in assorted learning experiences to practice positive character behaviors through classroom meetings and community commitments (Martinson, 2003).

Implementing Classroom Meetings

Edwards and Mullis (2003) recommend classroom meetings as another promising component of effective character education programming. Regular classroom meetings promote character education by developing cooperative and supportive classroom and school environments but are an underutilized strategy, especially in high schools (Edwards & Mullis, 2003). Classroom meetings provide opportunities for teachers and counselors to model prosocial skills and to enable students to practice positive social skills related to character development in authentic settings (Charney & Kriete, 2001; Dovre, 2007). During classroom meetings, counselors effectively encourage discussions while guiding students and teachers in positive communication and modeling prosocial group skills (Edwards & Mullis, 2003). When teachers facilitate classroom meetings, a school-wide sense of belonging and connection develops to support positive character development (Edwards & Mullis, 2003).

Other Classroom Practices

Lickona (1993) explains that comprehensive implementation of character education has other implications for classroom practices when teachers support the schools' mission and values of helping students to develop into caring citizens. He suggests that teachers must fully embrace their roles as mentors and caregivers while modeling and supporting appropriate interactions in the classroom. Involving students in establishing classroom rules, fostering a democratic environment, and creating a supportive and valued moral community offer effective ways to promote positive character (Charney & Kriete, 2001). Conflict resolution, cooperative learning, using the curriculum to present ethical issues and moral questions, and assigning writing, and conducting debates to promote reflection are additional ways to have each classroom comprehensively support character education (Lickona, 1993).

Although classroom teachers may adopt specific character education curricula, there are several other programming options. Components of character education can be integrated into the ongoing academic curriculum, teachers can develop caring classrooms and supportive learning environments, or teachers can adjust their instructional process to incorporate the skills of negotiating and conflict resolution (Zins et al., 2004). Character education may also be introduced as a part of the informal curriculum. In this process, instruction promoting character development may be encouraged in such settings as in the school cafeteria, on the playground, and during extracurricular activities (Zins et al., 2004).

Implementing Teacher-Counselor Consultation

Teacher-counselor consultation is another effective tool to use in schools and can incorporate the strengths, skills, and expertise of both teachers and counselors in promoting student, classroom, and school-wide character development (Sink, 2005). Sink (2005) suggests that this type of consultation provides an effective model for improving relationships between and among teachers and students that encourages a prosocial school environment. Counselors are skilled in effective communication and are educated to lead groups in practicing appropriate social and affective skills (Corey & Corey, 1997); counselors can be key personnel in positively impacting character education efforts. Clark and Amatea (2004) suggest that teachers need specific information regarding how school counselors can more effectively assist students and faculty, especially in prevention and developmental services. However, when there is an expectation that teachers and counselors will work collaboratively, time and space must be structured during the school day to facilitate these opportunities for promoting positive development in students (Amatea, Daniels, Bringman, & Vandiver, 2004).

SUCCESSFUL STRATEGIES FOR IMPLEMENTING CHARACTER EDUCATION PROGRAMS

Recommended strategies are suggested for practitioners interested in developing character education programs in their schools. In "Partnerships in Character Education State Pilot Projects, 1995–2001: Lessons Learned," the Office of Safe and Drug-Free Schools summarizes recommendations from federal grant recipients regarding successful implementation of character education in schools and communities (USDOE, 2008). Several of these strategies are also found in nationally recognized character education programs (Dovre, 2007) and will be reviewed in this section.

Comprehensive Programming

Perhaps the most important recommendation from states receiving Partnership in Character Education (PCE) pilot grants is that character education must be comprehensive and integrated into every facet of the school program to be effective (USDOE, 2008). Participants noted that the entire school climate and culture had to change in order to promote positive character development in students. In addition to supporting state academic standards and curricular outcomes, character education projects had to be integral components of the total school program with required participation from the entire school community (USDOE, 2008).

Dovre (2007) reviewed schools that had received national recognition for their character education programs and also found that effective programs in character education are comprehensive, involve all faculty and staff, and exemplify the vision of the director or principal. In these schools, character education can be found embedded in the broader learning environments through classroom meetings and discussions regarding issues and concepts of character and service learning (Dovre, 2007).

Cohen (2006) recommends implementing a comprehensive approach to character education and describes this approach as involving two core processes: (a) systematic efforts to develop safe, responsive, and caring schools and communities, and (b) social, emotional, ethical, and cognitive development processes appropriate for students and adults. The most effective efforts today "are characterized as being provided in more coordinated, sustained, and systematic ways using comprehensive multiyear, multicomponent approaches" (Zins et al., 2004, p. 8). In addition, a planned, coordinated, systematic, and ongoing approach to character development should begin in preschool and continue through high school (Greenberg et al., 2003).

There are some challenges to comprehensive programming for character education initiatives. Many schools currently implement a variety of different programming options that relate to character development such as conflict mediation, health promotion, risk-prevention, service learning, and positive school climates (Greenberg et al., 2003; Zins et al., 2004). "Schools nationally are implementing a median of 14 practices to prevent problem behavior and to promote safe environments" (Zins et al., 2004, p. 5). These efforts are often short-termed, fragmented, and disjointed, with little or no school-wide coordination, efficiency, or understanding of how each separate program contributes to student development or school climate (Cohen, 2006). If these programs are not monitored, evaluated, and/or improved, they will have a questionable impact on character development and are likely to be discontinued quickly (Greenberg et al., 2003).

Professional Development

Every state that received a PCE pilot grant emphasized the value of professional development regarding character education programming for all faculty and staff (USDOE, 2008). Education included disseminating information regarding quality character education programs, effective program assessment, and coordination of the character education program in alignment with state standards and the academic curricula (USDOE, 2008).

Professional development in character education is important because there are high expectations for teachers to serve as character educators (Milsom & Mehlig, 2002). Frequently teachers may not feel comfortable or competent teaching or discussing topics related to social and emotional learning. It is important to provide character education guidance for classroom teachers, since most teachers do not learn about character education in their teacher education programs or through school staff development opportunities (Jones, Ryan, & Bohlin, 1998; Lickona, 1993). A majority of school administrators surveyed in one study admitted that half of their faculty had not received any education in character education (Wood & Roach, 1999). Despite expressing widespread support for character education, most of the 600 colleges and universities surveyed also did not consider or make character education a curricular priority (Nielsen-Jones et al., 1999). Professional development and character education programming guidance must be offered to teacher candidates and faculty who are expected to serve as character educators.

Consensus Building and Collaboration

Research on effective programming for social and emotional education in schools indicates the importance of sustained and collaborative efforts to success of the program (Zins et al., 2004). Developing a collaborative climate of support allows all adults in schools to model important social and emotional skills for students while promoting a commitment for long-term implementation of the program (Kress & Elias, 2006). Howard and Solberg (2006) describe this collaborative implementation through a program that focuses on school success. School counselors meet with faculty, staff, and student services personnel monthly to coordinate the program, prepare interventions, gather feedback, and provide support. Regular meetings allow for long-range planning and encourage opportunities for student goals to be implemented successfully into each teacher's curriculum (Howard & Solberg, 2006).

Skaggs and Bodenhorn (2006) evaluated character education programs in five school districts. Their research indicates that more positive student behaviors were found in schools that implemented programs most effectively linked to positive commitment from school faculty and staff. Furthermore, enthusiastic personnel who were able to tailor the selected character education program to fit their schools' and communities' needs resulted in more positive results, while schools with district-mandated participation and a lack of staff support showed less positive results (Skaggs & Bodenhorn, 2006).

The states that implemented PCE pilot grants also found collaboration and consensus building to be important in the success of their character education programs (USDOE, 2008). In addition to promoting a sense of agreement among participants regarding what character traits were important to emphasize, collaboration promoted investment in the program for faculty and staff, allowing for agreement for implementing the new character education program (USDOE, 2008).

Partnerships

Involving parents and community members as partners in planning and implementation is another effective practice of successful character education programs (Kress & Elias, 2006). The PCE pilot grant recipients reported success with forming partnerships with parents and community members (USDOE, 2008). Each state used some type of steering committee, advisory council, or task force comprised of key community leaders, representatives from a wide array of businesses and agencies, as well as parent and student representation. Involving parents and the larger community created a sense of ownership of the character education programs and led to more successful program implementation (USDOE, 2008). Family involvement in some states included disseminating reports and newsletters to parents and guardians, inviting family members to participate in character education training and program delivery, and using parents and guardians as additional resources at school (USDOE, 2008).

Partnerships for community service and service learning programs are also enhanced through community collaboration. Schools with successful service learning programs promote meaningful parental involvement coupled with local business and community partnerships to enhance character development (Benninga et al., 2006). Skaggs and Bodenhorn (2006) found that community and staff support for character education produced a higher degree of program implementation and resulted in greater reductions of problem behaviors in students.

Program Planning and Evaluation

Historically, character education initiatives have been implemented to address a variety of students' needs including developmental issues such as career exploration, decision-making, and conflict resolution as well as prevention concerns related to alcohol and substance abuse, dropouts, pregnancy, and delinquency (Greenberg et al., 2003). Greenberg et al. (2003) point out that character education initiatives, when implemented without an understanding of the schools' cultures, missions, and priorities, are generally disruptive, short-lived, and ineffective. Effective character education is a process and should be an ongoing component of school programming rather than a quick fix. It is important for schools and school districts to construct long range plans and to spend several years in research, training, implementation, and incorporation of new character education programming. Leadership teams and administrative support must include support for preparation, financial resources, common time for planning and processing during implementation, and regular and ongoing assessment and evaluation with a sustainable commitment for continual reflection and revision (Greenberg et al., 2003).

PCE pilot grant recipients emphasized the importance of carefully designing or selecting a specific character education curriculum as another key component for successful program implementation (USDOE, 2008). In addition, PCE participants agreed that time constraints, budgetary restrictions, lack of commitment from key personnel such as administrators, and assessment concerns presented the major challenges to effective program planning, implementation, and evaluation (USDOE, 2008).

Webb and her colleagues (2005) highlight the importance of fidelity issues associated with implementation of any program, including thorough training, use of a manual for presentation, monitoring student attendance, and even peer coaching. Lewis (1998) cautions that schools may lose their institutional focus when they adopt specific character education curricula or teach character development as a stand-alone subject. In order to improve effectiveness, the total school program and community should demonstrate integrated character education values (Lewis, 1998). Selection of a program and use of a curriculum guide should not limit the implementation of a character education program to the time frame when lessons are presented or only to faculty and staff who facilitate the program (Bulach, 2002). Effective character education should be infused throughout the school day with important skills and values modeled and encouraged by everyone at the school.

Another consideration is the implementation of developmentally appropriate character education programs for students throughout their PK–12 school years. The majority of programs have been designed and implemented in elementary schools, while Leming (1993) points out that much of the current interest in character education results from the risk-taking actions of adolescents. He suggests that services, evaluation, and research regarding program implementation should be focused on high schools and adolescent students (Leming, 1993). PCE pilot grant recipients expressed interest in more effective character education programming options for both middle and high school students (USDOE, 2008). Clarifying how to coordinate several programs to provide continual PK–12 character education in schools is also important to consider (Greenberg et al., 2003).

FUTURE DIRECTIONS

Concerns related to effectively incorporating character education into U.S. schools include research on effective programs and responsibilities for schools of education in preparing educators to implement character education (Greenberg et al., 2003; Howard et al., 2004; Skaggs & Bodenhorn, 2006; Walberg, Zins, & Weissberg, 2004). These concerns and their importance to character education will be explored in this section.

Research

Although character education has been implemented in varying degrees across the United States, empirical research using an experimental design to assess program effectiveness has been limited. According to Skaggs and Bodenhorn (2006), many of the character education programs available for purchase and implementation have been reviewed via internal evaluations or have not undergone any academic review process or evaluation at all. In cases where evaluations have been completed, results often remain with the agency that provided grant funding for implementation (Skaggs & Bodenhorn, 2006). This lack of empirical data on effective programs makes it difficult for school planning or leadership team coordination to select appropriate programs and materials. In addition, character education programs with clear research supporting their effectiveness may not be readily adopted by schools, as educators and legislators may not support the research evidence as objective (Howard et al., 2004). Some school administrators select programs with clear empirical evidence of effectiveness, but school leaders neglect to implement the program with fidelity, which reduces program effectiveness (Greenberg et al., 2003)

The USDOE's emphasis on empirically supported data is also a challenge for educators implementing character education programs (Howard et al., 2004). It is often difficult to locate the required number of schools willing to implement a character education program as mandated by federal guidelines. It is even more difficult to have the requisite number of control schools that will not be able to implement the program for the two years of evaluation (Howard et al., 2004).

Greenberg and his colleagues (2003) suggest future research initiatives should include the development of brief, reliable, and valid instruments for evaluating both students and school environments as the lack of effective instrumentation hinders the systematic collection and review of data. Walberg and colleagues (2004) concur, adding the importance of developing tools to assess academic outcomes and the readiness of teachers, schools, and districts for implementing character education programs. The development of more comprehensive and effective measures will allow contrasts and comparisons among different character education programs and initiatives (Walberg et al., 2004). Cohen (2006) also recommends including action research models to measure the success of character education initiatives. When researchers and practitioners collaborate, investigators will better understand the school culture and practices while practitioners will learn how to more effectively assess their program implementation and interventions (Cohen, 2006).

Greenberg and his colleagues (2003) recommend that consortia be developed to focus on further illuminating effective school-based practices and to further forge the link between such practices and improved academic achievement. Such collaboration would benefit the implementation of large-scale randomized field trials that will provide greater evidence for the effectiveness and impact of character education programming (Walberg et al., 2004). Such large-scale efforts would allow researchers to explore differences in program impacts for differing conditions such as student age, demographics, and type of school (Walberg et al., 2004). Completing meta-analyses of current and future research would also allow investigators to better compare and contrast different character education programs, the importance of implementing with fidelity, and long- and short-term outcomes for different types of students (Walberg et al., 2004). In addition, cost-benefit analyses and other financial comparisons may be valuable for policymakers and educators operating with limited budgets (Walberg et al., 2004). Finally, case study analyses and qualitative investigations might prove beneficial in efforts to determine key barriers to successful character education program implementation (Walberg et al., 2004).

Responsibilities of Higher Education for Character Education

Although teacher educators indicate that they support preparing teacher candidates for character education, there is a lack of evidence that character education is being taught in colleges and universities (Nielsen-Jones et al., 1999). Teacher candidates wanting to teach high school subjects primarily focus on their academic discipline and the cognitive domain; the candidates rarely explore affective development and its connection with learning (Cohen, 2006). Milson and Mehlig (2002) point out the clear discrepancy between the lack of character education teacher candidates receive and the high expectations placed on classroom teachers to serve as character educators. Many educators are not comfortable and do not feel competent teaching character education due to a lack of education (Lickona, 1993). Furthermore, there is little research regarding appropriate curriculum and methods to meet the goal of infusing an awareness of character education into teacher education programs (Milson & Mehlig, 2002).

A gap exists between state departments of education which increasingly are adopting empirically supported character education guidelines, and the preparation and practices found in university schools of education, few of which are incorporating instruction regarding effective character education in their programs (Cohen, 2006). Walberg and colleagues (2004) suggest that the various constituents who influence teacher preparation collaborate to infuse character education into their schools of education. Efforts from such groups as schools of education, state departments of education, state legislators, accrediting agencies, and professional organizations could improve teacher candidate and classroom teacher education programs by incorporating character education programming (Walberg et al., 2004).

Establishing and modeling communication while fostering collaboration among faculty and classroom teachers enrolled in advanced programs can help establish a model for future professional collaboration (Clark & Amatea, 2004). Tobler and colleagues (2000) reviewed results from 207 character education programs and found that prevention programs offered by school counselors had more positive results than those offered by classroom teachers. This finding is not surprising as teacher candidates rarely receive theoretical or practical information regarding effective character education programming or social-emotional considerations in their courses (Cohen, 2006). Counselor education and teacher education departments should establish ongoing communication and connection early and throughout graduate programs to promote future collaboration between counselors and teachers (Clark & Amatea, 2004).

PK–12 schools should seek opportunities to partner with college and university faculty to promote best practices, evaluate effective programs, and contribute to the research related to character education (Fleming & Bay, 2004). Teacher educators can advise PK–12th grade administrators and faculty on planning, implementing, and evaluating effective character education programs; assist in developing effective research; and reporting results on program effectiveness to others. Teacher educators need to continue investigating promising programs and practices in an effort to produce evidence-based research that demonstrates the effects of character education (Fleming & Bay, 2004).

CONCLUSION

Educators have been given a great responsibility associated with the charge to promote character development in PK–12 students, considering the current social climate of increasing violence and reduced civility. Perhaps due to the routine of measuring academic achievement through high-stakes testing, character education programs are less clearly defined and effectively measured in schools. Teachers receive little formal education in character education; program implementation can be hit-or-miss and long-term efforts to sustain programming can be challenging to maintain.

Despite these concerns, there is clear support for comprehensive, collaborative, and sustained efforts in developing effective citizens who are capable of contributing to society in positive ways. To ensure the character development of all PK–12th grade students, it is imperative that educational goals and standards be revised to incorporate character education as an integral component of each and every school. Private organizations, university schools of education, state and federal governments, as well as communities, families, and schools share in the responsibility of promoting positive character development in all children.

APPLICATION ACTIVITIES

Activity 1

Go to the Character Education Partnership's website at www.character.org/site/c.ipIJKTOEJsG/b.3438707/. Use the Character Education Quality Standards to assess your institution's effectiveness in operationalizing the key components of character education programming (Character Education Partnership, 2008). Ask a colleague to complete the assessment and compare your results. What are areas of strength in your character education initiatives? What are areas for concern? Select one standard that needs to be more fully implemented and share three strategies that might be used to more fully incorporate this initiative.

Activity 2

Review the mission statement of your school, district, department, agency, or another program. Reflect on the ways in which this mission statement is or is not fully realized in the programs, policies, practices, and personnel actions of the organization. What are some of the ways in which the mission is effectively promoted? What changes might you suggest to more closely align the program with its stated mission?

Activity 3

Go to the Character Education Partnership's website at www.character.org/site/c.ipIJKTOEJsG/b.3438707/. Review the 11 Principles of Effective Character Education (Lickona, Schaps, & Lewis, 2007). Select a principle that was discussed in this chapter and identify how it is addressed at your institution. What recommendations do you have for further implementing this principle into your program?

Activity 4

Reflect on your personal educational experience and teacher education. What are some of the positive character traits that you were encouraged to develop during your educational experiences? How were the expectations transmitted and how successful were the efforts? If you had the opportunity, what might you say to your former teachers, professors, and mentors regarding your character development?

Activity 5

Consider one practice that you would be willing to incorporate in your class, school, or work setting in order to promote character development and education. What might make it challenging to sustain your efforts? What resources might enhance your ability to further character education in your community?

REFERENCES

Amatea, E. S., Daniels, H., Bringman, N., & Vandiver, F. M. (2004). Strengthening counselor teacher-family connections: The family-school collaborative consultation project. *Professional School Counselor, 8,* 47–55.

Anderson, D. R. (2000). Character education: Who is responsible? *Journal of Instructional Psychology, 27*(3), 139–142.

Areglado, R. J. (2001). Social and emotional learning: The future is now. In J. Cohen (Ed.), *Caring classrooms/intelligent schools: The social emotional education of young children* (pp. 183–194). New York: Teachers College Press.

Astor, R. A., & Benbenishty, R. (2005). *School violence in context: Culture, neighborhood, family, school, and gender.* New York: Oxford University Press.

Benninga, J. S., Berkowitz, M. W., Kuehn, P., & Smith, K. (2006). Character and academics: What good schools do. *Phi Delta Kappan, 87*(6), 448–454.

Brandt, R., & Wolfe, P. (1998). What do we know from brain research? *Educational Leadership, 56*(3), 8–13.

Brigman, G., & Campbell, C. (2003). Helping students improve academic achievement and school success behavior. *Professional School Counseling, 7,* 91–98.

Brigman, G., Webb, L. D., & Campbell, C. (2007). Building skills for student success: Improving the academic and social competence of students. *Professional School Counseling, 10*(3), 279–288.

Britzman, M. J. (2005). Improving our moral landscape via character education: An opportunity for school counselor leadership. *Professional School Counseling, 8,* 293–295.

Bulach, C. R. (2002). Implementing a character education curriculum and assessing its impact on student behavior. *The Clearinghouse, 79,* 79–83.

Campbell, C., & Brigman, G. (2005). Closing the achievement gap: A structured approach to group counseling. *Journal for Specialists in Group Work, 30,* 67–82.

Carns, A. W., & Carns, M. R. (1991). Teaching study skills, cognitive skills, and metacognitive skills through self-diagnosed learning styles. *Elementary School Guidance and Counseling, 38,* 341–346.

Character Education Partnership. (2008). *Character education quality standards.* Washington, DC: author. Retrieved from www.character.org/site/c.ipIJKTOEJsG/b.3438707/.

Charney, R., & Kriete, R. (2001). Creating a classroom community where social emotional learning thrives: The case of the "cool girls" list. In J. Cohen (Ed.), *Caring classrooms/intelligent schools: The social emotional education of young children* (pp. 77–84). New York: Teachers College Press.

Clark, M. A., & Amatea, E. (2004). Teacher perceptions and expectations of school counselor contributions: Implications for program planning and training. *Professional School Counseling, 8,* 132–140.

Cohen, J. (2006). Social, emotional, ethical, and academic education: Creating a climate for learning, participation in democracy and well-bring. *Harvard Educational Review, 76*, 201–237.

Corey, M. G., & Corey, G. (1997). *Groups: Process and practice*. Belmont, CA: Thompson Brooks/Cole.

Cummings, C., & Haverty, K. P. (1997). Praising healthy children. *Educational Leadership, 54*(8), 28–31.

Dodd, A. (2000). Making schools safe for all students: Why schools need to teach more than the 3Rs. *NASSP Bulletin, 84*(614), 25–31.

Dovre, P. J. (2007). From Aristotle to Angelou: Best practices in character education. *Education Next, 2007*(2), 38–45.

Edwards, D., & Mullis, F. (2003). Classroom meetings: Encouraging a climate of cooperation. *Professional School Counseling, 7*, 20–28.

Fleming, J. E., & Bay, M. (2004). Social and emotional learning in teacher preparation standards. In J. E. Zins, R. P. Weissberg, M. C. Wang, & H. J. Walberg (Eds.), *Building school success through social and emotional learning* (pp. 94–110). New York: Teachers College Press.

Greenberg, M. T., Weissberg, R. P., O'Brien, M. U., Zins, J., E., Fredericks, L., Resnik, H., & Elias, M. J. (2003). Enhancing school-based prevention and youth development through coordinated social, emotional, and academic learning. *American Psychologist, 58*, 466–474.

Hadley, H. R. (1988). Improving reading scores through a self-esteem intervention program. *Elementary School Guidance and Counseling, 22*, 248–252.

Howard, K. A. S., & Solberg, V. S. H. (2006). School-based social justice: The achieving success identity pathways program. *Professional School Counseling, 9*, 278–287.

Howard, M. B. (1993). Service learning: Character education applied. *Educational Leadership, 51*(3), 42–44.

Howard, R. W., Berkowitz, M. W., & Schaeffer, E. F. (2004). Politics of character education. *Educational Policy, 18*, 188–215.

Hyman, I., & Snook, P. (2000). Dangerous schools and what you can do about them. *Phi Delta Kappan, 81*, 489–501.

Jones, E., Ryan, K., & Bohlin, K. (1998). Character education and teacher education: How are prospective teachers being prepared to foster good character in students? *Action in Teacher Education, 20*, 11–28.

Jones, E., Ryan, K., & Bohlin, K. (1999). *Teachers as educators of character: Are the nation's schools of education coming up short?* Washington, DC: Character Education Partnership.

Jones, S. E., Fisher, C. J., Greene, B. Z., Hertz, M. F., & Pritzl, J. (2007). Healthy and safe school environments, part I: Results from the school health policies and programs study 2006. *Journal of School Health, 77*, 522–543.

Kohlberg, L. (1969). Stage and sequence: The cognitive-developmental approach to socialization. In D. A. Goslin (Ed.), *Handbook of socialization theory and research* (pp. 347–480). Chicago: Rand McNally.

Kress, J. S., & Elias, M. J. (2006). Building learning communities through social and emotional learning: Navigating the rough seas of implementation. *Professional School Counseling, 10*, 102–107.

Lee, R. S. (1993). Effects of classroom guidance on student achievement. *Elementary School Guidance and Counseling, 27*, 163–171.

Leming, J. S. (1993). In search of effective character education. *Educational Leadership, 51*(3), 63–71.

Lewis, A. C. (1998). Seeking connections through character. *Phi Delta Kappan, 80*, 99–100.

Lickona, T. (1993). The return of character education. *Educational leadership, 51*(3), 6–11.

Lickona, T., Schaps, E., & Lewis, C. (2007) *CEP's 11 Principles of Effective Character Education*. Washington, DC: Character Education Partnership. Retrieved from www.character.org/site/c.ipIJKTOEJsG/b.3438707/.

Martinson, D. L. (2003). High school students and character education: It all starts at Wendy's. *The Clearinghouse, 77*, 14–18.

Metlife. (2002). *The Metlife survey of the American teacher 2002 student life: School, home and community*. New York: author. Retrieved from www.metlife.com.

Milson, A., & Mehlig, L. M. (2002). Elementary school teacher's sense of efficacy for character education. *The Journal of Educational Research, 96*, 47–54.

New York State Education Department. (2001). *Project SAVE, Safe Schools against Violence in Education Act: Instruction in Civility, Citizenship and Character Education*. Retrieved from www.emsc.nysed.gov/deputy/Documents/character-ed.html.

Nielsen-Jones, R., Ryan, K., & Bohlin, K. (1999). *Teachers as educators of character: Are the nation's schools of education coming up short*? Washington, DC: Character Education Partnership.

Partnerships in Character Education (PAC). (2007). *FY 2007 Grant Awards*. Retrieved from www.ed.gov/programs/charactered/2007awards.html.

Pasi, R. J. (2001). A climate for achievement. *Principal Leadership, 2*(4), 17–20.

Rose, L. C., & Gallup, A. M. (2000). *The 32nd annual Phi Delta Kappa/Gallup Poll of the public's attitude toward the public schools*. Retrieved from www.pdkintl.org /kappan/kpol0009.htm.

Rose, L. C., & Gallup, A. M. (2007). The 39th Annual Phi Delta Kappa/Gallup poll of the public's attitude toward the public schools. *Phi Delta Kappa, 89*, 35–45.

Seitsinger, A. M. (2005). Service-learning and standards-based instruction in middle schools. *The Journal of Educational Research, 99*, 19–30.

Sink, C. A. (2005). Fostering academic development and learning: Implications and recommendations for middle school counselors. *Professional School Counseling, 9*, 128–135.

Skaggs, G., & Bodenhorn, N. (2006). Relationships between implementing character education, student behavior and student achievement. *Journal of Advanced Academics, 18*, 82–115.

Stott, K. A., & Jackson, A. P. (2005). Using service learning to achieve middle school comprehensive program goals. *Professional School Counseling, 9*, 156–159.

Theberge, S. K., & Karan, O. C. (2004). Six factors inhibiting the use of peer mediation in a junior high school. *Professional School Counseling, 7*, 283–290.

Tobler, N. S., Roona, M. R., Ochshorn, P., Marshall, D. G., Streke, A. V., & Stackpole, K. M. (2000). School-based adolescent drug prevention programs: 1998 meta-analysis. *Journal of Primary Prevention, 20*, 275–336.

Traiger, J. (1995). The time is now: Reflections on moral education. *Education, 115,* 432–434.
U.S. Department of Education (USDOE). (2001). *No Child Left Behind Act of 2001.* Retrieved from www.ed.gov/nclb/landing.jhtml.
U.S. Department of Education, Institute of Education Sciences, What Works Clearinghouse (2007). *WWC Topic Report: Character Education.* Retrieved June 1, 2008, from ies.ed.gov/ncee/wwc/reports/character_education/topic/index.asp.
U.S. Department of Education, Office of Safe and Drug-Free Schools, Character Education and Civic Engagement Technical Assistance Center. (2008). *Partnerships in character education, state pilot projects, 1995–2001: Lessons learned.* Retrieved June 7, 2008, from www.cetac.org/documents/Publications/DOE_StatePilot.pdf.
Walberg, H. J., Zins, J. E., & Weissberg, R. P. (2004). Recommendations and conclusions: Implications for practice, training, research, and policy. In J. E. Zins, R. P. Weissberg, M. C. Wang, & H. J. Walberg (Eds.), *Building school success through social and emotional learning* (pp. 209–217). New York: Teachers College Press.
Wang, M. C., Haertel, G. D., & Walberg, H. J. (1994). What helps students learn? Spotlight on student success. *Educational Leadership, 51,* 74–79.
Webb, L. D., & Brigman, G. A. (2006). Student success skills: Tools and strategies for improved academic and social outcomes. *Professional School Counseling, 10,* 112–120.
Webb, L. D., Brigman, G. A., & Campbell, C. (2005). Linking school counselors and student success: A replication of the student success skills approach targeting the academic and social competence of students. *Professional School Counseling, 8,* 407–413.
Welsh, W. N. (2000). The effects of school climate on school disorder. *Annals of the American Academy of Political and Social Science, 567,* 88–107.
Williams, M. (2000). Models of character education: Perspectives and developmental issues. *Journal of Humanistic Counseling, Education and Development, 39,* 32–40.
Wood, R. W., & Roach, L. (1999). Administrators' perceptions of character education. *Education, 120,* 213–217.
Zins, J. E., Bloodworth, M. R., Weissberg, R. P., & Walberg, H. J. (2004). The scientific base linking social and emotional learning to school success. In J. E. Zins, R. P. Weissberg, M. C. Wang, & H. J. Walberg (Eds.), *Building school success through social and emotional learning* (pp. 3–22). New York: Teachers College Press.

8

Affective Education through Best Practices and Conflict Resolution

Candace H. Lacey, Patrice R. LeBlanc, and Nancy L. Maldonado

ABSTRACT

This study investigated whether implementation of the "Peace Works" conflict resolution program reduced angry and aggressive behavior and increased prosocial behavior in students. Data were collected at four elementary schools and two middle schools, with equal numbers of treatment and control schools. Findings indicated that elementary treatment schools showed a significant decrease in hostile/irritable behaviors and a tendency to move in the appropriate directions to increase social competence. No significant changes were noted at the middle school level except for increases in interpersonal skills at the control school, which may have been due to the effects of simultaneous participation in other social and emotional learning programs. Best practices for teaching effectiveness incorporated within the "Peace Works" program are identified.

Affective education, or the processes of developing the social and emotional side of the learner, can be traced back to the Progressive Education Movement and John Dewey. Dewey's pedagogy focused on the development of skills extending from requisite knowledge and dispositions needed for effective participation in a democratic society, including solving problems in nonviolent ways and developing social and emotional growth in students (Cohen, 2006; Parkay & Hardcastle Stanford, 2007). Today, social and emotional learning (SEL) is a growing movement in education (Graczyk, Domitrovich, Small, & Zins, 2006). It is seen as a way "to improve social, emotional, and behavioral skills in children and youth, prevent risky behaviors, and promote engagement in learning and achievement" (Graczyk et al., p. 267). Early intervention to teach children the skills and dispositions for learning has become a policy focus (Fantuzzo et al., 2007) with social skills such as cooperation, engagement, and persistence being deemed as those necessary for learning (USDOHHS, 2000). SEL efforts in schools include character education and conflict resolution (Cohen, 2006). Interestingly, conflict resolution is viewed as a basic component of SEL programs, as well as bullying prevention (Cohen, Compton, & Deikman as cited in Cohen, 2006; McGrath, 2007).

Since violence in the United States has reached "epidemic proportions" and is "a significant aspect of the public school experience in America" (Yell & Rozalski, 2000, para. 2), SEL programs are being used as measures to combat school violence. In particular, research indicates that increasingly children are at risk for being involved in violence (Kramer, Jones, Kirchner, Miller, & Wilson, 2002; Opotow, Gerson, & Woodside, 2005; Werle, 2006). It is no surprise that both teachers and students feel that schools are unsafe places where violence can occur at any time (Browning, Cohen, & Warman, 2003; Flynt & Morton, 2004; Hanish & Guerra, 2000; Harris, 2007; Jenkins, 2007; Kramer et al., 2002; Stallworth-Clark, 2007; Werle, 2006). Associated with school safety is "peer victimization." Peer victimization is an outcome of intentional bullying that results in diminishing a child's sense of worth and acceptance (Brock, 2005). Peer victimization has been the focus of recent attention because of the association between victimization and school shootings and fatalities (Felix & McMahon, 2006). In addition, Werle reinforces the concept that bullying is related to violent crimes, citing the relationship between school shootings and prior victimization by bullies.

Fortunately, peace education "reforms counteracted the most prevalent form of school violence, bullying, that affects over five million elementary and junior high students a year and has played a role in most school shootings" (Burlach & Penland, as cited in Harris, 2007, p. 351). Through both prevention and intervention SEL programs, schools can make a difference (Brion-Meisels, Brion-Meisels, & Hoffman, 2007; Jenkins, 2007; Kramer et al., 2002.; Michael, 2000; Rowan, 2007; Skroban, Gottfredson, & Gottfredson, 1999; Smith, Schneider, Smith, & Ananiadou, 2004; Werle, 2006; Yoon, 2004). Kramer et al. (2002) state this well:

> Because one constant in the lives of most youth is school attendance, it is a natural setting in which teachers and school personnel have the opportunity to intervene when a child or adolescent exhibits potential signs of violence or appears to be at risk for other reasons. (para. 35)

Failing to teach social competence at a young age can perpetuate a cycle of violence (Corcoran & Mallinckrodt, 2000; Harris, 2007; Jenkins, 2007; Opotow et al., 2005). Thus, SEL programs hold promise for combating school violence. This chapter discusses a research study conducted on one such SEL program, "Peace Works," a conflict resolution program.

LITERATURE REVIEW

Social Competence

Much like Dewey, Jenkins (2007) notes that education has a social purpose: the creation of "active citizen-learners with the necessary skills and knowledge to understand, confront, resist, transform, and ultimately eliminate violence in all its multiple forms and manifestations" (p. 367). A part of the social purpose of education is the development of social competence in students. It is also a goal of SEL to enhance the emotional and social aspects of life in order to be "successful [in the] accomplishments of life tasks" (Harris, 2007, p. 351).

McKenzie (2004) discusses social competence under the umbrella of SEL, a construct commonly referenced as social-awareness, social problem solving, and emotional intelligence. However, the overall goal of social competence is to encourage prosocial behaviors. These behaviors "usually include the qualities of responsiveness, flexibility, empathy and caring, communication skills, a sense of humor (Bernard as cited in DeMar, 1997, p. 219). "Children's ability to form positive relationships with peers represents an important component of social development" (Newcomb & Bagwell, as cited in Lindsey, 2002, p. 145). In educational settings, being socially accepted is an important factor of adjustment. Furthermore, social success is related to academic success (Fan & Mak, 1998; McKenzie, 2004; Sandy, Bailey, & Sloane-Akwara, 2000; Stevahn, 1997, 2004; Stevahn, Johnson, Johnson, Oberle, & Wahl, 2000), while inadequate social success has been linked to delinquency (Loeber, 1985; McCay & Keyes, 2001), mental health problems (Browning et al., 2003; Felix & McMahon, 2006), and the development of antisocial behavior (Coie & Dodge, 1998; Felix & McMahon, 2006).

Conflict Resolution

According to Harris (2007, p. 351), "conflict-resolution education is one of the fastest-growing school reforms." These programs address mediation as well as conflict resolution. When effectively implemented, conflict resolution programs can increase prosocial skills while decreasing antisocial behaviors that are linked to school violence (Enger, LeBlanc, & Lacey, 2000; Ferber, 2007; Grossman et al., 1997; Lacey, 1999, 2000; Lacey & LeBlanc, 2000; LeBlanc & Lacey, 1999; Pellegrini & Bartini, 2000; Schellenberg, Parks-Savage, & Rehfuss, 2007; Stomfay-Stitz & Wheeler, 2007; Vestal & Jones, 2004).

Effective programs for prevention of violence include nine components: (1) taking a comprehensive approach that "includes family, peers, media, and community" (Dusenbury, Falco, Lake, Brannigan, & Bosworth, 1997, p. 410); (2) starting in primary grades; (3) developing interventions suited to developmental stages; (4) "promot[ing] personal and social competencies" (p. 411); (5) using varied, interactive, teaching techniques; (6) reflecting the ethnic/cultural identity of the recipients; (7) incorporating staff development to insure program fidelity; (8) designing activities to foster "positive school climate" including "effective classroom management strategies that promote good discipline" (p. 412); and (9) developing activities to create a climate in which the norm is peace—"against violence, aggression, and bullying" (p. 412). Many aspects of each of these nine components link to what teacher education refers to as best practices.

Best Practices for Teachers

Particularly since the passage of No Child Left Behind (USDOE, 2001), teachers are held accountable for using best practices in teaching. Best practices include strategies that have been researched and found to be effective in enhancing students' growth and development (Arends, 2007). For example, Stronge's (2002) compendium of research literature on effective teachers identifies many of these best practices, several of which are identified in the work of Dusenbury and colleagues (1997) (e.g., component numbers six and eight in the previous section). Other research on SEL programs identifies best practices as well, as educators understand that "techniques and instructional strategies have nearly as much influence on student learning as student aptitude" (Stronge, p. 44).

For example, several of Rowan's (2007) recommendations for teachers related to bullying correspond to best practices identified by Stronge (2002). Rowan recommends: (1) "reflect[ing] on classroom management practices"; (2) "promot[ing] nonviolence, respect, and service to others"; (3) "teach[ing] responsibility and teamwork"; and (4) "collaborating" (pp. 183, 185). In addition, Rowan's study suggests that effective classroom management strategies may reduce bullying. Therefore, she suggests that teacher preparation programs emphasize these strategies.

Another example of best practices to prevent violence is in Jenkins's (2007) work. At the Peace Education Center at Teachers College at Columbia University, educators are guided in "pedagogy of engagement" and learn the "power of nonviolence" (pp. 183–186). Again, the importance of pedagogy arises, connecting to Stronge's (2002) work that suggests effective teachers have "a broad repertoire of approaches" (p. 45).

The Peace Works Program

The Peace Education Foundation's (PEF) "Peace Works" program is a grade-level specific curriculum that teaches students the dispositions, behaviors, and skills necessary to resolve conflict peaceably. The focus of this program is to develop peaceable schools. To this end, the curriculum content is made up of six essential components, delineated in the PEF's White Paper (PEF, Content section, para. 1).

1. Community Building: Building trust, exploring common interests, and respecting differences
2. Developmentally Appropriate Rules: Establishing the framework for appropriate behavior and the associated skills, such as I-messages, listening, assertion, and problem-solving
3. Understanding Conflict: Defining conflict, the elements of conflict, escalation and de-escalation, different conflict management styles
4. Perception: Understanding different points of view, enhancing empathy, and increasing tolerance
5. Anger Management: Identifying the pros and cons of anger, triggers, anger styles, increasing tolerance of frustration, anger management plans
6. Communication skills: Incorporating I-messages and related basic skills of expressing feelings in order to help resolve conflicts constructively and peacefully

Based on the previous discussion of best practices, it is easy to see that many of the components of the "Peace Works" program draw on common best practices in education (e.g., Developmentally Appropriate Rules) that aid in effective classroom management.

The "Peace Works" curriculum is implemented in a model, teach, coach, encourage, and export methodology. Modeling is the first step since people tend to follow what they see demonstrated, even more than what is said to them. Next, the dispositions, behaviors, and skills are taught explicitly, reinforcing what the participants/students have seen modeled. Then, the participants/students are coached and encouraged to use what they learned. Finally, the participants/students export the dispositions, behaviors, and skills into real life situations. These varied teaching strategies make use of best practices in pedagogy. Additionally, through these strategies, conflict resolution moves beyond a program and becomes a process for peaceably resolving conflict. When implemented throughout a school, the result is a peaceable school where conflict resolution is part of the school climate or culture, a component of effective SEL programs.

The six components taught through the "Peace Works" program's materials relate to specific lessons with grade-level student workbooks and teachers' manuals. The lessons incorporate interesting stories and engaging activities (e.g., games and role-playing). For accurate implementation, the teacher teaches lessons a minimum of once per week, using the methodology of modeling, teaching, coaching, encouraging, and exporting.

The Current Study

Seeking to take a proactive approach in addressing the issues of school violence and bullying, the Peace Education Foundation and the Miami-Dade County Public Schools System applied for and received a two-year Allegany Foundation Grant to fund the implementation of the "Making Peace Work in the Miami-Dade County Public Schools" project. The "Peace Works" conflict resolution program was implemented in one region of the Miami-Dade County Public Schools. Two of the major goals of the project were to: (1) reduce students' aggressive behavior and (2) promote students' prosocial behavior through the use of conflict resolution. This chapter reports on the program results related to those goals.

With this primary goal serving as the project's focus, the following research questions guided this study. Does the "Making Peace Work in the Miami-Dade County Public Schools" project reduce angry and aggressive behaviors? Does the "Making Peace Work in Miami-Dade County Public Schools" project increase prosocial behavior?

METHODS

Design

In order to report outcomes related to student growth, a dominant-less dominant mixed method research design was used in this study (Creswell, 1994; Tashakkori & Teddlie, 1998). A parallel QUAN + qual design (Miller, 2003) was selected because the primary data for assessing outcomes related to students' growth were quantitative measures. The dominant quantitative portion of the design used an experimental pretest and posttest design with the school as the basis of randomization. This design ensured that gains made in students' prosocial skills and reduction in aggressive behavior were the result of the conflict resolution program and not the result of other factors (e.g., maturation), thus addressing the validity of results and findings.

The less dominant qualitative methods of interviews and observation served to obtain participant's perceptions of the program. The qualitative findings reported in this chapter help to enhance the findings of the quantitative data by elaborating on the project outcomes (Creswell, 1994).

Participants

The community where the project schools were located was considered semi-rural, comprised mostly of farms, and characterized as poor with many migrant workers. Eight of the region's elementary schools and two of the middle schools participated in the project. The participant schools were selected based on their similar demographic and economic characteristics allowing control of these factors as intervening variables in the project. Region level administrators in the district selected the ten participating schools.

Once the schools were chosen, they were randomly selected as treatment or control schools. Treatment schools received the conflict resolution training immediately, while control schools waited until the end of the project.

For the purpose of this analysis, the two control elementary schools and two elementary schools randomly selected from the treatment schools were used. The one treatment and one control middle school are also included in this analysis.

One exemplary teacher was identified at the third grade level in each of the treatment and control schools. Exemplary teachers were selected since these teachers are more self-actualized and have higher self-efficacy, thus they tend to be more persistent and successful at implementing change programs (Fullan, 2001).

At the beginning of the academic year, 100 elementary school students and 61 middle school students were enrolled in the classrooms presented in this analysis. Because of the transient nature of the area, final data sets were available for 73 elementary school students (42 in the treatment group and 31 in the control) and 48 middle school students (31 in the treatment group and 30 in the control group).

Data Sources and Collection

Data for this study were collected from multiple sources. To provide context, school level demographic data were gathered from the district's school profiles. Classroom teachers provided data related to students.

At the beginning of the school year, both treatment and control teachers were trained to complete the School Social Behavior Scales (SSBS) on their students (Merrell, 1993, 2002). The SSBS is a valid and reliable instrument used to measure students' prosocial skills and antisocial behavior. The SSBS includes 65 items on two scales (Social Competence, 32 items, and Antisocial Behavior, 33 items). Each of these scales contains three subscales. Interpersonal Skills, Self-Management Skills, and Academic Skills comprise the Social Competency Scale. Hostile-Irritable Behavior, Antisocial-Aggressive Behavior, and Demanding-Disruptive Behavior comprise the Antisocial Behavior Scale. Data were analyzed using paired sample t-tests to determine if any significant differences existed between the treatment and control schools on the instruments subscales.

In order to enhance the findings of the quantitative data, sets of questions or protocols were developed that prompted the participants to express their thoughts during focus groups and interviews. These probing questions were asked to elicit participants' experiences with the project (Silverman, 2006). Protocols remained flexible, iterative, and continuously in design (Rubin & Rubin, 2004) for effectiveness. While this chapter does not report on the qualitative data in-depth, the findings that are presented serve to clarify and/or explain the quantitative conclusions.

Procedures

As previously mentioned, exemplary teachers were selected in both treatment and control classrooms. The selection of exemplary teachers helped to control for effects of poor teacher self-efficacy, which has been found to impact the implementation of a conflict resolution program negatively (LeBlanc, Lacey, & Mulder, 1998).

The standards for selecting the exemplary teacher were based on a list of characteristics identified in a review of the literature. School principals and/or assistant principals used this list to identify the participating exemplary teachers. As an incentive, all of the participating teachers were awarded points toward renewal of their teaching certificates for their work on the project.

Project teachers were educated in the "Peace Works" curriculum in two sessions. The training encompassed the six essential components of the "Peace Works" program. The training methodology modeled the same strategies used in the "Peace Works" curriculum, based on the sequence of modeling, teaching, coaching, encouraging, and exporting. The agenda for each instructional session included an overview and goals; community building and motivational activities; instruction in the essential components using discussions, games, role plays, and student materials; time for questions and answers; and closure that included teacher reflection on learning from the session.

School sites were considered in the planning of the training. Sessions were coordinated to allow for use of teacher planning days scheduled for the start of the school year, large group sessions, and follow-up sessions to ensure accurate implementation of the conflict resolution program. Additional training was held for all personnel in the schools. Finally, train-the-trainer sessions were conducted to ensure that at least two people at each school could train other people within their schools.

Implementation teams for each school developed action plans for implementation, setting goals for their individual schools that they reported on at the end of the year. The team consisted of an assistant principal, classroom teachers, and support staff. To ensure fidelity of implementation, the teachers were responsible for teaching classroom lessons a minimum of once per week, using the methodology of modeling, teaching, coaching, encouraging, and exporting.

Just prior to the implementation of the conflict resolution curriculum, teachers completed the pre-SBSS for each of the students in the classroom. The teachers completed the post-SBSS on their students at the end of the school year in June, after having taught the curriculum throughout the year.

Interviews with school administrators and focus groups with project teachers were held midway through project implementation. Again, these findings serve only to support the quantitative data reported in this chapter.

Data Analysis

Class level quantitative data were analyzed using paired sample t-tests to determine if there was a significant difference between pre- and post-scores on the SSBS. To determine if reduction in students' aggressive behavior scores and increase in students' prosocial behavior scores were greater for the treatment group than for the control group, change scores were calculated. The researchers also reviewed interview transcripts in order to elaborate and further illustrate the quantitative findings (Creswell, 1994).

FINDINGS AND DISCUSSION

In order to increase the clarity of data interpretation from the SSBS, the reporting of results are organized by grade level. First, the elementary school classes' demographic results are reported. Second, the SSBS results on antisocial behaviors are presented. Next, SBSS social competency results are presented. Finally, change scores for treatment and control classes are discussed. Findings are presented in the same manner for the middle school classes.

Elementary Schools' Class Demographics

As previously mentioned, classroom level data were collected from the individual classroom teachers. The back of the SBSS had questions related to each student's demographics. Table 8.1 presents demographic data for the four elementary schools included in this study.

Of the teachers who reported student ages, the average age of the students in this study was 8.3 years. It should be noted, the teacher at CW Elementary failed to complete the age data. By ethnic breakdown, 7 percent (n= 3) were white/non-Hispanic students, 38 percent (n=16) were black students,

Table 8.1 Elementary Schools Treatment and Control Classes' Demographics

		Treatment Classes		Control Classes	
	Total	Class TF	Class TH	Class CC	Class CW
Number of Participants	73	19	23	20	11
Age					
8	39	10	16	13	
9	20	8	7	5	
Not reported	11				11
Gender					
Male	36	13	10	12	1
Female	35	6	13	8	8
Not reported	2				2
Ethnicity					
White/ Non-Hispanic	5	1	2	2	
Black	23	9	7	5	2
Hispanic	43	8	14	12	9
Other	2	1		1	
Special Programs					
ESE	1	1			
ESOL	11			11	
Speech	1				1

Note: This table was constructed using data provided by classroom teachers who completed the demographic portion of the SSBS. All classes were third grade.

and 52 percent (n=22) were Hispanic students. The control classes had 7 percent (n=2) white/non-Hispanic students, 22 percent (n=7) black students, and 68 percent (n=21) Hispanic students.

Elementary School Classes' SSBS Antisocial Behavior Results

There were no significant reductions or increases in the total antisocial behavior on any of the subscales for treatment Class TH or control Class CC. Lack of a consistent principal figure may have impacted the implementation of the program in Class TH. The school had three principals in three years, a dynamic that came to light during qualitative data collection.

Treatment Class TF showed significant reductions on the total antisocial behavior scale and on the hostile/irritable and demanding/disruptive subscales. Moderate to high effect sizes (*d*) are noted for each of these areas. Of particular importance to the impact of this program was the teacher. Her level of enthusiasm and expertise resulted in her being nominated and subsequently awarded the "Peace Educator of the Year" award from the Peace Education Foundation.

Control Class CW showed significant increases on the hostile/irritable behavior, antisocial/aggressive behavior, and demanding/disruptive behaviors subscales. These scores resulted in a significant increase in the total antisocial behavior scale.

When scores for the treatment schools were combined and compared to the combined scores for the control schools, treatment schools showed a significant decrease in hostile/irritable behaviors. Table 8.2 presents these findings.

Elementary School Treatment and Control Classes' SSBS Social Competence Results

Table 8.3 presents the changes that occurred in the treatment classes and the control classes related to social competence. The results indicate a significant increase in interpersonal skills for TF treatment class, with total social competency scores also improving significantly.

Interestingly, the one control class (CC) had significant increases in students' academic skills and self-management skills. These increases can be attributed to the exemplary teacher's use of positive approaches to discipline, including "Peace Works" peace education techniques that the teacher implemented on her own, which was another finding from the qualitative data.

Control class CW showed a significant decrease in academic skills. This result might be due to the high number of English speakers of other languages (ESOL) students in this class. Most of these children lived in homes where English was not spoken, and thus they might have been at a disadvantage when they came to school.

Change scores were calculated for the combined treatment classes and the combined control classes. While the only significant change was found in the decrease on hostile/irritable behavior subscale of the combined treatment classes ($p=.034$, $d=.512$), it is worthwhile to note that all change scores for the treatment classes showed a tendency to move in the appropriate directions. The control groups showed an opposite tendency with social competence skills declining across all scales and subscales while antisocial behaviors increased across all scales and subscales. Table 8.4 summarizes these findings.

Middle School's Class Demographics

As can be seen in table 8.5, the number of participants in the treatment and the control classes is approximately the same. The age of participants indicates that 88 percent of the control class was 11, while 74 percent of

Table 8.2 Elementary School Treatment and Control Classes' SSBS Antisocial Behavior Results

	N	M_{pre}	M_{post}	t	p	d
Hostile/Irritable						
Class TH (T)	23	20.96	21.13	.117	.908	
Class TF (T)	19	24.37	18.84	-3.452	.003*	.792
Class CC (C)	20	19.80	18.45	-1.243	.229	
Class CW (C)	11	22.73	28.91	2.712	.022*	.818
Treatment Total	42	22.50	20.10	-2.065	.045*	.322
Control Total	31	20.84	22.16	1.069	.293	
Antisocial/Aggressive						
Class TH (T)	23	13.39	13.83	.344	.734	
Class TF (T)	19	14.05	12.68	-1.895	.074	
Class CC (C)	20	12.80	12.95	1.62	.873	
Class CW (C)	11	13.91	19.55	2.350	.041*	.709
Treatment Total	42	13.69	13.31	-.494	.624	
Control Total	31	13.19	15.29	1.869	.071	
Demanding/Disruptive						
Class TH (T)	23	12.91	12.78	-.170	.867	
Class TF (T)	19	13.79	12.53	-2.135	.047*	.490
Class CC (C)	20	13.45	12.25	1.997	.060	
Class CW (C)	11	15.00	18.27	-.253	.048*	.679
Treatment Total	42	13.31	12.67	-1.284	.206	
Control Total	31	14.00	14.39	.522	.605	
Total Antisocial						
Class TH (T)	23	47.26	47.74	.141	.889	
Class TF (T)	19	52.21	44.05	-2.966	.008*	.681
Class CC (C)	20	46.05	43.65	-1.040	.312	
Class CW (C)	11	51.64	66.73	2.489	.032*	.750
Treatment Total	42	49.50	46.07	-1.484	.145	
Control Total	31	48.03	51.84	1.279	.211	

Note: * $p < .05$

the treatment class was 11, making the treatment class a slightly younger group. There were differences in gender, with the treatment school having more girls than boys. However, since the SSBS does not have different results by gender, any gender differences between the classes are not a concern.

By ethnic breakdown, the treatment class had 8 percent white/non-Hispanic students (n=2), 48 percent black students (n= 11), and 44 percent Hispanic students (n= 10). In the control class, 16 percent were white/non-Hispanic students (n=4), 20 percent were black students (n=11), and 60 percent were Hispanic students (n=15).

Table 8.3 Elementary School Treatment and Control Classes' SSBS Social Competence Results

	N	M_{pre}	M_{post}	t	p	d
Interpersonal Skills						
Class TH (T)	23	59.74	61.70	1.164	.257	
Class TF (T)	19	45.16	50.11	3.93	.003*	.778
Class CC (C)	20	42.65	44.10	.926	.366	
Class CW (C)	11	54.00	52.27	-.767	.461	
Treatment Total	42	53.14	56.45	2.896	.006*	.447
Control Total	31	46.68	47.00	.249	.805	
Self-Management Skills						
Class TH (T)	23	44.26	44.52	.282	.781	
Class TF (T)	19	41.00	43.00	1.498	.152	
Class CC (C)	20	32.60	35.05	2.201	.040*	.492
Class CW (C)	11	42.64	40.09	-1.430	.183	
Treatment Total	42	42.79	43.83	1.325	.192	
Control Total	31	36.16	36.84	.654	.518	
Academic Skills						
Class TH (T)	23	34.0	35.52	.883	.387	
Class TF (T)	19	31.79	32.95	1.261	.224	
Class CC (C)	20	24.95	27.45	2.440	.025*	.545
Class CW (C)	11	33.00	29.73	-2.663	.024*	.803
Treatment Total	42	33.38	34.36	1.496	.142	
Control Total	31	27.81	28.26	.486	.630	
Total Social Competence						
Class TH (T)	23	138.70	141.74	.918	.369	
Class TF (T)	19	117.95	125.63	2.466	.024*	.566
Class CC (C)	20	97.20	106.60	1.879	.076	
Class CW (C)	11	129.64	122.09	-1.668	.126	
Treatment Total	42	129.31	134.45	2.236	.031*	.345
Control Total	31	108.71	112.10	.879	.386	

Note: * p =.05

Middle School Classes' SSBS Antisocial Behavior Results

Table 8.6 reports the changes that occurred between the treatment school grade six class and the control school grade six class. The results indicate significant increases in hostile/irritable, antisocial/aggressive, and total antisocial behavior at the treatment school, TCD Middle. Since the teacher did not report the student participation in special programs (i.e., Exceptional Student Education, ESOL), it is difficult to understand the cause of this increase specifically. During interviews, the administrative team at the school described the program implementation as excellent and noted that the assistant principal

Table 8.4 Elementary School Treatment and Control Classes' Change Scores

	Treatment		Control				
	N	M_{change}	N	M_{change}	t	p	d
Antisocial Behavior							
Hostile/Irritable	42	-2.405	31	1.323	-2.163	.034*	.512
Antisocial/Aggressive	42	-.381	31	2.097	-1.883	.064	
Demanding/Disruptive	42	-.642	31	.387	-1.194	.237	
Total Antisocial	42	-3.429	31	3.807	-1.950	.055	
Social Competence							
Interpersonal Skills	42	3.310	31	.323	1.722	.089	
Self-Management	42	1.048	31	.677	.289	.773	
Academic	42	.976	31	.452	.477	.635	
Total Social Comp.	42	5.143	31	3.387	.413	.681	

Note: * $p < .05$

Table 8.5 Middle School Treatment and Control Classes' Demographics

	Total	Treatment Class TCM	Control Class CHM
Number of Participants	48	23	25
Age			
10	1	1	
11	39	17	22
12	7	4	3
Not reported	1	1	
Gender			
Male	22	7	15
Female	26	16	10
Ethnicity			
White/Non-Hispanic	6	2	4
Black	16	11	5
Hispanic	25	10	15
Other	1		1

Note: This table was constructed using data provided by classroom teachers who completed the demographic portion of the SSBS. All classes were sixth grade.

Table 8.6 Middle School Treatment and Control Classes' SSBS Antisocial Behavior Results

Behavior	N	M_{pre}	M_{post}	t	p	*d*
Hostile/Irritable						
Class TCD (T)	23	16.78	18.96	-2.071	.05*	.432
Class CHM (C)	25	17.24	17.28	-.026	.980	
Antisocial/Aggressive						
Class TCD (T)	23	10.65	12.83	-2.754	.012*	.574
Class CHM (C)	25	11.08	12.52	-1.322	.199	
Demanding/Disruptive						
Class TCD (T)	23	10.39	11.39	-1.973	.061	
Class CHM (C)	25	13.40	12.40	1.168	.254	
Total Antisocial						
Class TCD (T)	23	37.70	43.17	-2.527	.019*	.527
Class CHM (C)	25	41.72	42.24	-1.52	.889	

Note: * $p < .05$

monitored the implementation of the project closely. Perhaps the fact that these students were in sixth grade and new to the school caused them to exhibit behaviors which might mediate themselves as a result of long-term participation in the PEF program and natural maturation. Increases, though not statistically significant, also were noted at the control school, CHM Middle. In addition, this school had participated in the Comer Program for six years, which was a variable identified during the interview process. The Comer Program, or the School Development Program, is a school restructuring effort with a focus on a safe and respectful school climate (Aguilera, Crane, Hamer, Morrison, & Serano, 1998; McCollum, 1994).

Middle School Treatment and Control Classes' SSBS Social Competence Results

Table 8.7 indicates the changes that occurred between the treatment class and the control class in the sixth grade. TCD Middle School showed significant decreases in self-management skills, academic skills, and total social competence score. It is surmised that these negative results may be caused by the mobility of the students and the effect of transitioning to middle school.

Interestingly, there were significant increases in interpersonal skills at the control school (CHM Middle). This result may be explained by two factors discovered during the collection of qualitative data. First, the school partici-

Table 8.7 Middle School Treatment and Control Classes' SSBS Social Competence Results

	N	M_{pre}	M_{post}	T	p	d
Interpersonal Skills						
Class TCD (T)	23	54.96	52.65	1.590	.126	
Class CHM (C)	25	45.12	49.72	-2.447	.002*	.489
Self-Management Skills						
Class TCD (T)	23	43.43	38.96	3.887	.001*	.810
Class CHM (C)	25	43.56	40.52	1.581	.127	
Academic Skills						
Class TCD (T)	23	33.48	29.35	4.203	.000*	.876
Class CHM (C)	25	27.96	29.16	-1.055	.302	
Total Social Competence						
Class TCD (T)	23	131.87	120.96	3.406	.003*	.710
Class CHM (C)	25	116.52	119.40	-.620	.541	

Note: * p<.05

Table 8.8 Middle School Treatment and Control Classes' Change Scores

	Treatment		Control				
	N	M_{change}	N	M_{change}	t	p	d
Antisocial Behavior							
Hostile/Irritable	23	2.17	25	.04	1.120	.269	
Antisocial/Aggressive	23	2.17	25	1.44	.537	.594	
Demanding/Disruptive	23	1.00	25	-1.00	1.966	.055	
Total Antisocial	23	5.48	25	.52	1.203	.237	
Social Competence							
Interpersonal Skills	23	-2.30	25	4.60	-2.873	.006*	.830
Self-Management	23	-4.48	25	-3.04	-.642	.525	
Academic	23	-4.13	25	1.20	-3.519	.001*	1.017
Total Social Comp.	23	-10.91	25	2.88	-2.443	.019*	.694

Note: * p <.05

pated in the Comer Program for six years prior to the Grant project. And, second, there also are a peer mediation program run by a school counselor and an after-school program that teaches conflict resolution as part of the program. One or both of these programs could have impacted students' interpersonal skills.

CONCLUSION

Based on the results and findings, the "Peace Works" program appeared to make a positive impact on the treatment classes at the elementary school level. When scores for the treatment schools were combined, then compared and contrasted to the combined scores for the control schools, treatment schools showed a significant decrease in hostile/irritable behaviors. Additionally, the treatment classes' scores showed a tendency to move in the appropriate directions for social competence. However, the control classes showed an opposite tendency, with social competence skills declining across all scales and subscales, while antisocial behaviors increased across all scales and subscales. No significant changes were noted at the middle school level, with one exception. Increases occurred in Interpersonal Skills at the control school, which may have been due to the effects of simultaneous participation in other SEL programs. The findings at the elementary school level are supported by the SEL literature, with multiple studies indicating that conflict resolution programs can increase students' prosocial skills while decreasing their antisocial behaviors (Enger, LeBlanc, & Lacey, 2000; Ferber, 2007; Grossman et al., 1997; Lacey, 1999, 2000; Lacey & LeBlanc, 2000; LeBlanc & Lacey, 1999; Pellegrini & Bartini, 2000; Schellenberg, Parks-Savage, & Rehfuss, 2007; Stomfay-Stitz & Wheeler, 2007; Vestal & Jones, 2004).

As discussed previously, the "Peace Works" program makes use of many best practices for teacher effectiveness in enhancing students' growth and development. It may be that the findings identified in this study were influenced by the implementation of these best practices that are part of the "Peace Works" program. They are summarized here to help others who wish to implement conflict resolution programs for SEL.

1. Establish rules for effective classroom management that promote discipline (e.g., Rules for Fighting Fair) (Dusenbury et al., 1997; Rowan, 2007; Stronge, 2002).
2. Use varied, interactive, teaching strategies and materials (e.g., modeling, coaching, role playing) (Dusenbury et al., 1997; Jenkins, 2007; Stronge, 2002).
3. Develop social competence in students through teaching social skills (e.g., I-language) (Dusenbury et al., 1997; Rowan, 2007).

4. Build community, developing a positive school climate (e.g., respect diversity) (Dusenbury et al., 1997; Stronge, 2002).

APPLICATION ACTIVITIES

The authors recommend the following activities to enhance the information provided in this chapter.

1. Visit the Peace Education Foundation website at www.peace-ed.org to learn more about the "Peace Works" program in conflict resolution.
2. Visit the National Registry of Evidenced-based Programs and Practices at www.nrepp.samhsa.gov to learn more about violence prevention programs. Select a program and explain why it would be appropriate to your setting.
3. Visit the website www.casel.org to learn more about social and emotional learning. Review the standards and policies for SEL. Identify standards that would apply in your setting.

REFERENCES

Aguilera, L., Crane, P., Hamer, M., Morrison, M., & Serano, D. (1998). Comer schools: Are they recognizable through direct observation? Paper presented at the Annual Meeting of the American Educational Research Association, San Diego, CA (ERIC Document Reproduction Service No. ED420925).

Arends, R. I. (2007). *Learning to teach* (7th ed.). New York: McGraw-Hill.

Brion-Meisels, L., Brion-Meisels, S., & Hoffman, C. (2007). Creating and sustaining peaceable school communities. *Harvard Educational Review, 77*(3), 374–381.

Brock, S. E. (2005, August). *The nature and consequence of peer victimization.* Workshop presented at the annual convention of the American Psychological Association, Washington, DC. Retrieved July 15, 2008, from www.csus.edu/indiv/b/brocks/Workshops/APA/Peer%20Victimization.pdf.

Browning, C., Cohen, R., & Warman, D. M. (2003). Peer social competence and the stability of victimization. *Child Study Journal, 33*(2), 73–90.

Cohen, J. (2006). Social, emotional, ethical, and academic education: Creating a climate for learning, participation in democracy, and well-being. *Harvard Educational Review, 76*(2), 201–285.

Coie, J. D., & Dodge, K. A. (1998). Aggression and antisocial behavior. In W. Damon & N. Eisenberg (Eds.), *Handbook of child psychology: Vol. 3. Social, emotional, and personality development* (5th ed., pp. 779–862). New York: Wiley.

Corcoran, K., & Mallinckrodt, B. (2000). Adult attachment, self-efficacy, perspective taking, and conflict resolution. *Journal of Counseling & Development, 78*, 473–483.

Creswell, J. W. (1994). *Research design: Qualitative and quantitative approaches.* Thousand Oaks, CA: Sage.

DeMar, J. (1997). A school-based group intervention to strengthen personal and social competencies in latency-age children. *Social Work in Education, 19*(4), 219.

Dusenbury, L., Falco, M., Lake, A., Brannigan, R., & Bosworth, K. (1997). Nine critical elements of promising violence prevention programs. *The Journal of School Health, 67*(10), 409–414.

Enger, J., LeBlanc, P., & Lacey, C. (2000). *The 1999–2000 comprehensive after-school program (CAP) Evaluation*. Palm Beach County, FL: Palm Beach County Safe Schools Center.

Fan, C., & Mak, A. S. (1998). Measuring social self-efficacy in a culturally diverse student population. *Social Behavior and Personality, 26*(2), 131–144.

Fantuzzo, J. F., Bulotsky-Shearer, R., McDermott, P. A., McWayne, C., Frye, D., & Perlman, S. (2007). Investigation of dimensions of social-emotional classroom behavior and school readiness for low-income urban preschool children. *School Psychology Review, 36*(1), 44–62.

Felix, E. D., & McMahon, S. D. (2006). Gender and multiple forms of peer victimization: How do they influence adolescent psychosocial adjustment? *Violence and Victims, 21*(6), 707–725.

Ferber, L. (2007). On board the peace train. *The Advocate, 987*, 54–55.

Flynt, S. W., & Morton, R. H. (2004). Bullying and children with disabilities. *Journal of Instructional Psychology, 31*(4), 330–333.

Fullan, M. (2001). *The new meaning of educational change* (3rd ed.). New York: Teachers College Press.

Graczyk, P. A., Domitrovich, C. E., Small, M., & Zins, J. E. (2006). Serving all children: An implementation model framework. *School Psychology Review, 35*, 266–274.

Grossman, D. C., Neckerman, H. J., Koepsell, T. D., Liu, P.-Y., Asher, K. N., Beland, K., Frey, K., & Rivara, F. P. (1997). Effectiveness of a violence prevention curriculum among children in elementary school: A randomized controlled trial. *Journal of the American Medical Association, 277*, 1605–1611.

Hanish, L. D., & Guerra, N. G. (2000). The role of ethnicity and school context in predicting children's victimization by peers. *American Journal of Community Psychology, 28*(2), 201–223.

Harris, I. M. (2007). Peace education in a violent culture. *Harvard Educational Review, 77*(3), 350–355.

Jenkins, T. (2007). Rethinking the unimaginable: The need for teacher education in peace education. *Harvard Educational Review, 77*(3), 366–370.

Kramer, T. L., Jones, K. A., Kirchner, J. Miller, T. L., & Wilson, C. (2002). Addressing personnel concerns about school violence through education, assessment and strategic planning. *Education, 123*(2), 292–304.

Lacey, C. H., & LeBlanc, P. R. (1999). *Twenty-first century learning communities grant evaluation*. West Palm Beach, FL: Palm Beach County Safe Schools Center.

Lacey, C. H., & LeBlanc, P. R. (2000, April). Conflict resolution and at-risk students: Insights into a comprehensive after school program. Paper presented at the annual meeting of the American Educational Research Association, New Orleans, LA.

Lacey, C. H., & LeBlanc, P. R. (2000). *Evaluation of the 21st century learning community's grant*. West Palm Beach, FL: Palm Beach County Safe Schools Center.

LeBlanc, P., & Lacey, C. H. (1999). *Comprehensive after-school program (CAP) evaluation*. West Palm Beach, FL: Palm Beach County Safe Schools Center.

LeBlanc, P., Lacey, C., & Mulder, R. (1998). Conflict resolution: A case study of one high school class' experience. *Journal for Just and Caring Education, 4*(2), 224–244.

Lindsey, E. W. (2002). Preschool children's friendships and peer acceptance: Links to social competence. *Child Study Journal, 32*, 145–156.

Loeber, R. (1985). Patterns and development of antisocial child behavior. *Annals of Child Development, 2*, 77–116.

McCay, L. O., & Keyes, D. W. (2001/2002, Winter). Developing social competence in the inclusive primary classroom. *Childhood Education, 78*(2), 70–78.

McCollum, H. (1994). *School reform for youth at risk: Analysis of six change models. Volume 1: Summary and Analysis*. Department of Education, Washington, DC (ERIC Document Reproduction Service No. ED370201).

McGrath, M. J. (2007). *School bullying: Tools for avoiding harm and liability*. Thousand Oaks, CA: Corwin.

McKenzie, M. (2004). Seeing the spectrum: North American approaches to emotional, social, and moral education. *The Educational Forum, 69*(1), 79–90.

Merrell, K. W. (1993). Using behavior rating scales to assess social skills and antisocial behavior in school setting: Development of the School Social Behavior Scales. *School Psychology Today, 22*(1), 115–133.

Merrell, K. W. (2002). *School social behavior scales* (3rd ed.). Eugene, OR: Assessment-Intervention Resources.

Michael, K. (2000). *The gendered society*. London: Oxford University Press.

Miller, S. (2003). Impact of mixed methods and design on inference quality. In A. Tashakkori & C. Teddlie (Eds.), *Handbook of mixed methods in social & behavioral research*. Thousand Oaks, CA: Sage.

Opotow, S., Gerson, J., & Woodside, S. (2005). From moral exclusion to moral inclusion: Theory for teaching peace. *Theory into Practice, 44*(4), 303–319.

Parkay, F., & Hardcastle Stanford, B. (2007). *Becoming a teacher* (7th ed.). Boston: Allyn and Bacon.

Peace Education Foundation (PEF). (July, 2005). [White paper]. Retrieved from www.peaceeducation.org/research.html.

Pellegrini, A. D., & Bartini, M. (2000). An empirical comparison of methods of sampling aggression and victimization in school settings. *Journal of Educational Psychology, 92*, 360–366.

Rowan, L. O. (2007). Making classrooms bully-free zones: Practical suggestions for educators. *Kappa Delta Pi Record, 43*(4), 182–183, 185.

Rubin, H., & Rubin, I. (2004). *Qualitative interviewing: The art of hearing data*. Thousand Oaks, CA: Sage.

Sandy, V. S., Bailey, S., & Sloane-Akwara, V. (2000). Impact on students: Conflict resolution education's proven benefits for students. In T. S. Jones & D. Kmita (Eds.), *Does it work? The case for conflict resolution education in our nation's schools*. Washington, DC: CREnet.

Schellenberg, R. C., Parks-Savage, A., & Rehfuss, M. (2007). Reducing levels of elementary school violence with peer mediation. *Professional School Counseling, 10*(5), 475–481.

Silverman, D. (2006). *Interpreting qualitative data: Methods for analysing talk, text, and interaction* (3rd ed.). London: Sage.

Skroban, S. B., Gottfredson, D. C., & Gottfredson, G. D. (1999). A school-based social competency promotion demonstration. *Evaluation Review, 23*(1), 3–27.

Smith, J. D., Schneider, B. H., Smith, P. K., & Ananiadou, K. (2004). The effectiveness of whole-school anti-bullying programs: A synthesis of evaluation research. *School Psychology Review, 33*, 548–561.

Stallworth-Clark, R. (2007). The psychology of violence and peace. *Harvard Educational Review, 77*(3), 359–363.

Stevahn, L. (1997). Making meaning: Why integrating conflict resolution training into academic coursework enhances learning. Unpublished manuscript, University of Minnesota, Minneapolis.

Stevahn, L. (2004). Integrating conflict resolution training into the curriculum. *Theory into Practice, 43*(1), 50–58.

Stevahn, L., Johnson, D. W., Johnson, R. T., Oberle, K., & Wahl, L. (2000). Effects of conflict resolution training integrated into a kindergarten curriculum. *Child Development, 71*, 770–782.

Stomfay-Stitz, A., & Wheeler, E. (2007). Caring for each other in a peace club. *Childhood Education, 84*(1), 30–32.

Stronge, J. H. (2002). *Qualities of effective teachers*. Alexandria, VA: Association of Supervision and Curriculum Development.

Tashakkori, A., & Teddlie, C. (1998). *Mixed methodology: Combining qualitative and quantitative approaches*. Thousand Oaks, CA: Sage.

U.S. Department of Education (USDOE). (2001). *Executive summary of the no child left behind act*. Office of Elementary and Secondary Education. Retrieved from www.ed.gov/print/nclb/overview/intro/execsumm.html.

U.S. Department of Health and Human Services (USDOHHS). (2000). *Head Start child outcomes 2000 framework*. Administration for Children and Families, Head Start Bureau. Retrieved from www.hsnrc.org/CDI/pdfs/UGCOF.pdf.

Vestal, A., & Jones, N. A. (2004). Peace building and conflict resolution in preschool children. *Journal of Research in Childhood Education, 19*(2), 131–142.

Werle, G. D. (2006). Taking steps to promote safer schools. *The Journal of School Health, 76*(4), 156–168.

Yell, M. L., & Rozalski, M. E. (2000). Searching for safe schools: Legal issues in the prevention of school violence. *Journal of Emotional and Behavioral Disorders, 8*(3), 187–196.

Yoon, J. S. (2004). Predicting teacher interventions in bullying situations. *Education and Treatment of Children, 27*(1), 37–45.

9

Applying Principles of Invitational Education

Gail E. Young and Alex J. Tripamer

ABSTRACT

Given the opportunity to establish the philosophic culture when opening their new elementary school, the administration, faculty, and staff at Russell H. Emge Elementary School in O'Fallon, Missouri, chose to create a school culture based on principles of invitation education. This philosophic approach, grounded on affective education, features four tenets: trust, respect, optimism, and intentionality. The four tenets reach across all populations involved with the school supporting the beliefs that individuals should be personally inviting with oneself, personally inviting with others, professionally inviting with oneself, and professionally inviting with others. By concentrating on the five Ps: People, Places, Programs, Policies, and Processes through assorted affective approaches and strategies, everyone associated with the school increases one's invitation quotient.

Russell H. Emge Elementary School is located in O'Fallon, Missouri, about 30 miles west of St. Louis. The school opened in August 2002, in a school district that is student-centered, allowing for the inherent potential to create an inviting educational culture from the start. As a new school, the choice was made by the administration to embrace the principles outlined in invitational education. Each member of the administration, faculty, and staff was required to read the popular book "FISH!" (Lundin, Paul, & Christensen, 2000). This text provided the groundwork for creating a student-centered atmosphere, prompting the administration, faculty, and staff to delve deeply into invitational theory literature.

The elementary school personnel, as a whole, wanted to learn more about invitational theory and, perhaps more importantly, sought ways to implement invitational theory in the school. Invitational theory would become synonymous with the school culture. To this end, a "think tank" was started that included members of the administration, faculty, and staff, as well as several parents. Everyone spent time reading literature related to invitational education, brainstorming ideas that could be implemented that had both short-term and long-term outcomes, and putting plans into action.

Novak (1992) defines invitational education as an attempt to provide an integrative framework for constructing environments and cultures that extend and evaluate intentional messages and that affirm the uniqueness, possibilities, and dignity of everyone involved in the educative process. William Purkey and John Novak (1996) along with Betty Siegel (2003), founders of the invitational philosophy, generated many of the tenets outlined in invitational theory. The researchers have identified four basic assumptions associated with invitational education: "trust, respect, optimism, and intentionality" (Purkey & Novak, 1996, p. 50). Fully understanding all of the principles outlined in invitational education based on the research of Purkey, Siegel, and Novak presented a complex, yet insightful, challenge. This chapter highlights the endeavors documented by educators at Emge Elementary School in their attempt to make their school the most inviting place in town.

FOUR ELEMENTS OF INVITATIONAL EDUCATION

Intentionality

Intentionality is the key to being an inviting individual! Intentionality is doing things on purpose and making a conscious effort to behave in a certain way. Emge Elementary School teachers interact with students over 1,000 times a day; each interaction is embraced as another special opportunity for teachers to affect children positively. Teachers at Emge Elementary School start the day by greeting students at the doors. Many teachers admit that multitasking is a necessity for maintaining their effectiveness; however, at Emge Elementary School, teachers stop what they are doing and look directly at the students when they are speaking. Teachers demonstrate that they are sincerely interested in what students are saying, communicating with their words and actions that teachers are at school for the students. Teachers must ask themselves this simple question each day, "How can I leave every student I talk with today feeling better than they felt before our conversation?"

Trust

All individuals need to see themselves as responsible, capable, and valued. Trust is defined by Purkey and Novak (1996) as being nonjudgmental, respecting a student's confidentiality, and following through on agreements. At Emge Elementary School, trust is a core belief of the administration, faculty, and staff. Everyone adds or takes away from the learning atmosphere, which is why developing trust with the students is so important. Students need to know that they are understood and respected. What students share with faculty and staff is to be kept confidential, which means the information is not to be repeated in the faculty workroom and definitely not mentioned to other students. Also, it is extremely important to make one's verbal language match one's body language.

Respect

"Respect in the school means that whatever a classroom should be, it should not be a place where people are embarrassed, insulted, humiliated, or subjected to prejudice" (Purkey & Novak, 1996, p. 52). Emge Elementary School concentrates on the beliefs that people are able, valuable, and responsible. Invitational education emphasizes that people should be treated with mutual respect and shared responsibility (Riner & Mann, 2000, para. 9). It is important at school that the adults expect and model appropriate manners every day in every situation. For example, all adults must make concerted efforts to treat the substitute teachers with the utmost respect; that is thanking them for coming to the school, checking in on them and their classrooms throughout the day, inviting substitute teachers to sit with the team during lunch, and so forth. Another example of respect is that all students are greeted by their teachers every morning as the students enter their classrooms. Finally, the office staff must take pride in being overly courteous, caring, and attentive to the needs of students, parents, and teachers.

Optimism

"Optimism is the belief that people possess untapped potential in all areas of human endeavor" and that people also possess goodness and want to express it (Riner & Mann, 2000, para. 11). When interviewing teacher candidates to work at Emge Elementary School, it is more important to learn as much as possible about each candidate's affect. Candidates and teachers who overtly communicate a child-centered belief system and believe that all children are capable and worthwhile tend to fit in with the accepted culture of the school because of the overall optimistic view of the school staff. Another element in demonstrating optimism is the obligation of the staff to meet all of the needs of the students. After reading Sanborn's "The Fred Factor" (Sanborn, 2002), the school's faculty and staff began striving to make the school extraordinary by consistently thinking of what can be done to best serve the students. As all educators take on the current mandates of the No Child Left Behind Act (2001), all school personnel must remember that challenges, problems, and impossibilities can be invitations in disguise (Purkey, n.d.).

INCREASING ONE'S INVITATIONAL QUOTIENT

Living the invitational process involves orchestrating four basic areas: "(1) Being personally inviting with oneself. (2) Being personally inviting with others. (3) Being professionally inviting with oneself. (4) Being professionally inviting with others" (Purkey & Novak, 1996, p. 103). All school personnel are encouraged to think about their interactions related to each of these areas. The impetus is placed directly on each individual's own shoulders to model an invitational framework so students hear about the model and see the model in action. The following items frame the theory of becoming an invitational educator.

Be Personally Inviting with Oneself

One goal of the invitational theory is to enrich one's own life. Many times individuals become so consumed with their school responsibilities and their students that family and friends are neglected. School personnel even neglect themselves. Educators need to remember that they are people and not just teachers.

Here are some guidelines to be personally inviting with oneself.

- Be happy; hang around with happy people. Too many times individuals are drawn into the negativity that can spread in the teachers' workroom.
- Self-care is essential. To take care of others, one must take care of oneself first. It is like being on an airplane, the attendant announces that adults must cover their faces first with the oxygen masks and then attend to taking care of their children and families.
- Keep the child inside alive. Play is as vital to adults as it is to students. Educators are encouraged to get a hobby, exercise, and laugh. They should visit friends and use positive self-talk. There is a saying, "Live well, laugh often, and love much." Each individual must find his or her own joy in order to model the joy of living for others.
- Be open to invitations received from other individuals. Learn to say yes to your friends and yourself.

Be Personally Inviting with Others

Being inviting is a way of life, a way of being, and an attitude. It is giving one's full attention to the other person during every interaction. To be personally inviting with others means having a positive attitude whenever there is verbal and nonverbal dialogue with others.

Here are some guidelines to be personally inviting with others.

- Get to know your colleagues on a social basis. It is easier to share a difference of opinion once colleagues are also friends.
- Learn faculty and staff members' names, including all of the support staff members. Remember the school secretary, custodian, and cook run the school; they are people too and are a tremendous help to everyone.
- Celebrate other peoples' successes. Giving recognition and power to others is giving recognition and power to everyone.
- Form an active social committee in the school. Create and join the committee; membership will help individuals to know each other much faster.

Be Professionally Inviting with Oneself

Educators need to keep growing professionally. Education is ever changing and educators must be prepared for these changes.

Here are some guidelines to be professionally inviting with oneself.

- Learn new skills that will help professionally and will enrich one personally.
- Attend professional conferences.
- Write for publications.
- Try something new in the classroom.

Be Professionally Inviting with Others

Being professionally inviting with others requires thinking of others at all times. Educators benefit by creating learning environments and climates where students want to be and where they can learn. Invitational theory is based on the idea of human interaction, both positive and negative; the theory supports people in reaching their potential and their goals. Educators have the potential to make a huge impact on their students, their students' parents, their colleagues, and themselves.

Here are some guidelines to be professionally inviting with others.

- Teachers should call parents during the first week of school. This call may be the only positive one that the parents receive from the school. Calling parents also presents an opportunity to establish a rapport with the parents in preparation for times that the teacher may have to call parents another time later in the year.

- Send two letters to each student before the school year starts. One letter should be written to the students welcoming them to the school and the individual classroom. The other letter is addressed to the students' parents thanking them for sharing their children with the teacher and asking parents to tell the teacher about their child.
- Be positive and supportive of colleagues.
- Share ideas and give credit where credit is due.
- Protect your colleagues. Stop any unnecessary conversations about administration, faculty, staff, and volunteers.
- Remember what happens at the school, stays at the school.

THE FIVE "Ps" OF INVITATIONAL EDUCATION

Applying the principles of invitational education can best be described by looking at the five areas in any school: "People, Places, Programs, Policies, and Processes" (Purkey & Novak, 2008, p. 19). At Emge Elementary School, everyone is trying to use invitational theory in each of these areas.

People

All administrators, faculty, and staff remind and extend themselves to be friendly and courteous. Courtesy is particularly important when greeting substitute teachers. Substitute teachers are introduced during morning announcements as "Guest Teachers." The title of "Guest Teacher" recognizes them and also communicates to all faculty and staff that they need to be neighborly to substitute teachers. Students greet adults properly, using manners and proper social norms. All adults also use and model to students a collegial atmosphere where conversation among adults is upbeat, friendly, and full of laughter. Additionally, Educators of the Year are recognized by painting star-embossed paving bricks located near the entrance of the school. The bricks have the teachers' names listed and collectively make up our "Walk of Fame."

Places

The easiest way to begin making one's school an inviting place is to start with addressing the school environment. Several park benches and greenery have been placed in the foyer so parents have a place to sit while waiting for their children. The school office has a warm and comforting décor to greet students and parents. Teachers have created inviting classrooms by hanging curtains, using lamps to provide warm lighting, recognizing student achievement on bulletin boards, creating reading nooks, and so on.

Teachers are encouraged to display their college diplomas in their classrooms. Inspirational quotes and curtains hang in the workrooms. Wallpaper has been added to adult restrooms, and the entrance to the cafeteria has been painted and renamed "The Starlight Café."

Programs

Each grade level in the school hosts a special event, that is, Grandparents' Day, Mother's Day Tea, Family Math Night, and so forth, to include all students' families in the school experience. The Title I Reading Program is called "Star Reading" rather than remedial reading. Several classrooms have been grouped together with other grade levels for students to establish "Reading Pals" with younger and older students. The school has created an imaginary secret member, Ida Blue, who boosts morale by placing inspirational quotes and other "pick me-ups" in every faculty and staff member's mailbox from time to time.

Policies

School rules are written to convey positively worded language; specifically, rules avoid starting with the words "Do not . . ." The school has joined the efforts within the school district to raise awareness about bullying and treating one another with respect. The office staff uses warm greetings when answering the phone and interacting with students, parents, and teachers.

Processes

The day-to-day operations of the school function in as inviting a manner as possible. It is important that, as educators work in grade level meetings, leadership meetings, or faculty meetings, everyone practices using invitational theory as the basis for processing thoughts and exchanging ideas. A huge key to success is including the Parent Teacher Organization (PTO) in the vision of invitational education. Members of the PTO create inviting experiences for the students and families, that is, dinner nights, skate nights, movie nights, fall festival, fun fair, and so forth.

Summary

Emge Elementary School received the Inviting Schools Award in 2004. It is the belief of the administration, faculty, and staff that people both create and are created by their environment. The school's mission has been to accomplish high student achievement by providing the best education possible in the most inviting manner. It is important to the entire school community that, when visiting their school, one sees people greeted warmly, a neat physical appearance, and intentional acts of kindness toward all students. Emge Elementary School believes that the journey has only begun; and, with an emphasis on invitational education, the school culture will continue to be positive and child-centered.

CONCLUSION

Modeling the principles of invitational education, we invite and encourage all other schools to begin the journey of applying concepts of invitational education within their own contexts. In the most effective models, there is an emphasis for an entire school to make the total environment as inviting as possible with individual teachers and staff members making contributions in their classrooms.

The Inviting School Survey-Revised (IAIE, 2008) is an easy inventory designed to measure the degree to which schools are welcoming in the five basic areas: People, Places, Policies, Programs, and Processes. This survey is available online through the International Alliance for Invitational Education: www.invitationaleducation.net. A school-wide committee comprised of faculty members, support staff members, parents, students, and community members can use the results to ascertain strengths and weaknesses in each of these key areas and develop a plan to improve their school's invitational nature. To keep the process ongoing and to be professionally inviting with oneself and others, faculty and staff members should develop partnerships with colleagues that meet on a regular basis to discuss and share inviting ideas and experiences within the classroom.

In terms of an individual teacher's efforts to apply invitational education, teachers can keep a regular checklist using a class roster to monitor the genuine, positive comments made to each student. This checklist will ensure that teachers are intentional in their interactions with all students. Greeting each student warmly as they enter the classroom each morning and giving them an encouraging good-bye each afternoon are two simple methods for accomplishing this goal of maintaining positive student interaction. The teacher gives special attention to the physical environment of the classroom to make it as inviting as possible; that is, warm lighting, motivational posters, beanbag chairs, student work prominently displayed, and so forth.

As educators strive to create inviting environments for their students, it is equally important to remember that, while not all invitations will be accepted, educators should continue to extend invitations to their students and colleagues.

APPLICATION ACTIVITIES

The authors recommend the following activities to enhance the information provided in this chapter.

1. Think about your own time as a student in an elementary, middle level, or high school. What was inviting for you that teachers could and should replicate in today's schools and classrooms? What was uninviting that teachers should avoid?
2. Brainstorm a list of achievable school-wide activities that school representatives could organize to create an inviting school environment and build a sense of community.
3. Visit the website for the International Alliance of Invitational Education at www.invitationaleducation.net/.
4. Form a book club to read and study *The FISH Philosophy* (Charthouse Learning, 2008) at www.charthouse.com/content.aspx?name=home2 or *The Fred Factor* (The Fred Factor, n.d.) at www.fredfactor.com/.

REFERENCES

Charthouse Learning. (2008). *The FISH philosophy*. Retrieved from www.charthouse.com/content.aspx?name=home2.

International Alliance of Invitational Education (IAIE). (2008). *Inviting school survey* (Rev.). Retrieved from International Alliance of Invitational Education Website: www.invitationaleducation.net.

Lundin, S. C., Paul, H., & Christensen, J. (2000). *FISH!* New York: Hyperion.

No Child Left Behind Act, 20 USCS § 7231 (2001).

Novak, J. M. (Ed). (1992). *Advancing invitational thinking*. San Francisco: Caddo Gap Press.

Purkey, W. W. (n.d.). *Corollaries of invitational theory*. Unpublished manuscript, The University of North Carolina at Greensboro.

Purkey, W. W., & Novak, J. M. (1996). *Inviting school success*. Belmont, CA: Wadsworth.

Purkey, W. W., & Novak, J. M. (2008). *Fundamentals of invitational education*. Kennesaw: The International Alliance for Invitational Education.

Purkey, W. W., & Siegel, B. L. (2003). *Becoming an invitational leader: A new approach to professional and personal success*. Atlanta: Humanics Trade Group Publication.

Riner, P., & Mann, K. (2000). *An introduction to invitational education*. Retrieved from the International Alliance for Invitational Education website: www.invitationaleducation.net/ie/intro.ppt.

Sanborn, M. (2002). *The Fred factor*. Colorado Springs, CO: Waterbrook.

The Fred Factor. (n.d.). Retrieved from The Fred Factor Website: www.fredfactor.com/.

About the Contributors

Thomas E. Baker is professor of education at Austin College in Sherman, Texas. He earned a B.A. in history and English and an M.A.T. in social sciences from the University of Louisville. After teaching history and English in Kentucky high schools, he earned an Ed.D. in curriculum from Indiana University where he served as field liaison for the Alternative Schools Master's Degree Program. At Austin College, he has served as chair of the education department and director of the graduate program. He currently teaches courses in curriculum and instruction, secondary education, social studies methods, and foundations of education. He also supervises students in field experiences and coordinates secondary field placements. He served three terms on the editorial review board of *The Teacher Educator*. In May 2003, he received the award for outstanding scholarship in the social science division at Austin College.

Donna J. Dockery is an assistant professor of counselor education at Virginia Commonwealth University. After earning a degree in biology from the College of William and Mary, she worked as a science and mathematics teacher in an urban high school designed for economically disadvantaged adolescents with academic promise. She earned a master's degree in counselor education from Virginia Commonwealth University and worked for 15 years as a professional school counselor at an urban high school and a regional program for high-end learners. She earned her Ph.D. from the University of Virginia and is concerned with providing access and opportunities for all students and their families. Her research interests include multicultural counseling, issues of diversity, school climate and affective concerns, bullying prevention, and psychosocial needs of gifted learners.

Nancy P. Gallavan is professor of teacher education at the University of Central Arkansas. She specializes in performance-based assessments, curriculum development, social studies, and multicultural education. Nancy earned her Ph.D. from the University of Denver and her master's degree from the University of Colorado. Prior to joining UCA, Nancy was a faculty member at the University of Nevada, Las Vegas, preceded by 20 years of classroom teaching primarily in the Cherry Creek schools in Colorado. Nancy has more than 60 publications in various journals and chapters in books, recently authoring *Developing Performance-Based Assessments in Elementary Schools* and *Developing Performance-Based Assessment in Middle and Secondary Schools*. Nancy is active in the American Educational Research Association, the Association of Teacher Educators, the National Association for Multicultural Education, and the National Council for the Social Studies.

David W. Johnson is a professor of educational psychology at the University of Minnesota. He is codirector of the Cooperative Learning Center. He held the Emma M. Birkmaier Professorship in Educational Leadership at the University of Minnesota from 1994 to 1997 and the Libra Endowed Chair for Visiting Professor at the University of Maine in 1996–1997. He received the American Psychological Association's 2003 Award for Distinguished Contributions of Applications of Psychology to Education and Practice. In 2007 he received (with his brother Roger) the Brock International Prize in Education administered by the College of Liberal Studies at the University of Oklahoma. In 2008 he received the Distinguished Contributions to Research in Education Award from the American Education Research Association. He received his doctoral degree from Columbia University. He has authored over 500 research articles and book chapters. He is the author of over 50 books. He is a past editor of the *American Educational Research Journal*. For the past 40 years, Dr. Johnson has served as an organizational consultant to schools and businesses throughout the world. He is a practicing psychotherapist.

Roger T. Johnson is a professor of curriculum and instruction at the University of Minnesota. He is the codirector of the Cooperative Learning Center. He holds his doctoral degree from the University of California in Berkeley. In 2007 he received (with his brother David) the Brock International Prize in Education administered by the College of Liberal Studies at the University of Oklahoma. Dr. Johnson's public school teaching experience includes kindergarten through eighth grade instruction in self-contained classrooms, open schools, nongraded situations, cottage schools, and departmentalized (science) schools. At the college level, Dr. Johnson has taught teacher-preparation courses for undergraduate through Ph.D. programs. He has consulted with schools throughout the United States and Canada, Panama, England, Germany, Norway, Sweden, Finland, and New Zealand. Dr. Johnson is the author of numerous research articles, book chapters, and books. Nationally, Dr. Johnson is a leading authority on inquiry teaching and science education. He has served on task forces examining college policy, environmental quality, science education, math education, elementary education, and cooperative learning.

Candace H. Lacey is a program professor in the Educational Leadership Doctoral Program at Nova Southeastern University. Recent research interests and publications include peace education, social competence, and moral and ethical leadership. Her latest publications include *Teacher Values: Quantification and Explanation, Moral Leadership Defined,* and *Mentoring At-risk Adolescent Girls: Listening to Little Sisters.*

Patrice R. LeBlanc holds a doctoral degree in educational leadership from Boston University. She also holds degrees in counseling-psychology and special education. She worked in public schools for 15 years as a special education teacher, elementary teacher, and held various teacher leadership roles. She simultaneously served as an adjunct faculty member at two local colleges. In 1990, she became director of the Educational Leadership Program at Barry University. Currently, she is a professor at Nova Southeastern University in the Fischler School of Education, predominantly teaching undergraduate teacher candidates. Her research interests span multiple areas, with social and emotional learning as the central focus, and she has over 100 presentations and publications. She has been an active member in the Association of Teacher Educators for over 20 years.

Nancy L. Maldonado, Ph.D., is director of curriculum and instruction for Kaplan Virtual Education. She also teaches doctoral students for Nova Southeastern University. She has served as assistant professor of educational leadership at Barry University where she taught leadership, research, and philosophy of science. Dr. Maldonado's primary research interests and publications focus on moral leadership, ethics, and peace education.

Maria McKenna is currently a doctoral student in Educational Foundations at Saint Louis University. Before beginning her teaching career in higher education eight years ago, Ms. McKenna was a first and second grade teacher in Virginia. She earned a bachelor's degree in economics at the University of Notre Dame and continued her education in Chicago, earning a master's degree in education at Northwestern University. In the years following, she taught education courses at a variety of colleges and universities as a part-time instructor while attending to her growing family. She recently moved to South Bend, Indiana, with her husband and four children. Her research interests include social capital formation, peace education, and the sociology of education.

Richard D. Osguthorpe is an assistant professor in the College of Education at Boise State University. He received his Ph.D. in Educational Foundations and Policy from the University of Michigan, with emphases in philosophy of education, educational foundations, and moral education. He conducts research that combines conceptual analysis and empirical study, and his scholarly interests include the moral dimensions of teaching, the study of moral education and moral development in schools, the use of practical reason and practical argument in teacher development, and the pedagogy of educational foundations. He teaches foundations of education and philosophy of education courses in both the undergraduate and graduate programs, and he works as a liaison in partner schools.

Terrell M. Peace began his academic career with a degree in ceramic engineering from Clemson University. After having opportunities to teach during graduate school, he began preparation for a new career in education. Peace has spent the last 20 years in higher education and currently he is the director of graduate and undergraduate teacher education at Huntington University, Indiana. He has been active in the Association of Teacher Educators since 1989 and will serve as president of ATE in 2010–2011. In 2003, Peace was honored by the Indiana Association of Teacher Educators as the state's Outstanding Teacher Educator. Peace has also been closely involved with Kappa Delta Pi and has served as counselor of Huntington University's award-winning chapter since its charter in 2000.

Cheryl J. Rike is an assistant professor in the Early Childhood Program, Instruction and Curriculum Leadership Department in the College of Education at the University of Memphis. She spent 13 years teaching remedial reading and kindergarten in elementary schools. She was the principal of a public school early learning center for 10 years and has spent the last 10 years of her professional career teaching both undergraduate and graduate classes at the university level. Teacher dispositions and effective teaching form a large component on her research agenda. Other research interests include infant/toddler interactions and language development, teacher candidates' reflection as it affects professionalism, and the process of adult learners constructing their own knowledge. In 2000, Dr. Rike was awarded the Dean's Award for Excellence in Teaching in the College of Education, and in 2004, she received the Distinguished Teaching Award at the University of Memphis.

L. Kathryn Sharp is an instructor in the Early Childhood Program at the University of Memphis. She works with teachers in early childhood settings and leads professional development programs on literacy development, assessment and evaluation, classroom management, and the classroom environment. Previously, Dr. Sharp taught elementary school for six years and was a professional nanny. She is the faculty sponsor for the University of Memphis Association for the Education of Young Children, frequently reviews professional journal articles and texts, and continues her writing and research with Dr. Rike on teacher dispositions. Her other research interests include urban learning environments, teacher burnout, and early childhood literacy. In 2008 she was a finalist for the Distinguished Teaching Award and received the Department of Instruction and Curriculum Leadership's Excellence in Teaching Award.

Regina M. Ryel Thomason has been an educator for 30 years, teaching at the elementary, middle school, university, and community college levels. She received her Ed.D. from Texas A&M/Commerce and an M.S.E and B.S.E in health and elementary education, respectively, from Henderson State University. She has been a member of the Association of Teacher Educators since 1988, serving on numerous committees and as a member of the ATE Leadership Academy. She has also served as a keynote speaker at the Southern Regional Association of Teacher Educators and was recognized as Woman of the Year by the Alabama House of Representatives and Distinguished Alumnus from Texas A&M/Commerce. She has published numerous articles and book chapters. Most recently, Ryel Thomason was a corecipient of the National Innovation Award presented by the League of Innovations for an infused service, team-and technology-based curriculum at NorthWest Arkansas Community College in Bentonville, Arkansas, where she presently serves as program coordinator for teacher education and as a full-time faculty member.

Alex J. Tripamer is currently the principal at Emge Elementary School in O'Fallon, Missouri. He received his bachelor's degree in elementary education from the University of Nevada, Las Vegas, and began teaching in the Clark County School District. Upon moving to Missouri, he received a master's degree from Lindenwood College and a specialist's degree from Southern Illinois University, Edwardsville. Alex serves on the advisory board for the International Alliance for Invitational Education and is the chairperson for state/country coordinators for the Alliance. He enjoys spending time at his home in O'Fallon with his wife, Jorie, and their three children, Morgan, Dillon, and Logan.

Frances S. van Tassell taught in private and public schools in Alabama, Mississippi, Ohio, South Carolina, New York, and Oklahoma before beginning her career as a teacher educator in 1988. She has been a member of the faculty at the University of North Texas since 1993, serving in various roles. She teaches courses in curriculum and instruction and has served as program coordinator or lead advisor for programs within the Department of Teacher Education and Administration. She served as president of the Association of Teacher Educators in 2003–2004 and served two terms as chair of the UNT Faculty Senate, in 2004–2005 and 2005–2006. She has two adult children and two teenage grandsons and considers herself very fortunate to have these family members living nearby.

Gail E. Young recently retired as a teacher at Emge Elementary School. She enjoyed 23 years as a classroom teacher in grades two through five in Missouri and Colorado. She received her bachelor's degree from Maryville University and her master's degree from Webster University. She serves on the advisory board for the International Alliance for Invitational Education and is the Missouri State Coordinator for the Alliance. Now that she is retired, she and her husband travel and spend time with their children and grandchildren.